HarperCollins Publishers
Westerhill Rd, Bishopbriggs, Glasgow, G64 2QT

www.**fire**and**water**.com

First published 2001

© HarperCollins Publishers (text), 2001

Reprint 10 9 8 7 6 5 4 3 2 1 0

ISBN 0 00 710161 9

A catalogue reference for this book is available from The British Library

Consultant: Christian Salzedo

Photography: Gonzalo Corvalan

   With additional photography/material from:
      Keith Gibson (www.photosfromfrance.co.uk),
      Hôtel XII Apôtres, Contrexeville,
      Christopher Riches, Fiona Steel, The Printer's Devil,
      Artville (pp 91, 94, 95, 97, 98, 99 101, 102)
      Anthony Blake Photo Library (pp 92[tr, br], 93[tl], 94[tl], 95[mr],
      96[br], 97[ml], 98[tl], 100[mr], 103[bl], 104[tl, mr], 105[br, tl], 106[br])
   Wine material: Andrea Gillies
   Map: Heather Moore
Layout & Origination: The Printer's Devil, Glasgow

Other titles in the Collins Language Survival Guide series:
   Germany (0 00 710162 7)
   Spain (0 00 710164 3)
   Italy (0 00 710163 5)
These titles are also published in a CD pack containing a 50-minute CD
and Language Survival Guide.

Printed in Italy by Amadeus SpA

CONTENTS

USEFUL WEBSITES

Currency Converters
www.oanda.com
www.x-rates.com

Foreign Office Advice
www.fco.gov.uk/travel/
countryadvice.asp

Passport Office
www.ukpa.gov.uk

Health advice
www.thetraveldoctor.com
www.doh.gov.uk/traveladvice
www.doh.gov.uk/hat

Travel insurance
www.insurance.org.uk

Pets
www.maff.gov.uk/animalh/
quarantine

Weather
www.bbc.co.uk/weather

Railways
www.sncf.com

Tourism
www.francetourism.com *(French
Government Tourist Office)*
www.cybervasion.com/france
(Information on France)
www.la-cote-dazur.com *(French
Riviera)*
www.normandy-tourism.org
(Normandy regional site)
www.visit-alsace.com *(Alsace
regional site)*
www.paris-tours-guides.com
(Guided tours of Paris)
www.paris.org *(Paris site)*
www.parisfree.com
www.autoroutes.fr *(Traffic and
road conditions)*

Internet Cafés
www.cybercafes.com

Culture & Activities
www.louvre.fr/louvrea.htm *(Musée
du Louvre)*
www.chateaux-france.com
(chateaux)
www.barginginfrance.com *(canal
boats)*
www.canalsoffrance.com *(canal
boats)*
www.opera-de-paris.fr *(Paris
opera)*
www.zingueurs.com *(Bars with
music, theatre)*

Hotels
www.francehotelreservation.com
www.hotels-france.com
www.hotel-restaurant-fr.com

INTRODUCTION

As technology sweeps across the world, travellers aren't just faced with the prospect of speaking a foreign language – they also have foreign machines to contend with. Machines for parking, for dispensing cash, for buying tickets and food. Often there is nobody about to ask how they work. *Collins Language Survival Guides* address this problem by showing photographically signs and situations you might come across.

The things that throw you are often the ones that look familiar – such as buses, trains or phones – but which operate slightly differently.

There are usually codes to how things operate, and though you might not think you are aware of them, you are probably using them every day: the colour-coding for roads (blue for motorways, green for major roads, yellow for temporary signs) or when buying milk (generally blue for whole milk, green for semi-skimmed and red for skimmed). It's when these familiar codes don't work in the same way, that you feel slightly at a loss and probably more unsure than you need be. By making a note of how these types of things work and knowing a few keywords, you will feel much more confident.

The unique combination of practical information, photos and phrases found in this book provides the key to hassle-free travel and the colour-coding below shows how information is presented and how to access it as quickly as possible.

 General, practical information which will provide useful tips on getting the best out of your trip.

keywords ◀

these are words that are useful to know both when you see them written down or when you hear them spoken

droite
drwat
right

gauche
gohsh
left

key talk ▶

short, simple phrases that you can change and adapt to suit your own situation

excuse me!
s'il vous plaît!
seel voo play

where is...?
où est...?
oo ay...

how do I get to...?
pour aller à...?
poor a-lay a...

The **Food Section** allows you to choose more easily from what is on offer both for snacks and at restaurants.

The practical 5000-word English–French, French–English **Dictionary** means that you will never be stuck for words.

SPEAKING FRENCH

We've tried to make the pronunciation under the phrases as clear as possible by breaking the words up with hyphens, but don't pause between syllables.

The consonants are not difficult, and are mostly pronounced as in English: *b*, *d*, *f*, *k*, *l*, *m*, *n*, *p*, *s*, *t*, *v*, *x* and *z*. The letter *h* is always silent, and *r* should be pronounced at the back of the throat in the well-known French way, although an English 'r' will be understood. When *c* comes before the vowels *e* or *i* it is pronounced like 's'; otherwise it is a hard 'k'. Likewise, *g* before *e* or *i* is 'zh' like 's' in 'pleasure', not hard 'g'. The letter *ç* is pronounced the same as *s*; *q* is always like *k* in 'kick' (not the 'kw' sound in 'quick'); *ch* is 'sh'; *gn* is 'ny', something like the sound in 'onion'; and *w* is either 'v' or 'w'.

Final consonants, especially *s* and *n*, are often silent, but sometimes not, for example when the following word begins with a vowel – just follow the pronunciation guide.

The sound spelt **ou** in French is something like 'oo' in English, while the sound represented by **u**, which many English speakers have difficulty with, is not really so hard: simply round your lips as if about to say 'ee' but pronounce 'oo'. We use the symbol '<u>oo</u>' in the pronunciation guide.

There are two **o** sounds in French; one is something like the 'o' in English 'hope' and one something like 'hop'. We've represented the first by 'oh' and the second by 'o' in the transcriptions. Meanwhile 'uh' represents both the rounded sounds of **peu** *puh* and **peur** *puhr* and also the sound (like 'a' in English 'ago' or 'sofa') found in **je** *zhuh* and **se** *suh* and the first syllables of **retard** *ruh-tar* and **demain** *duh-mañ*. Look out for the following letter combinations: **au** and **eau** are 'oh'; **oi** is 'wa'; and **ui** is something like 'wee'.

There are various 'nasalised' vowels in French. When you see a 'ñ' you should nasalise the vowel before it rather than pronouncing an n. For example 'mañ' in the pronunciation guide represents 'm' plus the vowel in the well-known French words **fin** *fañ* or **rien** *ryañ*, rather than the sounds in English 'man'. The others are 'uñ' (as in **brun** *bruñ*) and 'oñ', which we use to cover the similar vowel sounds in **dans** *doñ* or **en** *oñ* or **blanc** *bloñk* and **mon** *moñ* or **blond** *bloñ*.

EVERYDAY TALK

*There are two forms of address in French, formal (**vous**) and informal (**tu**). You should always stick with the formal until you are on a first-name basis. For this book, we will use the formal.*

yes
oui
wee

no
non
noñ

ok/that's fine
très bien
tray byañ

please
s'il vous plaît
seel voo play

thank you
merci
mehr-see

thanks very much
merci beaucoup
mehr-see boh-koo

don't mention it
de rien
duh ryañ

that's very kind
c'est très gentil
say tray zhoñ-tee

hello
bonjour/salut
boñ-zhoor/sa-loo

goodbye
au revoir
oh ruh-vwar

good evening
bonsoir
boñ-swar

good night
bonne nuit
bon nwee

see you later
à plus tard
a ploo tar

excuse me!
excusez-moi
eks-koo-zay mwa

sorry!
pardon
par-doñ

I am sorry
je suis désolé
zhuh swee day-zo-lay

I don't understand
je ne comprends pas
zhuh nuh koñ-proñ pa

I don't know
je ne sais pas
zhuh nuh say pa

Addressing people

The French might seem rather formal with their frequent use of *Monsieur* and *Madame*, but it is simply a form of politeness. So although the phrases above do not indicate it, remember to add *Monsieur* or *Madame* when talking to someone. It doesn't matter that you don't know their name. It is what you will hear being used to you and will guarantee you a much smoother passage through France. The greeting *salut* is used more among young people and means both hello and goodbye.

excuse me!
pardon, Monsieur/Madame
par-don muhs-yuh/ma-dam

that is very kind of you
vous êtes très gentil
vooz et tray zhoñ-tee

hi, Christian
salut, Christian
sa-loo Christian

bye, Claudine
salut, Claudine
sa-loo Claudine

see you tomorrow
à demain
a duh-mañ

*The simplest way to ask for something in a shop or bar is by naming what you want and adding **s'il vous plaît**.*

1	**un** *uñ*
2	**deux** *duh*
3	**trois** *trwah*
4	**quatre** *katr*
5	**cinq** *sañk*
6	**six** *seess*
7	**sept** *set*
8	**huit** *weet*
9	**neuf** *nuhf*
10	**dix** *deess*

a ... please
un/une... s'il vous plaît
uñ/oon... seel voo play

a white coffee please
un crème s'il vous plaît
uñ krem seel voo play

a beer please
une bière s'il vous plaît
oon byehr seel voo play

a tea and 2 beers please
un thé et deux bières s'il vous plaît
uñ tay ay duh byehr seel voo play

the...
le/la/les...
luh/la/lay...

some...
du/de la/des...
doo/duh la/day...

the menu please
la carte s'il vous plaît
la kart seel voo play

the bill please
l'addition s'il vous plaît
la-dee-syoñ seel voo play

another/more...
encore du/de la/des...
oñ-kor doo/duh la/day...

another beer
encore une bière
oñkor oon byehr

some more tea
encore du thé
oñkor doo tay

2 more beers
encore deux bières
oñkor duh byehr

2 more coffees
encore deux cafés
oñ-kor duh ka-fay

3 tickets
trois billets
trwah bee-yay

4 ice creams
quatre glaces
katr glass

To catch someone's attention

To catch the attention of a passerby, you should begin your request with **Pardon, Monsieur/Madame** or **S'il vous plaît, Monsieur/Madame**. This will induce the right kind of mood. You should not take it for granted that they speak English and address them in English.

excuse me!
s'il vous plaît!
seel voo play

can you help me?
est-ce que vous pouvez m'aider?
ess kuh voo poo-vay may-day

do you know where...?
est-ce que vous savez où...?
ess-kuh voo savay oo...

how I get to...?
comment j'arrive à...?
ko-moñ zha-reev a...

*In French you can turn a statement into a question simply by changing the intonation and putting a question mark in your voice: **vous avez une chambre?***

est-ce que vous avez? **do you have...?**	**do you have a room?** est-ce que vous avez une chambre? *ess kuh vooz a-vay <u>oon</u> shombr*	
c'est combien? **how much?**	**how much is the ticket?** c'est combien le billet? *say koñ-byañ luh bee-yay*	**how much is the wine?** c'est combien le vin? *say koñ-byañ luh vañ*
je voudrais... **I'd like...**	**I'd like a red wine** je voudrais un vin rouge *zhuh voo-dray uñ vañ roozh*	**I'd like an ice-cream** je voudrais une glace *zhuh voo-dray <u>oon</u> glass*
j'ai besoin de... **I need...**	**I need a taxi** j'ai besoin d'un taxi *zhay buhz-wañ duñ taxi*	**I need to phone** j'ai besoin de téléphoner *zhay buhz-wañ duh te-le-fo-nay*
à quelle heure?/ quand? **when?**	**when does it open?** ça ouvre à quelle heure? *sa oovr a kel uhr*	**when does it close?** ça ferme à quelle heure? *sa fehrm a kel uhr*
	when does it leave? quand est-ce qu'il part? *koñt ess-keel par*	**when does it arrive?** quand est-ce qu'il arrive? *koñt ess-keel a-reev*
où? **where?**	**where is the bank?** où est la banque? *oo ay la boñk*	**where is the hotel?** où est l'hôtel? *oo ay loh-tel*
est-ce qu'il y a...? **is there...?**	**is there a market?** est-ce qu'il y a un marché? *ess keel ee a uñ mar-shay*	**where is there a market?** où est-ce qu'il y a un marché? *oo ess keel ee a uñ mar-shay*
il n'y a pas de... **there is no...**	**there is no bread** il n'y a pas de pain *eel nee a pa duh pañ*	**there is no soap** il n'y a pas de savon *eel nee a pa duh sa-voñ*
est-ce que je peux...? **can I...?**	**can I smoke?** est-ce que je peux fumer? *ess kuh zhuh puh <u>foo</u>-may*	**can I phone?** je peux téléphoner? *zhuh puh te-le-foh-nay*
	where can I buy milk? où est-ce que je peux acheter du lait? *oo ess kuh zhuh puh ash-tay <u>doo</u> lay*	
c'est...? **is it...?**	**is it expensive?** c'est cher? *say shehr*	**is it far?** c'est loin? *say lwañ*
j'aime... **I like...**	**I like red wine** j'aime le vin rouge *zhem le vañ roozh*	**I don't like cheese** je n'aime pas le fromage *zhuh nem pa luh fro-mazhh*

These are a small selection of very useful words to know.

keywords keywords keywords keywords

grand
groñ
large

petit
puh-tee
small

un peu
uñ puh
a little

ça suffit
sa soo-fee
that's enough

le/la plus proche
luh/la ploo prosh
the nearest

loin
lwañ
far

trop cher
troh shehr
too expensive

et
ay
and

avec/sans
a-vek/soñ
with/without

pour
poor
for

mon/ma/mes
moñ/ma/may
my

celui-ci/-là
suhl-wee-see/-la
this one/that one

tout de suite
toot sweet
straight away

plus tard
ploo tar
later

a large white coffee
un grand crème
oon groñd krem

a little please
un peu s'il vous plaît
uñ puh seel voo play

where is the nearest chemist?
où est la pharmacie la plus proche?
oo ay la far-ma-see la ploo prosh

is it far?
c'est loin?
say lwañ

it is too expensive
c'est trop cher
say troh shehr

is it engaged?
c'est occupé?
say o-koo-pay

a tea and a coffee
un thé et un café
uñ tay ay uñ ka-fay

with sugar
avec sucre
a-vek sookr

without sugar
sans sucre
soñ sookr

for me
pour moi
poor mwah

my passport
mon passeport
moñ pass-por

I'd like this one
je voudrais celui-ci
zhuh voo-dray suhl-wee-see

a small car
une petite voiture
oon puh-teet vwa-toor

that's enough thanks
ça suffit merci
sa soo-fee mehr-see

it is too small
c'est trop petit
say troh puh-tee

is it free?
c'est libre?
say leebr

a beer and a red wine
une bière et un vin rouge
oon byehr ay uñ vañ roozh

with cream
avec crème
a-vek krem

without cream
sans crème
soñ krem

for her/him
pour elle/lui
poor el/lwee

my keys
mes clés
may klay

I'd like that one
je voudrais celui-là
zhuh voo-dray suhl-wee-la

I need a taxi straight away
j'ai besoin d'un taxi tout de suite
zhay buh-swañ duñ tak-see toot sweet

I'll call you later
je vais vous appeler plus tard
zhuh vay vooz ap-lay ploo tar

It is always good to be able to say a few words about yourself to break the ice, even if you won't be able tell your life history. Remember there are different endings for male and female.

my name is...
je m'appelle...
zhuh ma-pel...

I am from...
je suis de...
zhuh swee duh...

I am on holiday
je suis en vacances
zhuh sweez oñ va-koñss

I am on business
je suis en voyage d'affaires
zhuh swee oñ vwa-yazh da-fehr

I am single
je suis célibataire
zhuh swee say-lee-ba-tehr

I am married
je suis marié(e)
zhuh swee mar-yay

I have a partner *(male)*
j'ai un ami
zhay uhn am-ee

I have a partner *(female)*
j'ai une amie
zhay oon a-mee

I am a widow
je suis veuve
zhuh swee vuhv

I am a widower
je suis veuf
zhuh swee vuhf

I am divorced
je suis divorcé(e)
zhuh swee dee-vor-say

I am separated
je suis séparé(e)
zhuh swee sep-a-ray

I have a child
j'ai un enfant
zhay uhn oñ-foñ

I have ... children
j'ai ... enfants
zhay ... oñ-foñ

I work
je travaille
zhuh tra-vye

I am retired
je suis en retraite
zhuh swee oñ ruh-tret

I am a student
je suis étudiant(e)
zhuh swee ay-tood-yoñ(t)

this is a beautiful country
c'est un très beau pays
say uñ tray boh pay-ee

I love your food
j'aime beaucoup le repas
zhem boh-koo luh ruh-pa

people are very kind
les gens sont très gentils
lay zhoñ soñ tray zhoñ-tee

see you next year!
à l'année prochaine!
a la-nay pro-shen

thank you very much for your kindness
merci beaucoup pour votre gentillesse
mehr-see boh-koo poor votr zhoñ-tee-ess

I have enjoyed myself very much
je me suis très bien amusé(e)
zhuh me swee tray byañ a-moo-zay

we'd like to come back
nous voudrions revenir
noo voo-dree-oñ ruh-vuh-neer

I'll write to you
je vais vous écrire
zhuh vay vooz ay-kreer

here is my address
voici mon adresse
vwa-see mon ad-dres

People are generally helpful and, if in the right mood, will do all they can to help you. You should always try to use your French, however bad!

excuse me!
s'il vous plaît!
seel voo play

can you help me?
pouvez-vous m'aider?
poo-vay voo may-day

I don't speak French
je ne parle pas français
zhuh nuh parl pa froñ-say

I am sorry, I did not know
pardon, je ne savais pas
par-doñ zhuh nuh sa-vay pa

I am lost
je me suis perdu(e)
zhuh muh swee pehr-doo

we are lost
nous nous sommes perdus
noo noo som pehr-doo

I have lost...
j'ai perdu...
zhay pehr-doo...

my money
mon argent
moñ ar-zhoñ

my tickets
mes billets
may bee-yay

my passport
mon passeport
moñ pass-por

I have left...
j'ai laissé...
zhay less-ay...

in the restaurant
dans le restaurant
doñ luh res-toh-roñ

on the train
dans le train
doñ luh trañ

I have missed...
j'ai manqué...
zhay moñ-kay...

my flight
mon avion
mon av-yoñ

the train
le train
luh trañ

my connection
ma correspondance
ma ko-res-poñ-doñss

someone has stolen...
on m'a volé...
on ma vo-lay...

my purse
mon porte-monnaie
moñ port-mo-nay

my wallet
mon portefeuille
moñ port-fuh-ee

my bag
mon sac à main
moñ sak a mañ

my traveller's cheques
mes travellers
may tra-vuh-lurh

I need to get to...
je dois aller à/au...
zhuh dwa a-lay a/oh...

how can I get there?
comment je peux y arriver?
ko-mañ zhuh puh ee a-ree-vay

my luggage hasn't arrived
mes bagages ne sont pas arrivés
may ba-gazh nuh soñ pa a-ree-vay

my case has been damaged
ma valise a été abîmée
ma va-leez a ay-tay a-bee-may

I need to go to hospital
je dois aller à l'hôpital
zhuh dwa a-lay a lo-pee-tal

I have no money
je n'ai pas d'argent
zhuh nay pa dar-zhoñ

my child is missing
mon enfant s'est perdu
moñ oñ-foñ say pehr-doo

he/she is ... old
il/elle a ... ans
eel/el a ... oñ

go away!
allez-vous-en!
a-lay-vooz oñ

that man is following me
cet homme me suit
set om muh swee

Although no-one wants to consider the possibility, you may come across the odd problem and it is best to be armed with a few phrases to help you cope with the situation.

there is no...
il n'y a pas de...
eel nee a pa duh...

there is no soap
il n'y a pas de savon
eel nee a pa duh sa-voñ

it is dirty
c'est sale
say sal

they are dirty
ils sont sales
eel soñ sal

it is broken
c'est cassé
say kass-ay

they are broken
ils sont cassés
eel soñ kass-ay

the ... does not work
le/la ... ne marche pas
luh/la ... nuh marsh pa

the ... do not work
les ... ne marchent pas
lay ... nuh marsh pa

the window doesn't open
la fenêtre n'ouvre pas
la fuh-netr noovr pa

the door doesn't close
la porte ne ferme pas
la port nuh fehrm pa

it is too noisy
il y a trop de bruit
eel ee a troh duh brwee

the room is too small
la chambre est trop petite
la shoñbr ay trop puh-teet

it is too hot
il fait trop chaud
eel feh troh shoh

it is too cold
il fait trop froid
eel feh troh frwa

it is too expensive
c'est trop cher
say troh shehr

I'd like another room
je voudrais une autre chambre
zhuh voo-dray oon otr shoñbr

I want to complain
je veux faire une réclamation
zhuh vuh fehr oon rek-la-mass-yoñ

where is the manager?
où est le directeur?
oo ay luh dee-rek-tuhr

we want to order
nous voudrions commander
noo vood-ree-yoñ ko-moñ-day

the service is very bad
le service est très mauvais
luh sehr-vees ay tray moh-vay

this dish is cold
ce plat est froid
suh pla ay frwa

this coffee is cold
ce café est froid
suh ka-fay ay frwa

there is a mistake
il y a une erreur
eel ee a oon e-ruhr

please check the bill
pouvez-vous vérifier l'addition?
poo-vay voo ve-ree-fyay la-dee-syoñ

this isn't what I ordered
ce n'est pas ce que j'ai commandé
suh nay pa suh kuh zhay ko-moñ-day

I want a refund
je veux être remboursé(e)
zhuh vuh etr roñ-boor-say

EVERYDAY FRANCE

The next four pages should give you an idea of the type of things you will come across in France.

▲ **OPEN**

Shops in France generally shut in the afternoon from about 12 noon to 2 pm. Food shops close at around 7.30 pm. Shops are usually closed on Sun and Mon mornings. There are no markets on Mon.

▼ **CLOSED**

FERMÉ

▲ **PULL**

HORAIRES
du LUNDI au VENDREDI
de 8 heures 45 à 12 heures 20
et de 14 heures à 17 heures

OPENING HOURS ▲

CAISSE

CASH DESK/PAY HERE ▲

◀ **PUSH HERE**

There are lottery draws on Wednesdays and Saturdays. ▼

Accueil

▲ **INFORMATION/RECEPTION**

do you sell...?
est-ce que vous vendez...?
ess-kuh voo voñ-day...

where can I get...?
où est-ce que je peux acheter...?
oo ess kuh zhuh puh ash-tay...

stamps
des timbres
day tañbr

plasters
du sparadrap
doo spa-ra-dra

phonecards
des télécartes
day te-le-kart

a map
un plan
uñ ploñ

Paying machines are becoming more widespread. You generally have to insert the banknotes face up and last. You will need notes that are in good condition and may have to persevere until the machine accepts them.

CANCEL
coins accepted
COINS
BANK CARD

▼ *local mail*   ▼ *mail for outside Paris and abroad*

▲ Postboxes are yellow.

ENTREE

▲ ENTRANCE
▼ EXIT

SORTIE

The tabac is a an extremely useful place. A café, it is open all day until about 8 pm. It sells cigarettes, envelopes, stamps, transport tickets and lottery tickets – signs outside indicate what you can buy. You can also bet on the horses!

lottery tickets

the red lozenge: sign of the tabac

travel cards in Paris

betting

excuse me...
pardon, Monsieur/Madame...
par-doñ muhs-yuh/ma-dam...

how does this work?
comment ça marche?
ko-moñ sa marsh

what do I have to do?
qu'est-ce qu'il faut faire?
kess keel foh fehr

what does that mean?
qu'est-ce que ça veut dire?
kess kuh sa vuh deer

talking

EN SERVICE

IN SERVICE ▲

▼ **OUT OF SERVICE**

HORS SERVICE

ENTRÉE INTERDITE

▲ **ENTRY PROHIBITED**

Service Non Compris

▲ **SERVICE NOT INCLUDED**

Tipping in France is not compulsory and should be simply an appreciation of good service. If you are having dinner in a restaurant, you might consider tipping the waiter 5–10% of the bill if you liked the service.

NO SMOKING ▼

Smoking is still popular in France and you might find it difficult to find non-smoking areas in bars and restaurants. Smoking is banned in most public places.

◀ The French can seem quite officious at times and they regard the British (or *rosbifs* as they are nicknamed) as having an eccentric or almost wacky streak.

ATTENDEZ LE SIGNAL POUR TRAVERSER

wait for the signal to cross

Bars and cafés are open throughout the day and close around 8 pm. Bars that open later tend to be shut during the day. You generally pay when you leave. It is cheaper to have a drink at the bar, *au comptoir*. ▶

can I smoke here?
est-ce que je peux fumer ici?
ess kuh zhuh puh <u>foo</u>-may ee-see

do you mind if I smoke?
ça vous dérange si je fume?
sa voo day-roñzh see zhuh <u>foom</u>

I don't smoke
je ne fume pas
zhuh nuh <u>foom</u> pa

please don't smoke
s'il vous plaît ne fumez pas
see voo play nuh <u>foo</u>-may pa

an ashtray, please
un cendrier s'il vous plaît
uñ soñd-ree-ay seel voo play

a non-smoking table, please
une table non-fumeur s'il vous plaît
<u>oon</u> tabl noñ-<u>foo</u>-muhr see voo play

*In Paris the scarcity of coin-operated toilets means that one has to rely on cafés, which are numerous, but where you almost always have to pay, one way or another, and where standards vary greatly. In big cafés you can go straight to the toilets, generally downstairs. The toilet door is coin-operated (it accepts 1- or 2-F coins). In standard cafés the toilets are for patrons only and you will be expected to buy a drink. Have it at the bar; here are a few of the cheapest suggestions: **un ballon de limonade** (lemonade), **un café** (espresso coffee), **un petit rouge/blanc** (a small glass of red/white wine). Insist on the **petit** bit, otherwise you get charged more.*

◀ ▲ TOILETS

LIBRÉ **occupé**

▲ FREE   ▲ OCCUPIED

▲ Don't be fooled by the letters: *c* is for *chaud*, hot; and *f* is for *froid*, cold.

MESSIEURS

▲ GENTS   ▼ LADIES

DAMES

eau non potable

▲ NOT DRINKING WATER

Lave Mains Séchage Intégré

▲ HANDWASH AND DRYER IN ONE

Les ENFANTS de moins de 10 ans doivent être accompagnés

◀ CHILDREN UNDER 10 MUST BE ACCOMPANIED

excuse me! where is the toilet?
s'il vous plaît où sont les toilettes?
see voo play oo soñ lay twa-let

do you have the key for the toilet?
est-ce que vous avez la clé pour les toilettes?
ess kuh vooz av-ay la klay poor lay twa-let

are their toilets for the disabled?
est-ce qu'il y a des toilettes pour handicapés?
ess keel ee a day twa-let poor oñ-dee-ka-pay

where can I change my baby?
où est-ce que je peux changer mon bébé?
oo ess kuh shuh puh shoñ-zhay moñ bay-bay

talking talking

vous êtes ici
you are here

◄ The dispenser on ► the side of the area map sells a portable copy of the map (*un plan*) for 5F.

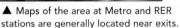
▲ Maps of the area at Metro and RER stations are generally located near exits.

talking talking talking

excuse me!
s'il vous plaît, Monsieur/Madame
seel voo play muhs-yuh/ma-dam

do you know where...?
est-ce que vous savez où...?
ess kuh voo sa-vay oo...?

how do I get to...?
pour aller à...?
poor a-lay a...

is this the right way to...?
c'est la bonne direction pour...?
say la bon dee-reks-yoñ poor...

do you have a map of the town?
est-ce que vous avez un plan de la ville?
ess kuh vooz a-vay uñ ploñ duh la veel

can you show me on the map?
pouvez-vous me montrer sur la carte?
poo-vay voo muh moñ-tray soor la kart

we're looking for...
nous cherchons...
noo shehr-shoñ...

where is...?
où est...?
oo ay...

is it far?
c'est loin?
say lwañ

a street directory
une répertoire des rues
ooñ rep-er-twar day roo

◀ White signs indicate local destinations.

porte
gate

gare
station

▲ In cities, street plates display the *arrondissement* (district) number at the top.

PEDESTRIANS ▲

▼ NO PEDESTRIANS

◀ EXIT

Pedestrian routes with symbol. Places of interest are signposted in brown and public services are in blue. ▼

poste de police
police station

bureau de poste
post office

hotel de ville
town hall

forum des halles
market hall

keywords keywords keywords keywords keywords keywords keywords

à droite
a drwat
to the right

à gauche
à gohsh
to the left

tout droit
too drwa
straight ahead

allez
a-lay
go

tournez
toor-nay
turn

rue
roo
street

place
plass
square

feux
fuh
traffic lights

église
eg-leez
church

première
pruhm-yehr
first

deuxième
duhz-yehm
second

loin
lwañ
far

près de
pray duh
near to

à côté de
a ko-tay duh
next to

en face de
oñ fass duh
opposite

jusqu'à
zhoos-ka
until

BANKS & MONEY

*Instead of the magnetic strip currently used on British credit cards, French credit cards carry a computer chip (**puce**) which contains the identity details of the cardholder. For this reason French card-reading machines may have difficulty reading the magnetic strip so make sure you have a contact number for your bank in case of problems. Note that most banks in France no longer accept Eurocheques. Many banks are not freely accessible and you have to go through a locked door. Once you have rung the bell, you will see either a red light indicating to wait, or a green light indicating that you should enter.*

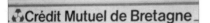

Crédit Mutuel de Bretagne

▲ Many banks can be identified by the word **Crédit**. Among the big French banks are **Crédit Lyonnais**, **Société Générale** and **BNP-Paribas**.

EN SERVICE — *in service*

▲ Cash dispensers are widely available. You will be able to carry out your transaction in English.

change ...

▲ You can change money in most post offices at competitive rates. This sign indicates this post office has a bureau de change.

wait (red light) — Attendez

come in (green light) — Passez

Sonnez

ring here — Ici

You will have to ring ▲ a bell and wait to be let into most banks.

MERCI D'ENTRER SEUL DANS CE SAS — *please enter one at a time*

no bike helmets to be worn

Locaux sous télésurveillance — *video surveillance in operation*

POUSSEZ — *push*

Nous vous accueillons
du lundi au jeudi
de 9h à 17h40
le vendredi
de 9h à 17h20

Du Lundi au Jeudi
de 8h50 à 17h15

Vendredi
de 8h50 à 16h45

Opening times may vary
from bank to bank.

▲ The French currency is the franc which breaks
down into 100 centimes.
Notes: 500F, 200F, 100F, 50F, 20F
Coins: 20F, 10F, 5F, 2F, 1F.
50 centimes, 20 c, 10 c, 5 c.
In Jan 2002 euro notes and coins will be introduced
and both the new currency and old national coins
and notes will be in circulation until end Feb 2002.

keywords keywords keywords

carte de crédit
kart duh kray-dee
credit card

distributeur
dees-tree-boo-tuhr
cash dispenser

code secret
kod suh-kray
PIN number

monnaie
mo-nay
change

insérez
añ-seh-ray
insert

tapez le montant
ta-pay luh moñ-toñ
press amount

billets
bee-yay
notes

espèces
ess-pess
cash

puce
poos
chip

talking talking talking

where is there...?
où est-ce qu'il y a...?
oo ess keel ee a...

a bank
une banque
oon boñk

a bureau de change
un bureau de change
uñ boo-roh duh shoñzh

where can I change money?
où est-ce que je peux changer de l'argent?
oo ess kuh zhuh puh shoñ-zhay duh lar-zhoñ

I would like small notes
je voudrais des petites coupures
zhuh voo-dray day puh-teet koo-poor

where is the nearest cash dispenser?
où est le distributeur le plus proche?
oo ay luh dees-tree-boo-tuhr luh ploo prosh

I want to change these traveller's cheques
je voudrais changer ces travellers
zhuh voo-dray shoñ-zhay say tra-vuh-luhr

the cash dispenser has swallowed my card
le distributeur a mangé ma carte
luh dees-tree-boo-tuhr a moñ-zhay ma kart

WHEN IS...?

*The 24-hour clock is used in timetables. With the 24-hour clock, the words half (**demie**) and quarter (**quart**) are not used.*

keywords keywords

matin
ma-tañ
morning

après-midi
a-pray mee-dee
afternoon

ce soir
suh swar
this evening

aujourd'hui
oh-zhoor-dwee
today

demain
duh-mañ
tomorrow

hier
yehr
yesterday

plus tard
ploo tar
later

tout de suite
toot sweet
straight away

maintenant
mañ-tuh-noñ
now

à dix-huit heures vingt-cinq
a deez-weet uhr vañ-sañk
at 18.45

à minuit
a meen-wee
at midnight

à ... moins le quart
a ... mwañ luh kar
at quarter to...

à vingt-quatre heures
a vañ-katr uhr

à vingt-trois heures
a vañ-trwaz uhr

à onze heures
a oñz uhr

à vingt-deux heures
a vañ-duhz uhr

à dix heures
a dees uhr

à vingt et une heures
a vañt ay oon uhr

à neuf heures
a nuhf uhr

à vingt heures
a vañt uhr

à huit heures
a weet uhr

à dix-neuf heures
a deez-nuhf uhr

à sept heures
a set uhr

à dix-huit heures
a deez-weet uhr

à ... moins vingt
a ... mwañ vañ
at twenty to...

talking

when is the next...?
quand part le prochain...?
koñ par luh pro-shañ...

train
train
trañ

bus
bus
boos

boat
bateau
ba-toh

at what time is...?
à quelle heure est...?
a kel uhr ay...

breakfast
le petit déjeuner
luh puh-tee day-zhu-nay

dinner
le dîner
luh dee-nay

when does the ... leave?
quand est-ce que le/la ... part?
koñt ess kuh luh/la ... par

when does the ... arrive?
quand est-ce que le/la ... arrive?
koñt ess kuh luh/la ... a-reev

when does the ... open?
le/la ... ouvre à quelle heure?
sa oovr a kel uhr

when does the ... close?
le/la ... ferme à quelle heure?
luh/la ... fehrm a kel uhr

keywords keywords keywords

lundi
luñ-dee
Monday

mardi
mar-dee
Tuesday

mercredi
mehr-kruh-dee
Wednesday

jeudi
zhuh-dee
Thursday

vendredi
voñ-druh-dee
Friday

samedi
sam-dee
Saturday

dimanche
dee-moñsh
Sunday

à midi
a mee-dee
at midday

à ... et quart
a ... ay kar
at quarter past...

à douze heures
a dooz uhr

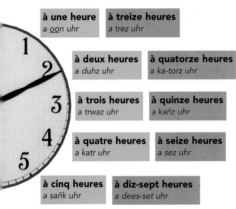

à une heure
a oon uhr

à treize heures
a trez uhr

à deux heures
a duhz uhr

à quatorze heures
a ka-torz uhr

à trois heures
a trwaz uhr

à quinze heures
a kañz uhr

à quatre heures
a katr uhr

à seize heures
a sez uhr

à cinq heures
a sañk uhr

à diz-sept heures
a dees-set uhr

à six heures
a sees uhr

à ... et demie
a ... ay duh-mee
at half past...

what time is it please?
il est quelle heure s'il vous plaît?
eel ay kel uhr seel voo play

what is the date?
quelle est la date d'aujourd'hui?
kel ay la dat doh-zhoor-dwee

it is the 8th May
nous somme le huit mai
noo som luh wee may

16 September 2002
le seize septembre deux mille deux
luh sez sept-toñbr duh meel duh

which day?
quel jour?
kel zhoor

which month?
quel mois?
kel mwa

talking

Timetables use the 24-hour clock. Bus and train timetables usually change once a year. French Summer Time starts on the last Sunday in March and ends on the last Sunday in October. France is always 1 hour ahead of the UK.

Janvier *Jan*
Février *Feb*
Mars *Mar*
Avril *Apr*
Mai *May*
Juin *Jun*
Juillet *Jul*
Août *Aug*
Septembre *Sep*
Octobre *Oct*
Novembre *Nov*
Décembre *Dec*

Service normal — *normal service*

Service du samedi et service réduit en vacances scolaires — *Saturday service & reduced service in school holidays*

Service des dimanches et fêtes — *Sunday & holiday service*

Pas de service — *no service*

Service été — *summer service*

lun *Mon*
mar *Tues*
mer *Wed*
jeu *Thur*
ven *Fri*
sam *Sat*
dim *Sun*

◀ Bus service key on timetable.

lignes en correspondance
connecting buses

vous êtes ici
you are here

Bus timetable (on bus stop) ▼

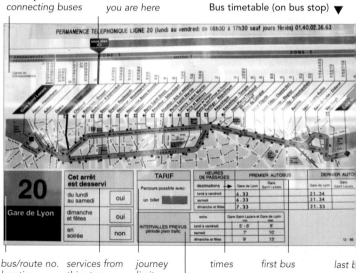

bus/route no. location

services from this stop
Mon-Sat: yes
Sun & hol: yes
eve: no

journey limit with 1 ticket

times

first bus

last bus

frequency in rush hour

Train timetable ▼

numéro de train notes à consulter		6115/4 1	534/5 TGV ♿♿	9536/7 2 TGV ♿♿	6132/3 3 ♿♿
Paris-Gare-de-Lyon	Dep				
Dijon-Ville	Dep	12.48			15.35
Chagny	Dep				
Chalon-sur-Saône	Dep	13.27			
Mâcon-Ville	Dep	13.55			
Satolas-TGV	Dep		15.14	15.14	
Lyon-Part-Dieu	Dep	14.39			17.13
Lyon-Perrache	Dep				
Vienne	Dep				
Valence-Ville	Dep	15.38	15,44	15.44	18.11
Montélimar	Arr				
Pierrelatte	Arr				
Orange	Arr				
Avignon	Arr		16.38	16.38	19.12

◀ This Paris-Avignon rail timetable runs from end of May to start of December.

trains run daily (dark background)

high-speed train: reservations necessary

| Trains circulant tous les jours (fond coloré) |
| — **TGV** Réservation obligatoire |
| ☾ Service nuit |

night service

Key to services ▼ ▶

JOURS DE CIRCULATION ET SERVICES DISPONIBLES

1. les sam.

2. jusqu'au 25 juin : les ven, sam, dim et fêtes sauf le 1er juin ; circule du 26 juin au 3 sept : tous les jours;du 8 sept au 3 nov : les ven, sam et dim;les 10, 17, 24 nov et 1er déc.

3. tous les jours sauf les 23 juil et 24 sept ⛌assuré certains jours-⛌ certains jours.

Days of operation and services available
1. Sundays
2. Until 25 Jun: Fri, Sat, Sun & hols exc. 1 Jun; 26 Jun-3 Sep: daily; 8 Sep-3 Nov: Fri, Sat, Sun; 10, 17, 24 Nov & 1 Dec.
3. Daily except 23 Jul & 24 Sep; refreshment trolley some days; reclining seats some days.

TICKETS

*Remember to try and begin your request with **Bonjour Monsieur** or **Bonjour Madame**. You should attempt to ask in French, even if you have to resort to English pretty quickly. Even though you might expect people working in such places to speak English, they will regard it as arrogant if you assume they do.*

Carte Orange ▶
Parisian travel
pass

*cut your photo
to fit and fix it
onto the white
square*

nom surname
prenom first name
fill in both
names in black
capital letters.

*logo of RATP,
Parisian trans-
port authority
(Travel tickets
and cards are
sold wherever
you see this
logo.)*

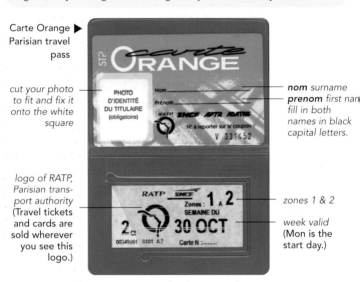

zones 1 & 2

*week valid
(Mon is the
start day.)*

Train tickets carry various information. ▼

**période de
pointe**
peak period

**à composter avant l'accès
au train** *validate ticket
before boarding train*

**conservez
tous vos billets**
retain all your tickets

2 adults

voit *coach*
place no
seat nos
non fum
no smoking

fenêtre
window
couloir
aisle

**découverte
à deux**
type of ticket

A/R A 2 obligatoire
*advance reservation
obligatory on TGV*

prix FRF, eur
*price in French
francs, euros*

A RATP transport ticket allowing travel in the Paris area. ▼

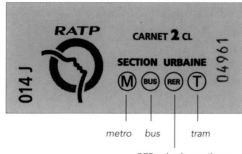

metro   bus   tram

RER suburban railway

A ticket like this bought in a book of 10 (*un carnet*), saves time and money: single tickets work out around 40% more expensive than when bought in a *carnet*.

Bus ticket for Boulogne-sur-Mer bought in a *carnet*. ▼

The ticket has been validated in the machine ▲
at the front of the bus (see page 28).
This stamps it and slices the corner off.

Reverse of the ticket ▼

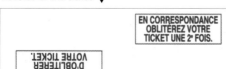

If you are catching a connection, remember ▲
to validate the ticket a second time
(it will slice off the opposite corner).

(see page 28)

keywords keywords keywords keywords

carnet
kar-nay
book of 10 tickets

ticket
tee-kay
bus/metro ticket

billet
bee-yay
ticket

aller simple
a-lay sañpl
single

aller-retour
a-lay ruh-toor
return

adulte
a-doolt
adult

enfant
oñ-foñ
child

étudiant
ay-tood-yañ
student

senior
sen-yor
over 60

handicapé
oñ-dee-ka-pay
disabled

famille
fa-mee
family

carte
kart
travel card/pass

PUBLIC TRANSPORT

*There is no zone system on Parisian buses. One ticket will get you to the end of the line or just one stop away. The bus timetable is posted in bus shelters (see pages 24-25). You have to stick your hand out if it is a request stop (**faire signe au machiniste**). If you haven't bought your ticket in advance, you can buy a single ticket from the driver (about 40% more expensive than when bought by the book, or **carnet**).There are 18 night-bus lines in Paris, indicated by letters. Night buses (**Noctambus** – a pun on **noctambule** meaning night-owl) operate 7 days a week from 1 am to 5.30 am. They serve Paris and its suburbs, up to 30 kms away from the city centre. On night buses you pay a fixed fare. Go to the back of the bus; do not block the entrance at the front and the exit in the middle.*

Bus stop for route numbers 39, 48, 95. Lines are colour-coded. ▼

The destination and route ▲ number appear at the front of the bus.

◄ *The bus stop location is indicated at the top of the stop.*

newsagent's sign

As well as in the tobaconist's and at metro booths, you can buy bus tickets from the newsagent's. ▶

26 Gare
        St-Lazare   Cours de
                               Vincennes **26**

▲ On all Parisian buses, the route
and the main districts served are also
indicated on the side of the bus.

The sign ▶
for the
night bus

les Noctambus   Gare de Nogent
                Le Perreux

Both regular and night buses stop here.

*validate
tickets
here
one by
one*

Validez ici
les billets
un par un

A typical ▶
bus stop found
outside Paris.

RⓞISSYBUS

▲ Ticket validating machine
This is located near the
front of the bus.

The bus to Roissy Airport. ▶

where do I catch a bus to...?
où est-ce que je prends le bus pour...?
oo ess kuh zhuh proñ luh boos poor...

is there a bus to...?
il y a un bus pour...?
eel ee a uñ boos poor...

which number goes to...?
quel numéro va à/au...?
kel noo-may-roh va a/oh...

does this bus go to...?
est-ce que ce bus va à/au...?
ess kuh suh boos va a/oh...

excuse me, is this a request stop?
s'il vous plaît, c'est un arrêt facultatif?
seel voo play say un a-ray fa-kool-ta-teef

which bus goes to the centre?
quel bus va au centre-ville?
kel boos va oh soñ-truh-veel

please tell me when to get off
pourriez-vous me dire quand descendre?
poo-ree-ay voo muh deer koñ day-soñdr

excuse me, I'm getting off!
pardon! je descends
par-doñ zhuh day-soñ

where do I catch the bus to the airport?
où est-ce que je prends le bus pour l'aéroport?
oo ess kuh zhuh proñ luh boos poor la-ehr-o-por

talking talking talking

*The Paris metro operates daily from 5.30 am to 12.30 at night and Paris' 6 main train stations connect to the metro system. There is a zone system (the centre of Paris is zone 1-3). The **Paris Visite carte** allows you to travel around for 1, 2, 3 or 5 days (with a reduced price for children between 4 and 11). It is a safe and fast way to travel, even late at night.*

▲ Metro signs ▼

Ticket barriers ▲

▲ Taxi ranks are located by metro stations.

▶ If the red disc lights up on the ticket barrier, seek assistance.

connecting lines (in orange)

CORRESPONDANCE
(M) (8) BALARD CRÉTEIL
(10) BOULOGNE GARE D'AUSTERLITZ
SORTIE

exit (in blue)

en cas d'affluence ne pas utiliser les strapontins

when crowded, do not use the foldable seats

RER is Paris' suburban train network, ▲ which is linked to the metro network (for instance, you'd take line A of the RER to go to Disneyland Paris, or line C or D to go to the *Stade de France*). You can take the RER with a standard metro/bus ticket as long as you don't leave zone 2, i.e. Paris *intramuros*. Some stations have disabled and pram access.

▲ When catching a metro, let people get out first, then go in and stand clear of the door. If travelling with a rucksack, take if off and move towards the back of the carriage where you won't be in the way of people getting on and off.

first train   *last train*

PREMIER TRAIN **DIRECTION** DERNIER TRAIN

5H41 (M) (6) 1H03

CHARLES DE GAULLE-ÉTOILE

Paris' 14 metro lines are called by their ▲ numbers as well as by their terminuses at each end.

where is the nearest metro station?
où est la station de métro la plus proche?
oo ay la stass-yoñ duh met-roh la ploo prosh

a carnet please
un carnet s'il vous plaît
uñ kar-nay seel voo play

a weekly card please
une carte hebdomadaire s'il vous plaît
oon kart eb-do-ma-dehr see voo play

have you a pocket map of the underground?
est-ce que vous avez un plan de poche du métro?
ess kuh vooz av-ay uñ ploñ duh posh doo met-roh

which station is it for...?
c'est quelle station pour...?
say kel stass-yoñ poor...

I want to go to...
je voudrais aller à/au...
zhuh vood-ray al-lay a/oh...

do I have to change?
est-ce qu'il faut changer?
ess keel foh shoñ-zhay

where do I change?
où est-ce qu'il faut changer?
oo ess keel foh shoñ-zhay

which line do I take?
je dois prendre quelle ligne?
zhuh dwah proñdr kel leen-yuh

in which direction?
dans quelle direction?
doñ kel dee-reks-yoñ

which stop is it for...?
c'est quel arrêt pour...?
say kel a-reh poor...

excuse me! this is my stop
s'il vous plaît! c'est mon arrêt
seel voo play say moñ a-reh

talking talking talking talking talking

*The train is not an especially cheap way to travel in France, but it's often the only one since coach companies cannot serve domestic destinations, only international ones (the SNCF has the monopoly on domestic transport). Several types of reduction are available under a scheme called **Découverte** (Discovery). You can get 25% off just by being over 60, being under 26, by travelling with at least one other person and at most eight others, accompanying (up to four people) a child under 12 years of age. Other reductions apply if you book your ticket eight days in advance or 30 days in advance. Train tickets are refundable, so if you decide you're not going to use them, just ask at the ticket window for your money back.*

Gare de PARIS-EST

▲ The logo for French railways and the name of the station

ACCUEIL - ORIENTATION

INFORMATION DESK ▲

▶ TICKETS FOR MAIN LINES

Billets Grandes Lignes

a single to...
un aller simple pour...
un a-lay sañple poor...

2 singles to...
deux allers simples pour...
duhz a-lay sañpl pour...

first class
première classe
pruhm-yehr klass

a return to...
un aller-retour pour...
un a-lay ruh-toor poor...

2 returns to...
deux aller-retour pour...
duhz a-lay ruh-toor poor...

second class
seconde classe
suh-goñd klass

a child's ticket to...
un billet enfant pour...
uñ bee-yay oñ-foñ poor...

2 senior tickets
deux billets senior pour...
duh bee-yay seen-yor poor...

do I have to pay a supplement?
je dois payer un supplément?
zhuh dwa pay-ay uñ soop-lay-moñ

do I need a reservation?
est-ce qu'il faut une réservation?
ess keel foh oon ray-zehr-vas-yoñ

do I have to change?
est-ce qu'il faut changer?
ess keel foh shoñ-zhay

I want to book...
je voudrais réserver...
zhuh voo-dray ray-zehr-vay...

2 seats
deux places
duh plass

a couchette
une couchette
oon koo-shet

smoking
fumeurs
foo-muhr

non-smoking
non-fumeurs
noñ foo-muhr

talking talking talking talking

◀ Validating machines are orange. You must validate (*composter*) your ticket before getting on the train and again for the return journey.

◀ Self-service ticket machine for main-line trains. There are separate machines for surburban trains (*billeterie banlieue*).

◀ LEFT-LUGGAGE LOCKERS

Consigne Automatique

Service Objets trouvés

▲ LOST & FOUND

DEPARTURES FOR SUBURBAN TRAINS ▼

départ
departure time

nature   *destination*   *voie*
type   destination   platform

DEPARTURES FOR MAIN-LINE TRAINS ▼

nature	départ	destination	voie		train n°	nature	départ	destination
	12·15	TROYES-CULMONT CHALINDREY			1845		13·13	TROYES-CHAUMONT-MUI
	12·17	DORMANS-REIMS-CHARLEVILLE MZ			67		13·47	STRASBOURG-PFORZHE
	12·51	METZ-FORBACH-KAISERSLAUTERN					•	LIMITE A STRASBOUR
	•	NEUSTADT-FRANCFORT			1909		14·30	NANCY-STRASBOURG
	13·06	CHALONS CH-NANCY-STRASBOURG					•	T

11:22

aller simple
a-lay sañpl
single

aller-retour
a-lay ruh-toor
return

réservation
ray-zer-va-syoñ
reservation

supplément
soo-play-moñ
reservation

période bleue
payr-yod bluh
off-peak rate

période normale
payr-yod nor-mal
standard rate

période de pointe
payr-yod duh pwañt
peak rate

couloir
kool-wahr
aisle

fenêtre
fuh-netr
window

fumeurs
foo-muhr
smoking

non-fumeurs
noñ foo-muhr
non-smoking

the train to…
le train pour…
luh trañ poor…

is this the train for…?
c'est le train pour…?
say luh trañ poor…

which platform does it leave from?
il part de quel quai?
eel par duh kel kay

this is my seat
c'est ma place
say ma plass

talking

TAXI

*You cannot hail taxis in the street – you will have to catch them at a stand. In Paris these are usually located near train stations and metro stations. Otherwise you will have to phone for a taxi. You can ask for a special price (**un forfait**) if you are going on a long journey (perhaps to the airport).*

◀ Paris taxi sign
A (white), B (orange) and C (green) lights correspond to the 3 different tariffs (see below). The taxi is free (*libre*) when the 'taxi' sign is lit and the A, B, C lights are off.

◀ Taxi meter (*le compteur*)

▲ Taxi stand

▶ Map showing different taxi tariff zones around Paris
Taxi tariff A corresponds to the white central zone (Paris *intramuros*); tariff B to the orange zone (the nearest suburbs) and tariff C to the green zone (the departments of Seine et Marne, Yvelines and Val d'Oise.)

where is the nearest taxi stand?
où est la station de taxi la plus proche?
oo ay la stass-yoñ duh tak-see la ploo prosh

to ... please
à ... s'il vous plaît
a ... seel voo play

how much is it to...?
c'est combien pour aller à...?
say koñ-byañ poor al-lay a...

please order me a taxi
pouvez-vous m'appeler un taxi?
poo-vay voo map-lay uñ tak-see

for now
pour maintenant
poor mañ-tuh-noñ

for ... o'clock
pour ... heures
poor ... uhr

can I have a receipt?
est-ce que je peux avoir un reçu?
ess kuh zhuh puh av-war uñ ruh-soo

keep the change
gardez la monnaie
gar-day la mo-nay

is there a special rate for the airport?
est-ce qu'il y a un forfait pour l'aéroport?
ess keel ee a uñ for-fay poor la-ehr-o-por

CAR HIRE

*To hire a car in France you have to be at least 21 and have held a driving licence for a year. If you are under 25 you might have to pay a young driver's supplement, depending on the type of car. Mileage (or **kilométrage**) is usually unlimited (**forfait kilométrage illimité**).*

LOCATION DE VEHICULES — vehicle hire

• **TOURISME** — cars

• **UTILITAIRES** — vans

I want to hire a car
je voudrais louer une voiture
zhuh voo-dray loo-ay oon vwa-toor

for one day
pour un jour
poor uñ zhoor

for ... days
pour ... jours
poor ... zhoor

I want...
je voudrais...
zhuh voo-dray...

a small car
une petite voiture
oon puh-teet vwa-toor

a large car
une grosse voiture
oon gross vwa-toor

a people carrier
un monospace
uñ mo-no-spass

an automatic
une automatique
oon oh-toh-ma-teek

how much is it?
c'est combien?
say koñ-byañ

is mileage included?
est-ce que le kilométrage est compris?
ess kuh luh kee-lo-me-trazh ay koñ-pree

I am ... old
j'ai ... ans
zhay ... oñ

here is my driving licence
voici mon permis de conduire
vwa-see moñ per-mee duh koñ-dweer

what is included in the price?
qu'est-ce qui est compris dans le prix?
kess kee ay koñ-pree doñ luh pree

where are the documents?
où sont les papiers?
oo soñ lay pap-yay

can you show me the controls?
vous pouvez me montrer les commandes?
voo poo-vay muh moñ-tray lay ko-moñd

what do we do if we break down?
qu'est-ce qu'il faut faire si la voiture tombe en panne?
kess keel foh fehr see la vwa-toor toñb oñ pan

we need a baby seat
nous avons besoin d'un siège pour bébés
nooz a-voñ buh-zwañ duñ syehzh poor bay-bay

DRIVING

*French drivers tend to be quite aggressive and the high incidence of road deaths has become a cause for national concern. Before you can get your driving licence in France, you have to be 18, have spent at least one year being accompanied by another driver (over 28 and a licence-holder for at least 3 years), and then have passed a practical test. There are speed restrictions for drivers who have held their licence for less than 2 years (110 km/h on motorways and 100 km/h on dual carriageways and 80 km/h on ordinary roads). Seatbelts are compulsory for both front and rear. Children under 10 should travel in the back, if possible. Babies and young children should be restrained appropriately, with a booster seat (**siège réhausseur**) or babyseat (**siège pour bébés**).*

Speed restrictions

built up area	50 km/h
ordinary roads	90 km/h
dual carriageway	110 km/h
motorway	130 km/h

(F)

French car ▲
nationality badge

French road signs
are colour-coded. ▼

Motorways

Primary routes

Local routes

Temporary routes

Places of interest

Direction indicators ▼

NORTH **Nord**

EAST

Ouest   ⊕   **Est**

WEST

Sud   SOUTH

◀ ROUTE
FOR HEAVY
VEHICLES

we are going to...
nous allons à...
nooz a-loñ a...

is the road good?
est-ce que la route est bonne?
ess kuh la root ay bon

is the pass open?
est-ce que le col est ouvert?
ess kuh luh kol ay oo-vehr

which is the best route?
quelle est le meilleur itinéraire?
kel ay luh may-yuhr ee-tee-nay-rehr

can you show me on the map?
pouvez-vous me montrer sur la carte?
poo-vay voo muh mon-tray soor la kart

do we need snow chains?
est-ce qu'il faut des chaînes?
ess keel foh day shen

talking

ROAD CLOSED DETOUR ▲
Follow the yellow detour signs
to rejoin your route.

GIVE WAY ▲   **SLOW DOWN** ▲

The traffic on
the roundabout
has priority.
◀ **YOU DO NOT
HAVE PRIORITY**

◀ Warning that
the crossroads
(*carrefour*) is a
roundabout (in France roundabouts
are fairly new).

◀ **LORRY EXIT**

▼ **SCHOOL EXIT**

**ROAD LIABLE
▼ TO FLOODING**

▼ **DANGER**

Signs on entering ▲
and leaving town ▼

is this the road to…?
c'est bien la route de…?
say byañ la root duh…

how do I get to…?
pour aller à…?
poor a-lay a…

I am sorry, I did not know
je suis désolé, je ne savais pas
zhuh swee day-zo-lay zhuh nuh sa-vay pa

do I have to pay the fine straight away?
est-ce qu'il faut payer l'amende tout de suite?
ess keel foh pay-ay la-moñd toot sweet

talking

*Although some portions of motorways are free around cities, you have to pay a toll if travelling over long distances. You get a ticket when you join the motorway. On leaving it you hand the ticket in at the **station péage** and the amount to pay is flashed up on an illuminated sign. Remember it is the front passenger who pays if you have a right-hand-drive car. Take care over speeding: limits are lowered in wet weather – by 20 km/h on motorways and 10 km/h on other roads.*

◀ Motorway signs are blue; local signs are white

inner ring-road

Motorway junction/exit ▼

The motorway routes ▲ signposted here are toll-paying (*péage*).

Motorway emergency phone ◀

Motorway ▶
services are
located every
30–40 km.

▲ STOP
TOLL STATION

Toll station ▲

If you break down on the motorway

If you break down on the motorway, first you should put on your hazard lights and place the warning triangle about 30 m behind the car. You should alert the police on emergency number 17 stating your exact location. If you are using an emergency SOS phone (located every 2 km along the motorway) they will know your location. The police will arrange for a recovery vehicle to come to you.

my car has broken down
ma voiture est en panne
ma vwa-toor ay oñ pan

what do I do?
qu'est-ce que je dois faire?
kess kuh zhuh dwa fehr

I am on my own (female)
je suis seule
zhuh swee suhl

my children are in the car
mes enfants sont dans la voiture
mayz oñ-foñ soñ doñ la vwa-toor

the car is near junction number...
la voiture est près de la sortie numéro...
la vwa-toor ay pray duh la sor-tee noo-may-roh...

it's a blue Fiat Uno
c'est une Fiat Uno bleue
say ooñ fee-at oo-noh bluh

registration number...
numéro d'immatriculation...
noo-may-roh dee-mat-ree-koo-las-yoñ...

In Paris, parking generally is not free. Outside Paris, in many towns, parking is only allowed on one side of the road. The system is that for the first 15 days of the month, parking is on the side of the road with odd house numbers. During the second half of the month, parking is on the even-numbered-house side.

◀ **PAYING**
Most of the time, parking is not free.

wherever you see this sign there will be some kind of parking restriction

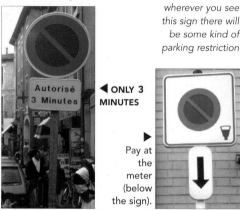

Autorisé 3 Minutes

◀ **ONLY 3 MINUTES**

▶
Pay at the meter (below the sign).

SUR LE TROTTOIR

NO PARKING ▲ ON THE PAVEMENT

Parking meter ▶

insert money

parking fee payable

daily 9 am to 12 and 2 pm to 7 pm except Sat, Sun, public holidays and the month of Aug

rates

8-hour time limit

residents pay by card (they get one at city hall)

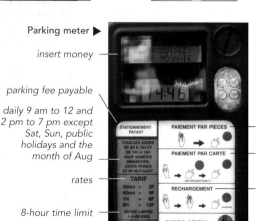

STATIONNEMENT PAYANT

TOUS LES JOURS DE 9H A 12H ET DE 14H A 19H SAUF SAMEDIS DIMANCHES, JOURS FERIES ET MOIS D'AOUT

TARIF

20mn	2F
40mn	4F
1H	6F
8H	12F

DUREE LIMITEE A 8 HEURES

RESIDANTE PAIEMENT PAR CARTE

PAIEMENT PAR PIECES

PAIEMENT PAR CARTE

RECHARGEMENT

ANNULATION

CET APPAREIL NE REND PAS LA MONNAIE
DROIT DE STATIONNEMENT EXCLUSIF DE TOUTE GARANTIE
EN CAS DE PANNE UTILISER L'APPAREIL VOISIN, MERCI

VILLE DE MONTROUGE

paying with coins

paying with a card

recharging (residents can insert coins to credit their card with more money)

cancel

OPEN 24 HOURS ▼

▲ Newer parking machines take notes and let you choose the language for your transaction.

▲ Don't be fooled: *libre* means there are spaces, not that parking is free.

▲ CAR PARK FULL

◀ Disabled parking places ▼

vehicle exit

no parking

NO PARKING ON SATURDAYS, MARKET DAY ▼

I am looking for a car park
je cherche un parking
zhuh shehrsh uñ par-keeng

can I park here?
est-ce que je peux me garer ici?
ess kuh zhuh puh muh ga-ray ee-see

the ticket machine doesn't work
l'horodateur ne marche pas
lo-ro-da-tuhr nuh marsh pa

do I need to pay?
il faut payer?
eel foh pay-ay

how long for?
pour combien de temps?
poor koñ-byañ duh toñ

talking

Petrol stations in small towns are generally manned and closed Sundays and in the evenings. The big towns have 24-hour petrol stations and you can buy petrol at some large supermarkets.

◀ Petrol pumps are colour-coded. You will find the pump number at the side.

TURN OFF ENGINE ▲

Colour-coding ▶ matches the pump handle: green for unleaded (*sans plomb*), blue for super and yellow for diesel.

Diesel is also known as *gazoil* or *gazole*. ▶

Sans Plomb 98	F/L	**7,99**
Super	F/L	**8,39**
Gazole	F/L	**5,99**

is there a petrol station near here?
est-ce qu'il y a une station-service près d'ici?
ess keel ee a oon stass-yoñ sehr-vees pray dee-see

fill it up please
le plein s'il vous plaît
luh plañ see voo play

300 francs worth of unleaded petrol
trois cents francs d'essence sans plomb
trwa soñ froñ dess-oñss soñ ploñ

I'd like to wash the car
je voudrais laver la voiture
zhuh voo-dray la-vay la vwa-toor

pump number...
pompe numéro...
poñp noo-may-roh...

how much is that?
c'est combien?
say koñ-byañ

talking

*You should carry a red warning triangle in case of breakdown.
It is also compulsory to carry a first-aid kit in the car. You will
have no trouble in France finding a **garage** to do repairs.*

Choose the car-
wash programme
you want. ▶

Multiprogrammes

3 Prélavage mousse - Lavage -
Rinçage - Cire lustrante - Séchage
Lavage Châssis

*foam prewash -
wash - rinse - wax -
dry - chassis wash*

2 Prélavage mousse - Lavage -
Rinçage - Cire lustrante - Séchage

*foam prewash -
wash - rinse -
wax - dry*

1 Lavage Rinçage - Séchage

wash - rinse - dry

I have broken down
je suis en panne
zhuh swee oñ pan

the car won't start
la voiture ne démarre pas
la vwa-toor nuh day-mar pa

I have a flat tyre
j'ai un pneu crevé
zhay uñ pnuh kruh-vay

the battery is flat
la batterie est à plat
la ba-tree ay a pla

I need tyres
j'ai besoin de pneus
zhay buh-zwañ duh pnuh

I have run out of petrol
je suis en panne d'essence
zhuh swee oñ pan dess-oñs

where is the nearest garage?
où est le garage le plus proche?
oo ay luh ga-razh luh ploo prosh

something is wrong with...
il y a un problème avec ...
eel ee a uñ pro-blehm a-vek...

the ... is not working
le/la ... ne marche pas
luh/la ... nuh marsh pa

the ... are not working
les ... ne marchent pas
lay ... nuh marsh pa

can you repair it?
est-ce que vous pouvez le réparer?
ess kuh voo poo-vay luh ray-pa-ray

how long will it take?
ça va être combien de temps?
sa va etr koñ-byañ duh toñ

when will it be ready?
il sera prêt quand?
eel suh-ra pray koñ

how much will it cost?
combien ça va coûter?
koñ-byañ sa va koo-tay

can you replace the windscreen?
pouvez-vous changer le pare-brise?
poo-vay voo shoñ-zhay luh par-breez

please check...	**the oil**	**the water**	**the tyres**
vous pouvez vérifier...	l'huile	l'eau	les pneus
voo poo-vay ve-ree-fyay...	*lweel*	*loh*	*lay pnuh*

talking talking talking talking talking talking

SHOPPING

Many shops are closed on Sundays and Monday morning. There are no markets on Mondays. Shops generally open at 9 am and close for lunch around 1 pm. Business resumes between 2 and 4 pm and the shops stay open until 8 pm.

boulangerie
boo-loñzh-ree
baker's

boucherie
boosh-ree
butcher's

charcuterie
shar-koot-ree
delicatessen

épicerie
ay-pees-ree
grocer's

alimentation générale
a-lee-moñ-tass-yoñ zhay-nay-ral
food shop

pâtisserie
pa-teess-ree
cake shop

supermarché
soo-pehr-marsh-ay
supermarket

diététique
dee-ay-tay-teek
health food

pharmacie
far-ma-see
pharmacy

▲ *Alimentation générale* is the classic corner shop. It stays open late and on Sun and is generally open when everything else is closed. It sells drinks (including alcohol), fruit and veg, bread and all kind of things. These shops are handy but their prices are about 20–30% dearer than supermarkets.

◄ The pharmacy symbol. You can buy nappies and baby food here but it tends to be more expensive than at the supermarket.

SHUT FOR A ►
SHORT WHILE

FERMETURE MOMENTANÉE

◄ Remember that the *tabac*, identified by the red lozenge, provides an indispensable service: as well as being a café, it sells stamps, envelopes, metro tickets and a host of other things.

Boucherie

Butcher's ▲

Pâtés, sausages, ham
▼ and other pork products

Charcuterie

*Supermarkets are generally open from 8.30 am to 8.30 pm Monday to Friday and 8.30 am to 8 pm on Saturday. They are shut on Sundays. Among the big chains are **Géant**, **Intermarché**, **Cora** and **Carrefour**. Most products are cheaper than in smaller shops. Postcards are also much cheaper than in tourist shops. You can also get petrol at many of the larger ones.*

◀ You must weigh fruit and veg before taking it to the till. The machine issues the price ticket which you stick to the bag or item. An alphabetical list of fruit and veg on the machine has pictures to identify each item. ▼

▲ **Géant** supermarket ad. Heading for Lorient on **Route nationale** 165, take **Parc des Expositions** exit.

milk

sauces

◀ You need a 10F coin to release the trolley.

where can I buy...?	**batteries**
où est-ce que je peux acheter...?	des piles
oo ess kuh zhuh puh ash-tay...	*day peel*

a tin-opener
un ouvre-boîtes
un oovr-bwat

do you have...?
est-ce que vous avez...?
ess kuh vooz a-vay...

how much is it?
c'est combien?
say koñ-byañ

I am looking for...
je cherche...
zhuh shehrsh uñ ka-doh...

a present
un cadeau
uñ ka-doh

a good wine
un bon vin
uñ boñ vañ

is there a market?
est-ce qu'il y a un marché?
ess keel ee a uñ mar-shay

which day?
quel jour?
kel zhoor

can I pay with this card?
je peux payer avec cette carte?
zhuh puh pay-ay a-vek set kart

talking talking talking

*Quantities are expressed in kilos and grams. **Une livre** (meaning pound) is very frequently used in markets and shops but it refers to half a kilo, i.e. 500g. In everyday language, **une livre**, and **une demi-livre** (roughly equivalent to 1lb and 1/2 lb) are often preferred to 500g (**cinq cents grammes**) and 250g (**deux cent cinquante grammes**). And they are easier to say! Remember to begin any shopping requests with **Bonjour Monsieur** or **Bonjour Madame**, as the French do.*

The standard French stick is a **baguette**. The thinner version is **une ficelle**, the fatter version **un pain**. Some bakers specialise in different types of bread: **seigle** (rye), **complet** (wholemeal), **châtaignes** (chestnut) and **olives** (olive).

▲ Bread is bought freshly baked, whether from the local food shop, the baker's or the supermarket. Bakers bake at least twice a day and they also sell snacks.

◀ Milk comes in the three varieties: wholemilk **entier**, semi-skimmed **demi-écrémé**, and skimmed **écrémé**.

There are over 350 varieties of French cheeses (one for every day of the year). If you want to buy cheese at the **fromager**, you could ask, pointing to the one you want, **un morceau de ce fromage, s'il vous plaît**.

◀

MADE WITH UNPASTEURISED MILK

▲ Nearly everything is sold by the kilo, but you buy ham by the slice, *à la tranche*.

▲ Eggs are sometimes sold individually, *à la pièce*.

PRODUIT DE L'AGRICULTURE BIOLOGIQUE

6 Œufs Biologiques

PRODUIT DE L'AGRICULTURE BIOLOGIQUE

▲ Organic eggs.

CERTIFIÉ

AB

AGRICULTURE BIOLOGIQUE

◀ Sign for organic produce

A EMPORTER

▲ TAKE-AWAY

Valeurs nutritionnelles moyennes pour 100g
Av. nutritional values per 100g ▼

energy (calories)	Valeur énergétique	64 kcal (271 kJ)
protein	Protéines	3,15g
carbohydrates	Glucides	4,9g
fat	Lipides	3,6g

a piece of that cheese
un morceau de ce fromage
uñ mor-soh duh suh froh-mazh

a little more
un peu plus
uñ puh plooss

a little less
un peu moins
uñ puh mwañ

that's fine thanks
ça suffit merci
sa soo-fee mehr-see

10 slices of ham
dix tranches de jambon
dee troñsh duh zhoñ-boñ

thick slices
des tranches épaisses
day troñsh ay-pess

thin slices
des tranches fines
day troñsh feen

a carton of milk
un carton de lait
uñ kar-toñ duh lay

a bottle of mineral water
une bouteille d'eau minérale
oon boo-tay doh mee-neh-ral

still	**sparkling**
plate	gazeuse
plat	*gaz-uhz*

a tin of...
une boîte de...
oon bwat duh...

a jar of...	**a packet of...**
un pot de...	un paquet de...
uñ poh duh...	*uñ pa-kay duh...*

a bottle of...
une bouteille de...
oon boo-tay duh...

that is everything thanks
c'est tout merci
say too mehr-see

a plastic bag please
un sac en plastique s'il vous plaît
uñ sak oñ plas-teek see voo play

*If you want some of something, change **le** to **du**, **la** to **de la** and **les** to **des**. If you want low fat versions, look out for the words **diet**, **light** and **minceur**. The word for frozen is **surgelé**.*

Everyday Foods l'épicerie *lay-pees-ree*

bread	le pain *pañ*
bread stick	la baguette *ba-get*
bread roll	le petit pain *puh-tee pañ*
sliced bread	le pain en tranches *pañ oñ troñsh*
butter	le beurre *buhr*
cereal	les céréales *say-ray-al*
cheese	le fromage *fro-mazh*
chicken	le poulet *poo-leh*
coffee	le café *ka-fay*
cream	la crème *krem*
crisps	les chips *sheeps*
eggs	les œufs *uh*
fish	le poisson *pwas-soñ*
flour	la farine *fareen*
ham *(cooked)*	le jambon cuit *zhoñ-boñ kwee*
ham *(cured)*	le jambon cru *zhoñ-boñ kroo*
herbal tea	la tisane *tee-zan*
honey	le miel *myel*
jam	la confiture *koñ-fee-toor*
juice	le jus de fruits *zhoo duh frwee*
margarine	la margarine *mar-ga-reen*
marmalade	la confiture d'orange *koñ-fee-toor do-roñzh*
meat	la viande *vyoñd*
milk	le lait *lay*
mustard	la moutarde *moo-tard*
oil	l'huile *weel*
orange juice	le jus d'orange *zhoo do-roñzh*
pasta	les pâtes *pat*
pepper	le poivre *pwavr*
rice	le riz *ree*
salt	le sel *sel*
sugar	le sucre *sookr*
stock cube	le bouillon cube *boo-yoñ koob*
tea	le thé *tay*
tomatoes *(tin)*	la boîte de tomates *bwat duh to-mat*
tuna *(tin)*	la boîte de thon *bwat duh toñ*
vinegar	le vinaigre *vee-negr*
yoghurt	le yaourt *ya-oort*

The best place to buy fresh fruit and vegetables is the local market. There is no market on Mondays.

Fruit	les fruits *frwee*
apples	les pommes *pom*
apricots	les abricots *a-bree-ko*
bananas	les bananes *ba-nan*
cherries	les cerises *suh-reez*
figs	les figues *feeg*
grapefruit	le pamplemousse *poñ-pluh-moos*
grapes	le raisin *ray-zañ*
lemon	le citron *seet-roñ*
melon	le melon *muh-loñ*
nectarines	les nectarines *nek-ta-reen*
oranges	les oranges *o-roñzh*
peaches	les pêches *pesh*
pears	les poires *pwahr*
pineapple	l'ananas *ana-na*
plums	les prunes *proon*
raspberries	les framboises *froñ-bwaz*
strawberries	les fraises *frez*
watermelon	la pastèque *pas-tek*

Vegetables	les légumes *leay-goom*
artichokes	les artichaux *ar-tee-shoh*
aubergines	les aubergines *oh-ber-zheen*
asparagus	les asperges *asperzh*
carrots	les carottes *ka-rot*
cauliflower	le chou-fleur *shoo-fluhr*
celery	le céleri *say-luh-ree*
courgettes	les courgettes *koor-zhet*
cucumber	le concombre *koñ-kombr*
French beans	les haricots verts *a-ree-koh vehr*
garlic	l'ail *eye*
leeks	les poireaux *pwa-roh*
lettuce	la laitue *lay-too*
mushrooms	les champignons *shoñ-pee-nyoñ*
onions	les oignons *on-yoñ*
peas	les petits pois *puh-tee pwa*
peppers	les poivrons *pwa-vroñ*
potatoes	les pommes de terre *pom duh ter*
radishes	les radis *ra-dee*
spinach	les épinards *ay-pee-nard*
spring onions	les ciboules *see-bool*
tomatoes	les tomates *to-mat*
turnip	les navets *na-vay*

*There are a number of good French department stores. Look out for **Printemps**, **Monoprix** and **Galeries Lafayette**. They are generally open from about 9.30 am to 7 pm, Monday to Saturday with late-night shopping on Thursdays.*

grand magasin
groñ ma-ga-zañ
department store

sous-sol
soo-sol
basement

rez-de-chaussée
ray-duh-shoh-say
ground floor

premier étage
pruhm-yehr ay-tazh
first floor

rayon
ray-oñ
department

électroménager
el-ek-troh-meh-na-zhay
electrical goods

bijouterie
bee-zhoo-tree
jewellery

femme
fam
ladies'

homme
om
men's

enfant
oñ-foñ
children's

◀ SALES EVERYTHING MUST GO

SOLDES TOUT DOIT DISPARAITRE *de* -20% *à* -50% SOLDES

Department store: *Galeries Lafayette* ▶

SPECIAL OFFERS ▶

talking

which floor is...?
quel étage est...?
kel ay-tazh ay...

the lingerie department
le rayon lingerie
luh ray-oñ loñzh-ree

the shoe department
le rayon chaussures
luh ray-oñ shoh-soor

the food department
le rayon alimentation
luh ray-oñ a-lee-moñ-tass-yoñ

Women's clothes sizes

UK/Australia	8	10	12	14	16	18	20	22
Europe	36	38	40	42	44	46	48	50
US/Canada	6	8	10	12	14	16	18	20

Men's clothes sizes (suits)

UK/US/Canada	36	38	40	42	44	46
Europe	46	48	50	52	54	56
Australia	92	97	102	107	112	117

Shoes

UK/Australia	2	3	4	5	6	7	8	9	10	11
Europe	35	36	37	38	39	41	42	43	45	46
US/Canada women	4	5	6	7	8	9	10	11	12	-
US/Canada men	3	4	5	6	7	8	9	10	11	12

Children's Shoes

UK/US/Canada	0	1	2	3	4	5	6	7	8	9	10	11
Europe	15	17	18	19	20	22	23	24	26	27	28	29

do you have size...?
est-ce que vous avez la taille...?
ess kuh vooz a-vay la tye...

do you have this in my size?
est-ce que vous avez ça dans ma taille?
ess kuh vooz a-vay sa doñ ma tye

it is too big
c'est trop grand
say troh groñ

I'm just looking
je regarde seulement
zhuh ruh-gard suhl-moñ

do you have a smaller/larger size?
vous l'avez en plus petit/grand?
voo lav-ay oñ ploo puh-tee/groñ

can I try this on?
est-ce que je peux l'essayer?
ess kuh zhuh puh leh-say-ay

shoe size...
la pointure...
la pwañ-toor...

I take size...
je fais du...
zhuh fay doo...

it is too small
c'est trop petit
say troh puh-tee

where are the changing rooms?
où sont les cabines d'essayage?
oo soñ lay ka-been deh-say-yazh

do you have it in other colours?
vous avez ça dans d'autres coloris?
vooz a-vay sa doñ dotr ko-lo-ree

talking talking talking

*You can buy stamps at the **tabac** or at the post office. In Paris and big towns, the post office is open 8 am to 7 pm Monday to Friday and until 12 pm on Saturdays. In smaller towns the hours may be reduced, so the morning is the best time to go.*

▲ Logo of the French Post Office

French letter boxes are yellow. ▲

▼ Parisian letter-boxes have two slots.

Paris & region

elsewhere in France & abroad

last collection 4 pm weekdays 1 pm Sat

nearest post office

where is the post office?
où est la poste?
oo ay la post

do you sell stamps?
est-ce que vous vendez des timbres?
ess kuh voo voñ-day day tañbr

10 stamps please
dix timbres s'il vous plaît
dee tañbr see voo play

for postcards
pour carte postales
poor kart pos-tal

for letters
pour lettres
poor letr

to Europe
pour l'Europe
poor luh-rop

to America
pour les États-Unis
poor layz ay-ta oo-nee

to Australia
pour l'Australie
poor lo-stra-lee

I want to stay this registered
je voudrais l'envoyer en recommandé
zhuh voo-dray loñ-vwa-yay oñ ruh-kom-oñ-day

I want to send this parcel
je voudrais envoyer ce colis
zhuh voo-dray oñ-vwa-yay suh ko-lee

fast mail
poste prioritaire
post pree-o-ree-tehr

surface
par voie normale
par vwa nor-mal

airmail
par avion
par av-yoñ

talking talking

◀ Stamp machine selling books of 10 3F stamps. One stamp carries a letter or postcard within Europe.

INFORMATION ▲

COUNTERS ▼

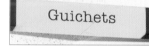

▲ Self-service franking machine
Instructions are in English as well as French.

keywords

pellicule
pe-lee-kool
film

pile
peel
battery

en mat
oñ mat
mat

en brillant
oñ bree-yoñt
glossy

caméscope
kam-eh-skop
camcorder

cassettes
kas-set
tapes

I want to buy film
je voudrais acheter des pellicules
zhuh voo-dray ash-tay day pel-lee-kool

tapes for this camcorder
des cassettes pour ce caméscope
day kass-et poor suh kam-e-skop

a colour film
une pellicule couleur
oon pe-lee-kool

with ... pictures
de ... vues
duh ... voo

a slide film
une pellicule pour diapositives
oon pe-lee-kool poor dee-a-po-zee-teev

24
vingt-quatre
vañ-katr

36
trente-six
troñt-sees

can you develop this film?
est-ce que vous pouvez développer cette pellicule?
ess kuh voo poo-vay dayv-lo-pay set pe-lee-kool

when will the photos be ready?
quand est-ce que les photos seront prêtes?
koñt ess kuh lay foh-toh suh-roñ pret

can we take pictures here?
est-ce qu'on peut prendre des photos ici?
ess koñ puh proñdr lay foh-toh ee-see

could you take a picture of us?
est-ce que vous pourriez nous prendre en photo?
ess kuh voo poo-ree-ay noo proñdr oñ foh-toh

talking talking talking talking talking

PHONES

*Coin phones are extremely scarce. The numerous phone boxes all operate with a phonecard, **une télécarte**, which you can buy in metro stations, in **tabacs** or at the Post Office. Cheap rates with French Telecom are from 7 pm to 8 am during the week, and from 2 pm on Saturday and on Sunday (you get 50% extra time).*

▲ Variety of phonecards

Public phone
Many public phones also work with credit cards. ▶

talking talking talking talking

do you sell phonecards?
est-ce que vous vendez des télécartes?
ess kuh voo voñ-day day te-le-kart

a phonecard please
une télécarte s'il vous plaît
oon te-le-kart seel voo play

Mr Lebrun please
Monsieur Lebrun s'il vous plaît
muh-syuh luh-bruñ seel voo play

can I speak to Paul?
je peux parler à Paul?
zhuh puh par-lay a paul

I'd like an outside line please
je voudrais la ligne s'il vous plaît
zhuh voo-dray la leen-yuh see voo play

I'd like to make a reverse charge call
je voudrais téléphoner en PCV
zhuh voo-dray te-le-fo-nay oñ pay-say-vay

what is your phone number?
quel est votre numéro de téléphone?
kel ay votr noo-may-ro duh te-le-fon

the smallest amount
le minimum
luh mee-nee-muhm

extension...
le poste...
luh post...

this is Caroline
c'est Caroline à l'appareil
say caroline a la-pa-ray

hello? *(on phone)*
allô?
a-loh

my number is...
voici mon numéro...
vwa-see moñ noo-may-ro...

◀ Instructions for use and emergency numbers are translated into English at some call boxes. You can make phone calls and also receive them. The number of the phonebox is on the top line.

Pick up the receiver first then insert a phonecard or credit card, or dial the free emergency number. ▼

décrochez
pick up

swipe your
credit card here

insert your
phonecard
here

télécarte
te-le-kart
phonecard

numéro vert
noo-may-ro vert
freephone

indicatif
een-dee-ka-teef
dialling code

renseignements
roñ-sen-yuh-moñ
directory
enquiries

pages jaunes
pazh zhohn
yellow pages

annuaire
a-noo-ehr
phone directory

I will call back
je vais rappeler
je vay rap-lay

later
plus tard
ploo tar

tomorrow
demain
duh-mañ

do you have a mobile?
vous avez un portable?
vooz a-vay uñ por-tabl

when can I call you?
quand est-ce que je peux vous téléphoner?
koñt ess kuh zhuh puh voo te-le-fo-nay

what is your mobile number?
quel est le numéro de votre portable?
kel ay luh noo-may-roh duh votr por-tabl

my mobile number is...
mon numéro de portable est...
moñ noo-may-roh duh por-tabl ay

Internet cafés are not very common. You generally pay by the hour. There are internet consoles in some post offices and at RER stations.

keywords keywords keywords

aide
ed
help

ordinateur
or-dee-na-tuhr
computer

mot de passe
mo duh pass
password

cliquez ici
klee-kay ee-see
click here

mise à jour
meez a zhoor
updated

écran
ay-krañ
screen

arrobase
a-ro-baz
at (@)

◄ Internet café
You go in and pay
for time online.

talking talking talking

what is your e-mail address?
quelle est votre adresse e-mail?
kel ay votr ad-ress e-mel

my e-mail address is...
mon adresse e-mail est...
moñ ad-ress e-mehl ay...

caroline.smith@anycompany.co.uk
caroline point smith arrobase anycompany point co point uk
caroline pwañ smith a-ro-baz anycompany pwañ co point uk

can I send an e-mail?
je peux envoyer un e-mail?
zhuh puh oñ-vwa-yay un e-mel

it is not working
ça ne marche pas
sa nuh marsh pa

did you get my e-mail?
est-ce que vous avez reçu mon e-mail?
ess-kuh vooz av-ay ruh-soo moñ e-mel

how much is it for one hour?
c'est combien pour une heure?
say koñ-byañ poor <u>oon</u> uhr

▲ You can access the internet in some larger post offices.

▲ The French word for @ is **arrobase**.

souris
soo-ree
mouse

tapis de souris
ta-pee duh soo-ree
mouse mat

site web
seet web
website

point
pwañ
dot

recherche
ruh-shehrsh
search

retour à
ruh-toor a
return to

icône
ee-kon
icon

keywords keywords keywords

send faxes — **Fax** Emission/Réception — receive faxes

I want to send a fax
je voudrais envoyer un fax
zhuh voo-dray oñ-vwa-yay uñ faks

do you have a fax?
est-ce que vous avez un fax?
ess-kuh vooz av-ay uñ faks

can I send a fax from here?
est-ce que je peux envoyer un fax d'ici?
ess kuh zhuh puh oñ-vwa-yay uñ faks dee-see

can I receive a fax here?
je peux recevoir un fax ici?
zhuh puh ruh-suh-vwar uñ faks ee-see

how much is it to send a fax?
c'est combien pour envoyer un fax?
say koñ-byañ poor oñ-vwa-yay uñ faks

what is your fax number?
quel est votre numéro de fax?
kel ay votr noo-may-roh duh faks

there is a problem with your fax
il y a un problème avec votre fax
eel ee a uñ prob-lehm a-vek votr faks

did you get my fax?
est-ce que vous avez reçu mon fax?
ess kuh vooz av-ay ruh-soo moñ faks

talking talking talking

OUT & ABOUT

*Tourist offices are known as **Offices de Tourisme** and **Syndicats d'initiative**. Most towns will have one and they can help with accommodation, what is on in the area, local transport and places to eat.*

▲ Tourist information

Paris sign indicating place of historic interest. ▶

caveau dégustation wine-tasting cellars

Musée
- **Collections**
- **Atelier Brancusi**

Muncipal museums close on Mon. National museums close on Tue (except Musée d'Orsay, Trianon Palace and Versailles), so check before you set off. For national museums there is an entrance fee (sometimes they are free on Sun). They are free for under 18s and there are reductions for 18–25-year-olds and for over 60s. Most towns have municipal museums offering free Sun admission. Under 7s and over 60s go free.

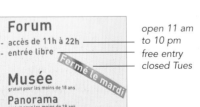

Forum
- accès de 11h à 22h
- entrée libre

Fermé le mardi

Musée
gratuit pour les moins de 18 ans

Panorama
gratuit pour les moins de 18 ans

Expositions

open 11 am to 10 pm
free entry
closed Tues

Most towns generally have a guide to the area. It is full of useful information such as emergency numbers for police, doctor, dentist and hospital; and details of on hotels, restaurants, shops, sporting activities, etc. ▶

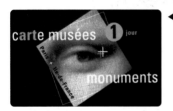

◀ Museum card

In Paris, the Parisian transport authority (RATP) organizes bicycle rentals and guided rides at many metro stations. Follow the *Roue Libre* sign.
▶

◀ *Randonnée en roller* RATP-organized rollerblade tours start at *Place de la Bastille* at 10 pm every Fri night and also on Sun afternoons.

keywords keywords keywords

animation
a-nee-mass-yoñ
show

exposition
eks-poh-zee-syoñ
exhibition

randonnée
roñ-don-ay
trek, ramble

dégustation
deh-goo-stass-yoñ
wine tasting

foire
fwar
fair

église
ay-gleez
church

cathédrale
ka-tay-dral
cathedral

château
sha-toh
castle

hôtel de ville
oh-tel duh veel
town hall

talking talking talking

where is the tourist office?
où est le syndicat d'initiative?
oo ay luh sañ-dee-ka dee-nees-ya-teev

do you have...?
vous avez...?
vooz a-vay...

a map of the town
un plan de la ville
uñ ploñ duh la veel

leaflets in English
des brochures en anglais
day broh-shoor on oñ-glay

we want to visit...
nous voudrions visiter...
noo vood-ree-yoñ vee-zee-tay...

is it open to the public?
c'est ouvert au public?
say oo-vehr oh poob-leek

when can we visit the...?
quand est-ce qu'on peut visiter...?
koñt ess koñ puh vee-zee-tay...

when does it close?
ça ferme à quelle heure?
sa fehrm a kel uhr

are there any sightseeing tours?
est-ce qu'il y a des visites guidées?
ess keel ee a day vee-zeet gee-day

*You will be able to find out about sporting activities from the local tourist office. They will also be listed in the local **Guide pratique et touristique**.*

▼ Beach information board

unsupervised beach

no nudism

🛁	**Baignade**	*swimming*
	Pêche	*fishing*
	Piscine découverte	*open-air pool*
🎾	**Tennis**	*tennis*
🏇	**Equitation**	*horse-riding*
🚶	**Randonnée pédestre**	*trekking*
⛷	**Ski de fond**	*cross-country skiing*
🛶	**Canoë-kayak**	*canoeing*
🧗	**Escalade**	*rock climbing*
	Spéléologie	*potholing*

▲ Leaflets detail local sporting facilities.

Initiation
BEGINNERS ▲

LOCATION
FOR HIRE ▲

Piscine
SWIMMING ▲
POOL

▼ Details of the swimming pool

PISCINE ....
Boulevard de l'Europe   ✆ 03 84 24 27 94
Bassin couvert, bassin olympique en plein air, pataugeoire et fosse à plongeons.

covered pool   *open-air olympic pool*   *paddling pool*   *diving pool*

where can we...?
où est-ce qu'on peut...?
oo ess koñ puh...

how much is it to...?
c'est combien pour...?
say koñ-byañ poor...

per hour/day
par heure/jour
par uhr/zhoor

is there a swimming pool?
est-ce qu'il y a une piscine?
ess keel ee a oon pee-seen

where can we...?
où est-ce qu'on peut faire...?
oo ess koñ puh fehr...

play tennis
jouer au tennis
zhoo-ay oh ten-eess

hire bikes
louer des vélos
loo-ay day vay-loh

can we hire skis?
on peut louer des skis?
oñ puh loo-ay day skee

is it dangerous to swim here?
c'est dangereux de nager ici?
say doñ-zhuh-ruh duh na-zhay ee-see

windsurf
du surf
doo suhrf

play golf
jouer au golf
zhoo-ay oh golf

go riding
faire du cheval
fehr doo shuh-val

waterski
du ski nautique
doo skee noh-teek

where can we hire a beach umbrella?
où est-ce qu'on peut louer un parasol?
oo ess koñ puh loo-ay uñ pa-ra-sol

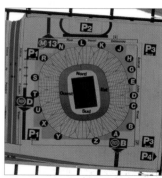

VENTE BILLETS

▲ Tickets at football stadium

Stadium seating plan ▲

LE PLUS BEAU LIEU DE RENCONTRE

ENTREE ACREDITES

▲ Season ticket entrance

OBJETS INTERDITS

**ARMES
COUTEAUX
BOUTEILLES EN VERRE**

ET TOUS OBJETS CONTONDANTS

▲ FORBIDDEN OBJECTS: GUNS,
KNIVES, GLASS BOTTLES

Stade de France flags ▲

we'd like to go to a football match
nous voudrions aller à un match de football
noo vood-reè-yoñ a-lay a uñ match duh foot-bol

who is playing?
qui joue?
kee zhoo

where can we get tickets?
où est-ce qu'on peut avoir des billets?
oo ess koñ puh av-war day bee-yay

how do we get to the stadium?
pour aller au stade?
poor a-lay oh stad

what time is the match?
à quelle heure commence le match?
a kel uhr koh-moñss luh match

talking

ACCOMMODATION

*French hotels operate a star system (1- to 4-star, and luxury). You can get great value from 1-star hotels. Increasingly, there is bed & breakfast (**chambre d'hôte** or **chambres chez l'habitant**).*

▲ The number 2000 indicates that this hotel has received classification for that particular year.

You won't have to hand in your passport, but you may be asked to fill in a *Fiche d'etranger* form giving your passport number. ▶

FICHE D'ÉTRANGER
CH. N°
NOM : *Name in capital letters / Name in Druckschrift* (*écrire en majuscules*)
Nom de jeune fille : *Maiden Name / Mädchenname*
Prénoms : *Christian Names / Vornamen*
Date de naissance : *Date of birth / Geburtsdatum*
Lieu de naissance : *Place of birth / Geburtsort*
Domicile habituel : *Permanent address / Gewöhnlicher Wohnort*
Profession : *Occupation / Beruf*
Nationalité : *Nationality / Nationalität*
Passeport n° : *Pass / Ausweis*
Date d'arrivée en France : *Date of arrival in France / Einreisedatum in Frankreich*
Date probable de sortie : *Probable date of your way out / Voraussichtliches Ausreisedatum*
le
Signature : *Unterschrift :*
Nombre d'enfants de moins de 15 ans accompagnant le voyageur / *Accompanying children under 15 / Zahl der begleitenden Kinder unter 15 Jahren*
Modèle déposé ORLAND - Réf. ORL. 298 (01.96) - distribué par JurisFormulaires

Booking in advance

You can contact the hotel direct buy you will be required to pay a deposit (arrhes) of approximately 25% of the bill. This is non-refundable if you cancel your booking.

I would like to book a room
je voudrais réserver une chambre
zhuh vood-ray ray-zayr-vay <u>oo</u>n shoñbr

a single/a double
pour une personne/deux personnes
poor <u>oo</u>n pehr-son/duh pehr-son

for ... nights
pour ... nuits
poor ... nwee

from ... to...
du ... au...
<u>doo</u> ... oh...

I will fax to confirm
je confirme par fax
zhuh koñ-feerm par faks

my name is ...
je m'appelle ...
zhuh ma-pel...

my credit card number is...
voici le numéro de ma carte de crédit...
vwa-see luh noo-may-ro duh ma kart duh kray-dee...

I will arrive at...
j'arrive à...
zha-reev a...

◀ Some places detail on boards exactly what you can expect to pay. ▶

room from 230f to 290f breakfast 28f

our rooms have shower, en-suite toilet, direct-dial phone, colour TV

from Jun to Sep restaurant service

CHAMBRES CHEZ L'HABITANT

SITUATION NOM	LITS 90 *=120	LITS 140 *=160	TARIFS nuit	semaine	Aménagements - Services J = Jardin C = cour T = Terrasse TV= Télévision ANCV= Chèques Vacances
Lavande		2	290	2030	Dans l'ancien château de Bessas
Hellebore	1		290	2030	4 chambres classées *3 Epis Prestige*.
Santoline	3		290	2030	*PISCINE*, Cour, prix pour 2 pers Petits déj. compris.
Eglantine	1		290	2030	Salon, terrasse jardin, ANCV.
Les Monteils	1		260	1820	Salon TV, J, C, Petits Déj. compris. SE & WC privés.
	1		260	1820	Chambres classées *3 Epis*, Rivière à 500 m. ANCV
Mas des	1		220	1400	*PISCINE* communes aux 6 chambres, jardin - terrasse.
Roches	2		220	1400	Certaines chambres sont équipées de SE & WC privés, d'autres avec SE & WC communs.
	2	1	200	1260	Le petit déjeuner est à la demande, les chambres sont classées *1 Clé*. ANCV.
	2	1	360	2520	Le prix est ici indiqué pour 4 personnes, chambre *2 Clés*.

◀ Leaflet detailing facilities at *Chambres chez l'habitant* (bed & breakfasts).

do you have a room for tonight?
est-ce que vous avez une chambre pour ce soir?
ess kuh vooz av-ay <u>oo</u>n shoñbr poor suh swar

with twin beds
avec deux lits
a-vek duh lee

a single room
pour une personne
poor <u>oo</u>n pehr-son

a double room
pour deux personnes
poor duh pehr-son

a family room
pour une famille
poor <u>oo</u>n fa-mee

with ensuite bath
avec bain
a-vek bañ

with shower
avec douche
a-vek doosh

with a double bed
avec un grand lit
a-vek uñ groñ lee

for tonight
pour ce soir
poor se swar

for one night
pour une nuit
poor <u>oo</u>n nwee

for... nights
pour ... nuits
poor ... nwee

how much is it per night?
c'est combien par nuit?
say koñ-byañ par nwee

is breakfast included?
le petit déjeuner est compris?
luh puh-tee day-zhuh-nay ay koñ-pree

how much is half board?
c'est combien la demi-pension?
say koñ-byañ la duh-mee poñ-syoñ

I'd like to see the room
je voudrais voir la chambre
zhuh voo-dray vwar la shoñbr

what time should we check out?
à quelle heure est-ce qu'il faut quitter la chambre?
a kel uhr ess-keel foh kee-tay la shoñbr

▲ You will find all sorts of accommodation on offer in tourist areas.

- **16 appartements**
  1 à 4 personnes
  low season — Basse saison :
  1960 F la semaine
  high season — Haute saison :
  2205 F la semaine

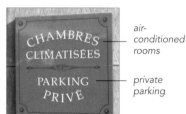

air-conditioned rooms

private parking

◀ Rubbish is collected from street bins daily. Recycling bins are often available. This one takes all types of glass (*verre*).

Students' rooms to let ▼

RECOMMANDATIONS

items left in vehicles in this car park by their owners are left at their own risk

LES OBJETS (bagages, vêtements, matériels,...) LAISSÉS PAR LEURS PROPRIETAIRES DANS LES VEHICULES GARES SUR CE PARKING LE SONT SOUS LEUR PROPRE RESPONSABILITÉ.

we recommend to our customers to check that their car boots are locked and that nothing of value is left inside the car

NOUS RECOMMANDONS A NOS CLIENTS DE VERIFIER QUE LES PORTIERES DE LEURS VEHICULES SONT SOIGNEUSEMENT VERROUILLÉES ET DE VEILLER A NE LAISSER AUCUN OBJET DE VALEUR A L'INTERIEUR DE CEUX-CI.

valuable items can be left at the hotel reception

LES OBJETS DE VALEUR PEUVENT ETRE CONFIES A LA RECEPTION DE L'HOTEL.

REMERCIEMENTS

LA DIRÉCTION

Hotel parking ▶

▲ Youth hostels (*Auberges de la Jeunesse*) are signposted locally.

▲ The symbol of the French Youth Hostel Federation.

▲ Separate areas for laundry and washing-up are clearly signposted. ▼

► INFORMATION/ RECEPTION

SHOWERS ▲
8.30 AM TO 10.30 AM
5.30 PM TO 7.30 PM

can you show us how this works?
est-ce que vous pouvez nous montrer comment ça marche?
ess kuh voo poo-vay noo moñ-tray koh-moñ sa marsh

how does … work?	**the cooker**	**the washing machine**
comment fonctionne…?	la cuisinière	la machine à laver
ko-moñ foñks-yon…	*la kwee-zeen-yehr*	*la ma-sheen a la-vay*
	the dishwasher	**the microwave**
	le lave-vaisselle	le micro-ondes
	luh lav-ve-sel	*luh mee-kro-oñd*

who do we contact if there are problems?
qui faut-il contacter s'il y a un problème?
kee foht-eel koñ-tak-tay seel ee a uñ prob-lem

there is/are no…   **the sink is blocked**
il n'y a pas de…   l'évier est bouché
eel nee a pa duh…   *lay-vyay ay boo-shay*

where do I leave the rubbish?
où est-ce que je dois mettre la poubelle?
oo ess kuh zhuh dwa metr la poo-bel

we'd like an extra key
nous voudrions une autre clé
noo voo-dree-oñ oon otr klay

talking talking talking talking talking

CAMPING

lessive
less-eev
washing powder

savon
sa-voñ
soap

ouvre-boîtes
oovr-bwat
tin-opener

tire-bouchon
teer-boo-shoñ
corkscrew

allumettes
a-<u>loo</u>-met
matches

bougies
boo-zhee
candles

bouteille de gaz
boo-tay duh gaz
gas cylinder

◀ CAMPING
ON THE
FARM

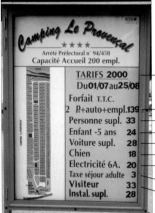

◀ Campsites
display prices
and are
star-rated.

Camping Le Provençal
★★★★
Arrêté Préfectoral n° 94/450
Capacité Accueil 200 empl.

	TARIFS 2000 Du01/07au25/08	
Forfait T.T.C.		
2 P+auto+empl.	139	2 people & car & caravan
Personne supl.	33	extra person
Enfant -5 ans	24	child under 5
Voiture supl.	28	extra car
Chien	18	dog
Electricité 6A.	20	electricity
Taxe séjour adulte	3	adult tax per day
Visiteur	33	visitor
Instal. supl.	28	

tariffs for 2000

FULL ▶

COMPLET

is there a campsite near here?
est-ce qu'il y a un camping près d'ici?
ess keel a uñ koñ-peeng pray dee-see

have you any vacancies?
est-ce que vous avez des places?
ess kuh vooz av-ay day plass

we want to stay for … nights
nous voudrions rester … nuits
noo voo-dree-oñ res-tay … nwee

how much is it…?
c'est combien…?
say koñ-byañ…

per tent
pour une tente
poor <u>oon</u> toñt

per caravan
pour une caravane
poor <u>oon</u> ka-ra-van

is there a restaurant on the campsite?
est-ce qu'il y a un restaurant dans le camping?
ess keel a uñ res-to-roñ doñ luh koñ-peeng

can we have a more sheltered site?
est-ce que nous pouvons avoir un emplacement plus abrité?
ess kuh noo poo-voñ av-war un oñ-plass-moñ plooz ab-ree-tay

can we camp here overnight?
est-ce qu'on pourrait camper ici cette nuit?
ess koñ poo-ray koñ-pay ee-see set nwee

LAUNDERETTES

◀ Launderette and dry cleaning

◀ Most launderettes are self-service and entirely automatic; there is no-one to attend to the customer.

LESSIVES A MAIN INTERDITES

◀ HAND WASHING FORBIDDEN

▼ WASHING INSTRUCTIONS

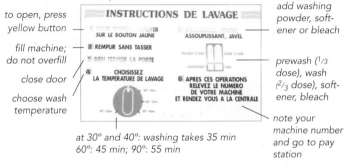

INSTRUCTIONS DE LAVAGE

to open, press yellow button

fill machine; do not overfill

close door

choose wash temperature

add washing powder, softener or bleach

prewash ($1/3$ dose), wash ($2/3$ dose), softener, bleach

note your machine number and go to pay station

at 30° and 40°: washing takes 35 min
60°: 45 min; 90°: 55 min

Payment centre ▶

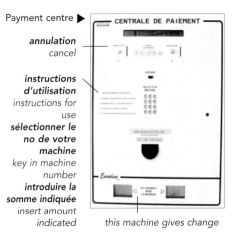

CENTRALE DE PAIEMENT

annulation
cancel

instructions d'utilisation
instructions for use

sélectionner le no de votre machine
key in machine number

introduire la somme indiquée
insert amount indicated

this machine gives change

SPECIAL NEEDS

Facilities for the disabled are gradually improving, but it is still quite difficult to get around using public transport.

ÊTES-VOUS SÛR
QUE CES PLACES
VOUS SOIENT RÉSERVÉES ?

EMPLACEMENTS
RÉSERVÉS

Are you sure these places are reserved for you?

disabled parking

TARIFS REDUITS

▲ Reduced tariffs for disabled (*handicapé*) and children (*enfants*)

▼ Disabled access

TOILETTES
LAVATORY
TOILETTEN

◀ Disabled toilet

are there any disabled toilets?
est-ce qu'il y a des toilettes pour handicapés?
ess keel a day twa-let poor oñ-dee-ka-pay

is there a wheelchair-accessible entrance?
est-ce qu'il y a une entrée pour les fauteuils roulants?
ess keel ee a oon oñ-tray poor lay foh-tuhy roo-loñ

is it possible to visit ... with a wheelchair?
est-ce qu'on peut visiter ... en fauteuil roulant?
ess koñ puh vee-zee-tay ... oñ foh-tuhy roo-loñ

is there a reduction for the disabled?
est-ce qu'il y a une réduction pour les handicapés?
ess keel ee a oon ray-dooks-yoñ poor lay oñ-dee-ka-pay

I need a bedroom on the ground floor
j'ai besoin d'une chambre au rez-de-chaussée
zhay buhz-wañ doon shoñbr oh ray-duh-shoh-say

I use a wheelchair
je suis en fauteuil roulant
zhuh swee oñ foh-tuhy roo-loñ

where is the lift?
où est l'ascenseur?
oo ay lass-oñ-suhr

WITH KIDS

In general, French children tend to go to bed early because they start school early in the morning. Public transport is free for under 4s; between 4 and 12, children pay half fare.

Key to ▶ minimum age for play areas

INFORMATION

Cette aire de jeux est mise librement à la disposition des enfants.

Les enfants sont placés sous la surveillance de leurs parents ou des personnes qui en ont la garde.

Un symbole indique **l'âge minimal** des enfants auxquels chaque jeu est destiné.

2 years — 2 ans 3 ans 6 ans 11 ans — 11 years

3 years 6 years

talking talking

is it safe for children?
c'est sans danger pour les enfants?
say soñ doñ-zhay poor layz oñ-foñ

where can I change the baby?
où est-ce que je peux changer le bébé?
oo ess kuh zhuh puh soñ-zhay luh bay-bay

do you have...?
est-ce que vous avez...?
ess kuh vooz a-vay...

a high chair
une chaise de bébé
oon shehz duh bay-bay

a cot
un lit d'enfant
uñ lee doñ-foñ

do you sell...?
est-ce que vous vendez...?
ess kuh voo voñ-day...

baby wipes
des lingettes
day lañ-zhet

nappies
des couches
day koosh

is there a children's menu?
est-ce que vous avez un menu pour les enfants?
ess kuh vooz av-ay uñ muh-noo poor layz oñ-foñ

is there a play park near here?
est-ce qu'il y a un aire de jeux près d'ici?
ess keel ee a un ehr duh zhuh pray dee-see

HEALTH

*Make sure you take your stamped E111 form (available from post offices) and if you require treatment look for a doctor who is **conventionné** (i.e. working within the French national health system). You must get a signed statement of your treatment in order to reclaim expenses. Remember that the pharamacist is also qualified to give advice.*

◀ Pharmacies operate a night duty rota. You can get details from pharmacies themselves, or if you are unable to find one, the police will be able to give details

GP's ▶
consulting
details

DOCTEUR PAUL-LOUIS RAMOND

DIPLOME DE LA FACULTE DE MEDECINE DE PARIS

MEDECINE GENERALE

adults and children — ADULTES - ENFANTS

Conventionné means there is no charge over the statutory fee fixed by the French state health service. — CONVENTIONNE

fourth floor left — 4ᵉᵐᵉ ETAGE GAUCHE   Tel. 01.45.42.18.23

CONSULTATIONS

LUNDI MERCREDI et VENDREDI de 15ᴴ30 a 17ᴴ30
MARDI et JEUDI de 17ᴴ30 a 19ᴴ30
SAMEDI de 10ᴴ a 12ᴴ

sur rendez-vous by appointment — OU SUR RENDEZ-VOUS

house calls — VISITES A DOMICILE

where is the nearest chemist?
où est la pharmacie la plus proche?
oo ay la far-ma-see la ploo prosh

have you something for...?
est-ce que vous avez quelque chose contre...?
ess kuh vooz av-ay kel-kuh shohz koñtr...

diarrhoea	**a headache**
la diarrhée	le mal de tête
la dee-ar-ay	*luh mal duh tet*

I need aspirin
j'ai besoin d'aspirine
zhay buh-swañ das-pee-reen

this bite is infected
cette piqûre est infectée
set pee-koor ay añ-fek-tay

sunburn
les coups de soleil
lay koo duh so-lay

flu
la grippe
la greep

I have a temperature
j'ai de la fièvre
zhay duh la fyehvr

talking talking talking

CONSULTATIONS
DU **LUNDI** AU **JEUDI** 9ᴴ 10ᴴ ET 15ᴴ 19ᴴ
VENDREDI   9ᴴ 10ᴴ ET 14ᴴ 16ᴴ

◀ *Consultations* means that no appointment is necessary to see a doctor. You walk in and wait in the wating room, *la salle d'attente*.

I feel ill
je me sens mal
zhuh muh soñ mal

he/she feels ill
il/elle se sent mal
eel/el suh soñ mal

I need a doctor
j'ai besoin d'un médecin
zhay buhz-wañ duñ mayd-sañ

we need a doctor to come out
il faut que le médecin vienne
eel foh kuh luh mayd-sañ vyen

can you call a doctor?
vous pouvez appeler un médecin?
voo poo-vay ap-lay uñ mayd-sañ

my child is ill
mon enfant est malade
mon oñ-foñ ay ma-lad

I have a pain here
j'ai mal ici
zhay mal ee-see

I am on this medication
je prends ces médicaments
zhuh proñ say may-dee-ka-moñ

I am pregnant
je suis enceinte
zhuh swee oñ-sañt

I am on the pill
je prends la pilule
zhuh proñ la pee-lool

I am breastfeeding
j'allaite mon enfant
zha-let moñ oñ-foñ

I have cystitis
j'ai une cystite
zhay oon sees-teet

I'm diabetic
je suis diabétique
zhuh swee dee-a-beh-teek

I am allergic to...
je suis allergique à...
zhuh sweez al-ehr-zheek a...

I have high blood pressure
j'ai de la tension
zhay duh la toñss-yoñ

my blood group is...
mon groupe sanguin est...
moñ groop soñ-gañ ay...

I need a receipt for my insurance
il me faut un reçu pour mon assurance
eel muh foh uñ ruh-soo poor moñ a-soo-roñss

I need a dentist
j'ai besoin d'un dentiste
zhay buhz-wañ duñ doñ-teest

I have toothache
j'ai mal aux dents
zhay mal oh doñ

my filling has come out
le plombage est parti
luh ploñ-bazh ay par-tee

can you repair my dentures?
vous pouvez réparer mon dentier?
voo poo-vay ray-pa-ray moñ doñt-yay

I need a temporary filling
j'ai besoin d'un plombage momentané
zhay buhz-wañ duñ ploñ-bazh moh-moñ-tan-ay

I have an abscess
j'ai un abcès
zhay un ab-seh

talking talking talking talking talking talking talking

If you require hopsital treatment your E111 form should cover you for 75% of the cost. You pay the balance and also a fixed daily hospital charge. (These are not refundable.)

▲ Emergency entrance for maternity cases

▼ X-RAY DEPARTMENT

▲ **ACCIDENT & EMERGENCY**
Calls for an ambulance are free from any phone, so you can phone from a call box, even if it accepts only cards. Just lift the receiver and dial 15.

▲ The law forbids smoking in all parts of the hospital.

If you need to go to hospital

will I/he/she have to go to hospital?
est-ce qu'il faudra aller à l'hôpital?
ess keel foh-dra a-lay a lop-ee-tal

to the hospital please
à l'hôpital s'il vous plaît
a lop-ee-tal seel voo play

I need to go to casualty
je dois aller aux urgences
zhuh dwa a-lay ohz oor-zhoñss

must I stay in bed?
est-ce que je dois rester au lit?
ess kuh zhuh dwa res-tay oh lee

when are the visiting hours?
quelles sont les heures de visite?
kel soñ layz uhr duh vee-zeet

where is the hospital?
où est l'hôpital?
oo ay lop-ee-tal

which ward?
quel service?
kel sehr-veess

• **can you explain what is the matter?**
vous pouvez m'expliquer le problème?
voo poo-vay meks-plee-kay luh prob-lehm

EMERGENCY

*The emergency number is 17. You will see either **Police** or
Gendarmerie (in smaller towns and villages). You should
report all thefts or crimes to them.*

▲ Fire station

Local police ▼

Police
◀ station

help!
au secours!
o suh-koor

can you help me?
vous pouvez m'aider?
voo poo-vay mah-day

please call...
s'il vous plaît! appelez...
seel voo play ap-lay...

the police
la police
la po-leess

an ambulance
une ambulance
oon oñ-boo-loñss

fire!
au feu!
o fuh

please call the fire brigade!
s'il vous plaît! appelez les pompiers!
seel voo play ap-lay lay poñ-pyay

my ... has been stolen
on m'a volé mon/ma...
oñ ma vo-lay moñ/ma...

I want to report a theft
je veux signaler un vol
zhuh vuh seen-ya-lay uñ vol

here are my insurance details
voici mon assurance
vwa-see moñ a-soo-roñss

please give me your insurance details
votre assurance s'il vous plaît
votr a-soo-roñss seel voo play

where is the police station?
où est la gendarmerie?
oo ay la zhoñ-darm-ree

I would like to phone...
je voudrais appeler...
zhuh voo-dray ap-lay...

my car has been broken into
on a forcé ma voiture
on a for-say ma vwa-toor

I need a report for my insurance
il me faut un constat pour mon assurance
eel muh foh uñ koñ-sta poor mon a-soo-roñss

talking talking talking talking talking talking

FOOD AND DRINK

FRENCH FOOD

i The French take their food very seriously, and what they eat largely depends upon what is available locally and in season. In Brittany you find fresh fish and superb seafood. In Normandy, the abundance of dairy produce means that the cooking is rich in butter and cream. And many of the dishes make use of the locally grown apples: either in the form of cider or **calvados** (brandy made from apples). You can get an idea of the different dishes from the map on page 88. Some of the greatest chefs have come from France and French cuisine is very much sauce-based. It is worth trying to familiarise yourself with the various sauces are as they will appear time and time again on menus.

au **comptoir** at the counter

à emporter take-away

Typical **bistro** with blackboard menu. ▶

where can we have a snack?
où est-ce qu'on peut manger un petit quelque chose?
oo ess koñ puh moñ-zhay puh-tee kel-kuh shoz

can you recommend a good local restaurant?
pouvez-vous nous recommander un bon restaurant?
poo-vay voo noo ruh-ko-moñ-day uñ boñ res-to-roñ

are there any vegetarian restaurants?
est-ce qu'il y a des restaurants végétariens?
ess keel ee a day res-to-roñ vay-zhay-ta-ryañ

do we need to book?
est-ce qu'il faut réserver une table?
ess keel foh ray-zehr-vay oon tabl

what do you recommend?
qu'est-ce que vous me recommandez?
kess kuh voo muh ruh-ko-moñ-day

how do we get to the restaurant?
pour aller au restaurant?
poor a-lay oh res-to-roñ

▲ MIXED HAM, BUTTER AND GRUYÈRE CHEESE SANDWICHES 25F

La boulangerie (baker's) is a great place for snacks. Bakers bake bread at least twice a day and with a bit of luck you will be able to get your *baguette* or *ficelle* fresh from the oven.

◀ Brasserie

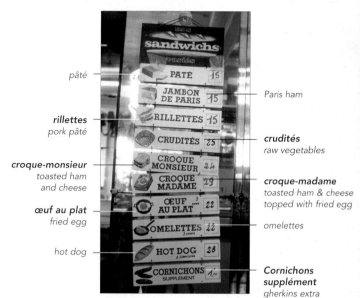

pâté	PATE 15
	JAMBON DE PARIS 15 — Paris ham
rillettes pork pâté	RILLETTES 15
	CRUDITÉS 25 — **crudités** raw vegetables
croque-monsieur toasted ham and cheese	CROQUE MONSIEUR 24
	CROQUE MADAME 29 — **croque-madame** toasted ham & cheese topped with fried egg
œuf au plat fried egg	ŒUF AU PLAT 22
	OMELETTES 22 — omelettes
hot dog	HOT DOG 28
	CORNICHONS SUPPLEMENT 1 — **Cornichons supplément** gherkins extra

▲ Types of sandwiches available in a French café.

*Bars often serve food, perhaps a dish of the day, **plat du jour** (served only at lunchtime), toasted cheese-and-ham sandwiches, **croque-monsieur** (**croque-madame** has a fried egg on top) or sandwiches. Food is usually reasonably priced and available throughout the day.*

◀ You can buy sweet and savoury pastries from the *boulangerie* as well as sandwiches and drinks, since many *boulangeries* are also *pâtisseries* (cake shops).

Pâtisseries sell mouth-watering specialities. ▶

talking talking talking

I'd like a ... please
je voudrais un/une ... s'il vous plaît
zhuh voo-dray uñ/oon ... seel voo pleh

a white coffee un crème *uñ krem*	**a large white coffee** un grand crème *uñ groñ krem*
a decaff coffee un déca *uñ day-ka*	**a hot chocolate** un chocolat chaud *uñ sho-ko-la shoh*
a tea with milk un thé au lait *uñ tay oh lay*	**a half of lager** un demi *uñ duh-mee*
an orange juice un jus d'orange *uñ zhoo do-roñzh*	**an apple juice** un jus de pomme *uñ zhoo duh pom*
a red wine un vin rouge *uñ vañ roozh*	**a white wine** un vin blanc *uñ vañ bloñ*

a bottle of mineral water
une bouteille d'eau minérale
oon boo-tay doh mee-nay-ral

sparkling	still
gazeuse	plate
gaz-uhz	*plat*

◀ *Crêpes* (pancakes, sweet or savoury) are a popular snack.

◀ Waffles

◀ Ice-cream parlour
If you want a cone, ask for *un cornet*. One scoop is *une boule*, two scoops are *deux boules*.

You can generally buy fresh bread from the *alimentation* ◀ *générale*.

keywords keywords keywords

menthe
moñt
mint

framboise
fromb-waz
raspberry

fraise
frez
strawberry

cassis
ka-sees
blackcurrant

citron
see-troñ
lemon

ananas
a-na-na
pineapple

pêche
pesh
peach

pistache
pee-stash
pistacchio

noisette
nwa-zet
hazelnut

raisin
reh-zañ
grape

can we eat here?
est-ce qu'on peut manger ici?
ess koñ puh moñzhay ee-see

what can we eat?
qu'est-ce qu'on peut manger?
kess koñ puh moñ-zhay

do you have a dish of the day?
est-ce que vous avez un plat du jour?
ess kuh vooz avay uñ pla doo zhoor

what is the dish of the day?
quel est le plat du jour?
kel ay luh pla doo zhoor

what sandwiches do you have?
qu'est-ce que vous avez comme sandwichs?
kess kuh vooz avay kom soñd-weech

I'd like ice-cream
je voudrais une glace
zhuh voo-dray oon glass

what flavours do you have?
qu'est-ce que vous avez comme parfums?
kess kuh vooz a-vay kom par-fuñ

talking talking talking

Sunday lunch is often a time for families to eat out. You should book to be sure of getting a table. In smaller towns, restaurants tend to shut on Sunday evenings.

◀ Opening times in a restaurant window Note that it is closed on Sun.

59F**90**
Boisson non comprise

▲ *Drink not included* Check what is and is not included in the price of your meal.

▼ Kids' meal served in a supermarket café.

à la cafétéria

Spécial enfants

menu

hamburger or	1 steak haché ou
3 fish fingers	3 bâtonnets de colin pané,
chips, 1 dessert	des frites, 1 dessert,
1 drink	1 boisson,
1 toy	1 gadget,
1 surprise	1 surprise !

25F*

BÔTAKADO

GRATUIT LE MARDI SOIR°

free on Tuesday evenings

I would like to book a table
je voudrais réserver une table
zhuh voo-dray ray-zehr-vay oon tabl

for 4 people
pour quatre personnes
poor katr pehr-son

for tonight
pour ce soir
poor suh swar

for tomorrow night
pour demain soir
poor duh-mañ swar

for lunch
pour le déjeuner
poor luh day-zhuh-nay

at 12.30
à midi et demi
a mee-dee ay duh-mee

at 19.30
à dix-neuf heures trente
a dees nuhf uhr troñt

at 8 o'clock
à vingt heures
a vañt uhr

in the name of Smart
au nom de Smart
oh noñ duh Smart

smoking/non-smoking
fumeur/non-fumeur
foo-muhr/noñ-foo-muhr

Bank card payment terminal.
▼ Many restaurants use this

little
portable
device.
If you use
Switch,
you may
be asked
to key in
your PIN
number.

▶ Restaurant
bill for a
prix fixe
(set price)
meal for
four.

Restaurant
Chez Maitre Paul
J.F DEBERT
12 , rue Monsieur le Prince
75006 PARIS
Tél : 01.43.54.74.59   Fax : 01.46.34.58.33
RC : 388 495 335 00019
Ouvert tous les jours

TABLE NO :   3

Date: 29/10/10
Serveur No: 2 Nbre Couverts->   4
Facture No: 7

4	Menu à 165 frs	660,00
1	Trousseau M.T	140,00
2	Eau minerale	44,00
1	Arbois chardonn	140,00
4	Cafe	68,00

TOTAL NET: 1052,00

Dont T.V.A. :   164,98

Total en EUROS...: 160,39

dont TVA
of which
VAT

total in euros

---

the menu please
le menu s'il vous plaît
luh muh-noo seel voo pleh

the wine list please
la carte des vins s'il vous plaît
la kar day vañ seel voo play

I'd like the menu at ... francs
je voudrais le menu à ... francs
zhuh voo-dray luh muh-noo a ... froñ

do you have a children's menu?
est-ce que vous avez un menu pour les enfants?
ess kuh vooz avay uñ muh-noo poor layz oñ-foñ

for a main dish I will have...
comme plat principal je prends...
kom pla prañ-see-pal zhuh proñ...

what vegetarian dishes do you have?
qu'est-ce que vous avez comme plats végétariens?
kes kuh vooz a-vay kom pla vay-zhay-ta-ryañ

what cheeses do you have?
qu'est-ce que vous avez comme fromages?
kes kuh vooz a-vay kom fromazh

what desserts do you have?
qu'est-ce que vous avez comme desserts?
kess kuh vooz a-vay kom day-sehr

some tap water please
de l'eau s'il vous plaît
duh loh seel voo play

some more bread please
encore du pain s'il vous plaît
oñ-kor doo pañ seel voo play

the bill please
l'addition s'il vous plaît
la-dee-syoñ seel voo play

talking talking talking talking talking

Carte *Menu*
POTAGES *soups*

ENTRÉES *starter*

POISSONS *fish*

FRUITS DE MER *seafood*

VIANDES *meat*

GIBIER et VOLAILLE *game and poultry*

LÉGUMES *vegetables*

FROMAGES *cheeses*

DESSERTS *sweet*

BOISSONS *drinks*

◀ The various courses you will find on any restaurant menu.

dish of the day
fish
or meat
or poultry
garnit
with vegetables &
French fries

Plat du Jour à 50 F
poisson
ou viande } garnis
ou volaille

Menu 1 à 95 F
au choix:
Pâté croûte avec crudité
Crudités de Saison
Pâté de Campagne et crud
Spaghetti à la forestière
Salade Portugaise

au choix:

starter

Poulet rôti
Boeuf Bourguignon
Côte de Porc grillée
Saucisse sicilienne
ou
Plat du Jour

main course

dish of the day

Tous ces plats sont ga

Plateau de Fromages
ou
Dessert du Jour

cheese platter
or
dessert of the day

En supplé
Café, Infusion,

to end the meal
(not included in the price)

Menu à prix fixe
set-price menu ▶

*By law, restaurants have to exhibit their menus outside. There are often two or three menus at different prices and a list of **à la carte** dishes. It is more expensive to select from the à la carte menu. The service charge is 15%. Service is included unless you see it stated (**service non compris**).*

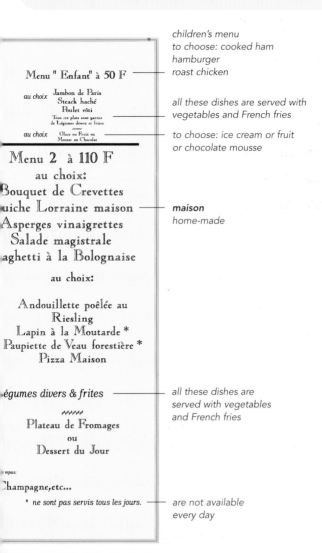

children's menu
to choose: cooked ham
hamburger
roast chicken

Menu " Enfant" à 50 F

au choix   Jambon de Paris
        Steack haché
        Poulet rôti
     Tous ces plats sont garnis
     de Légumes divers et frites

all these dishes are served with vegetables and French fries

au choix   Glace ou Fruit ou
        Mousse au Chocolat

to choose: ice cream or fruit or chocolate mousse

Menu 2 à 110 F
au choix:
Bouquet de Crevettes
Quiche Lorraine maison
Asperges vinaigrettes
Salade magistrale
Spaghetti à la Bolognaise

maison
home-made

au choix:

Andouillette poêlée au Riesling
Lapin à la Moutarde *
Paupiette de Veau forestière *
Pizza Maison

Légumes divers & frites

all these dishes are served with vegetables and French fries

Plateau de Fromages
ou
Dessert du Jour

repas:

Champagne, etc...

* ne sont pas servis tous les jours.

are not available every day

CHOOSING WINE

France is awash with cheap wine, some of it as low as 8F a bottle. Walk right on past these, because the very best tactic in France is to stick to what you would pay at home rather than going for the cheapies; superb wine can be had for 40 or 50F. The best advice for bargain hunters is to find a reputable local **cave** *(winery shop), where it's possible to taste before buying; it's usually safer to spend 20 or 30F a bottle here. If in doubt, stick to reds for safety, and pick out the* **domaine-** *or* **château-***bottled wines.*

This label is marked **Appellation Contrôlée**. *This is the French system that guarantees the origin of a wine from a demarcated area – in this case, Côtes de Bourg.*

1996

Château de Passedieu

CÔTES DE BOURG
APPELLATION CÔTES DE BOURG CONTRÔLÉE

JEAN-PIERRE DUBOIS, PROPRIETAIRE ⟨⟩ A BAYON · GIRONDE · FRANCE

MIS EN BOUTEILLE AU CHATEAU
PAR S.V. GRANDSCHATEAUX 33560 FRANCE

12 % vol.   PRODUCE OF FRANCE   75 cl

L 1689   CREATION RAPAT 13

alcohol content 12% 11.5% is average; 14% is a pretty heavy wine

bottled at the château

cuvée
koo-vay
vintage

rouge
roozh
red

blanc
bloñ
white

mousseux
moo-suh
sparkling

brut
broo
very dry

sec
sek
dry

demi-sec
duh-mee sek
sweet

doux
doo
very sweet

▲ Côtes de Bourg is a Bordeaux wine. Be sceptical about bargains from the Bordeaux region unless you really know your onions. Avoid fancy labels at low prices, particularly from the Médoc. For earlier drinking and lower prices look out for St Emilion, Côtes de Castillon, Côtes de Blaye, Côtes de Francs and Côtes de Bourg (above). Nearby ACs Côtes de Duras and Pecharmant (Bergerac) are also good. For whites choose Pessac-Léognan; for sweet whites St Croix du Mont.

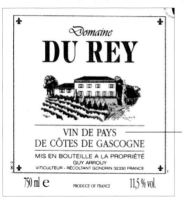

Vin de pays simply means the wine has come from one area and has not been blended. *Vin de table* or *vin ordinaire* indicates that the wine has been blended. These wines are often sold in plastic bottles.

Rhône has some snob ACs, but on the whole is still seriously underrated. Herby, sunkissed Syrah blends can match the reds of Burgundy and Bordeaux at about half the price. Alongside the famous names like Hermitage and Côte-Rôtie are others which dipped out of favour but have now cleaned up their act

and in many cases taken on New World methods. Châteauneuf-du-Pape is one of these though there are still too many overcooked, tired and flabby examples on sale. Côtes du Rhone Villages is increasingly reliable. Try also: Vacqueyras, Gigondas. White is very risky unless it's Hermitage or Condrieu.

the wine list please
la carte des vins s'il vous plaît
la kart day vañ seel voo play

can you recommend a good wine?
vous pouvez nous recommander un bon vin?
voo poo-vay noo ruh-ko-moñ-day uñ boñ vañ

a bottle of wine	**red**	**white**	**rosé**
une bouteille de vin	rouge	blanc	rosé
oon boo-tay duh vañ	*roozh*	*bloñ*	*ro-zay*

a carafe of wine   **a glass of wine**
un pichet de vin   un verre de vin
uñ pee-shay duh vañ   *uñ vehr duh vañ*

what liqueurs do you have?
qu'est-ce que vous avez comme liqueurs?
kess kuh vooz a-vay koñ lee-kuhr

◀ Champagne is good value on home ground and the supermarkets all have a good selection.

Calvados, apple brandy from Normandy. This regional speciality is used for cooking as well as drinking. See page 88. ▶

◀ Wine tasting is a fun way of buying wine. Try a sample or to and buy a bottle or case (if you really like it), but don't feel you have to.

VENEZ VISITER NOTRE CAVE —— *come and visit our cellars*
OUVERTE TOUS LES JOURS —— *open every day*
DÉGUSTATION - VENTE —— *wine tasting – sale*

Cave Wine cellar ▶

*When you ask for a **bière** in France, you will be served lager.
If you want an ale or bitter, you should ask for **bière brune**.
Draught beer will come as a **demi** (half pint approx.); you would
not normally get a pint of beer in France as they tend to drink in
halves. It can be quite expensive to drink out in France.*

There are a number of smallish brewers in the
northern-most part of France near to Belgium.
Bière de Garde is the term used to refer to them
becasue they were traditionally unfiltered and
designed to mature further in the bottle when laid
down in the cellar.

◀ Ch'ti: pale-coloured with
a fruity aroma.

Jenlain: ▶
light red colour
with a sharp
aroma; a full-
bodied, slightly
tart beer.

half a pint of lager
un demi
uñ duh-mee

a French lager
une bière française
oon byehr froñ-sez

do you have any ales?
est-ce que vous avez des bières brunes?
ess kuh vooz a-vay day byehr broon

t
a
l
k
i
n
g

FLAVOURS OF FRANCE

Calvados
brandy made from cider
sole normande
sole cooked in a cread, cider and shrimp sauce
moules marinières
mussels cooked in white wine
tripes à la mode de Caen
tripe cooked with vegetables, herbs, cider and Calvados
tarte normande
apple tart

seafood
coquilles Saint-Jacques
scallops cooked in their shell with a breadcrumb and cheese topping
homard à l'armoricaine
lobster cooked with onions, tomatoes and wine
cotriade
fish stew
crêpes
sweet and savoury pancakes

charcuterie
pork produce
rillettes
pâté made from pork
truffiat
potato cake

Poitou/Aquitaine/Périgord
pâté de foie gras
goose liver pâté
truffes
truffles, i.e. mushrooms
cèpes
wild mushrooms
anguilles
eels

perdreau à la catalane
partridge cooked in orange juice and peppers
grabure
bean, meat and vegetable stew
mouton à la catalane
mutton and ham stewed in wine and garlic

truffade
potato pie with garlic and cheese
tourte à la viande
veal or pork pie
potée auvergnate
cabbage and meat soup
truffade
potato pie with garlic and cheese

NOR
PAS-C
CALA

•Caen
NORMANDIE

ILE D
FRAN
Paris

•Brest
BRETAGNE

•Rennes

PAYS-DE-
LA-LOIRE

VAL-DE-LOIR

•Nantes

•Tours

•Orléa

POITOU-
CHARENTES

•Limoges

LIMOUSIN

•Bordeaux

AQUITAINE

MIDI-PYRÉNÉES

•Toulouse

influenced by the whole of French cusine
charcuterie
pork specialities

carbonnade
braised beef
veau flamande
veal cooked with dried apricots and prunes
Champagne

choucroute
sauerkraut
quiche lorraine
flan with egg and diced bacon
baeckoffe
hotpot of pork, mutton and beef baked with potato layers
kugelhopf
hat-shaped sugar-covered cake
kirsch
eau de vie made with cherries

bœuf bourgignon
beef cooked in burgundy, mushrooms and onions
coq au vin
chicken cooked in red wine
escargots
snails
matelote
fresh-fish stew

Lille

PICARDIE

LORRAINE
•Nancy ALSACE

CHAMPAGNE-
ARDENNE
Strasbourg •

Mulhouse •
FRANCHE-
BOURGOGNE COMTE

•Clermont-
Ferrand
•Lyon
RHÔNE-ALPES

AUVERGNE
•Grenoble

PROVENCE
Nice •
LANGUEDOC- CÔTE
ROUSSILLON D'AZUR
•Montpellier Aix-en-Provence
Marseille
•Toulon

•Perpignan

CORSE

Bastia

Ajaccio

gratinée lyonnaise
clear soup with eggs flavoured with port and served with French bread and grated cheese
pommes lyonnaise
potatoes fried with onions
fondue
melted cheese dish into which bread is dipped
poulet célestine
chicken cooked in wine with mushrooms, tomatoes and cream

Côte d'Azur/Provence
bouillabaisse
rich, saffron seafood soup
pissaladière
kind of flan with onions, anchovies and black olives
salade niçoise
salad of green beans, anchovies, black olives and green peppers
tomates à la provençale
grilled tomatoes steeped in garlic
aïoli
garlic mayonnaise
pistou
garlic, basil and olive oil sauce

civet de langouste
crayfish cooked in wine and garlic
cassoulet
bean stew with pork or mutton and sausages
escargots
snails

baccala fritta
dried salt cod fried Corsican-style
sanglier
wild boar

*There are times when you may not be able to eat some
things. It is as well to warn the waiter before you choose.*

talking talking talking talking talking

I'm vegetarian
je suis végétarien(ne)
zhuh swee vay-zhay-tay-ryañ(-ryeñ)

I don't eat meat/pork
je ne mange pas de viande/porc
zhuh nuh moñzh pa duh vyoñd/pork

I don't eat fish
je ne mange pas de poisson
zhuh nuh moñzh pa duh pwa-soñ

I'm allergic to shellfish
je suis allergique aux crustacés
zhuh swee a-lehr-zheek oh kroo-ta-say

I am allergic to peanuts
je suis allergique aux cacahuètes
zhuh swee a-lehr-zheek oh ka-ka-wet

I can't eat raw eggs
je ne peux pas manger les œufs crus
zhuh nuh puh pa moñ-zhay layz uh kroo

I am on a diet
je suis au régime
zhuh swee oh ray-zheem

I can't eat liver
je ne peux pas manger de foie
zhuh nuh puh pa moñ-zhay duh fwah

I don't drink alcohol
je ne bois pas d'alcool
zhuh nuh bwa pa dal-kol

what is in this?
quels sont les ingrédients?
kel soñ lay añ-gra-dyoñ

is it raw?
c'est cru?
say kroo

is it made with unpasteurised milk?
c'est fait avec du lait cru?
say fay a-vek doo lay kroo

frit
free
fried

en croûte
oñ kroot
in pastry

darne
darn
steak or fillet

rôti
ro-tee
roast

en daube
oñ dohb
casseroled

farci
far-see
stuffed

grillé
gree-yay
grilled

fumé
foo-may
smoked

fricassé
free-ka-say
stewed

mariné
ma-ree-nay
marinated

hâché
a-shay
minced

au four
oh foor
baked

garni
gar-nee
served with veg

bleu
bluh
very rare

MENU READER

A

...à l'/à la/au/aux in the style of
   au feu de bois cooked over a wood fire
   au four baked
   au porto in port
abats offal, giblets
abricot apricot
Abricotine liqueur brandy with apricot flavouring
acajou cashew nut
agneau lamb
aïado roast shoulder of lamb stuffed with garlic and other ingredients
aiglefin haddock
aïgo bouïdo garlic soup
ail garlic
aile wing
aïoli rich garlic mayonnaise originated in the south and gives its name to the dish it is served with: cold steamed fish and vegetable stew. The mayonnaise is served on the side
airelles bilberries, cranberries
alicot puréed potato with cheese
allumettes very thin chips
amande almond
arête fish bone
argumes citrus fruit
arlésienne, à l' with tomatoes, onions, aubergines, potatoes and rice
armagnac fine grape brandy from the Landes area
armoricaine, ...à l' cooked with brandy, wine, tomatoes and onions
ananas pineapple
anchoïade anchovy paste usually served on grilled French bread
anchois anchovies
andouille, andouillette spicy tripe sausage
anglaise, ...à l' poached or boiled
anguille eel

anis aniseed
arachide peanut (uncooked)
araignée de mer spider crab
artichaut artichoke
   artichauts à la barigoule artichokes in wine, with carrots, garlic, onions
   artichauts châtelaine artichokes stuffed with mushrooms
asperge asparagus
aspic de vollaille chicken in aspic

asperge

assiette dish, platter
   assiette anglaise plate of assorted cold meats
   assiette de charcuterie plate of assorted sausages
   assiette de crudités selection of raw vegetables served with a dip
   assiette de pêcheur assorted fish
aubergine aubergine
   aubergines farcies stuffed aubergines
aurin grey mullet
auvergnat, ...à l' with cabbage, sausage and bacon
avocat avocado

B

babas au rhum rum baba
baccala frittu dried salt cod fried Corsica style
Badoit mineral water, very slightly sparkling

baeckoffe hotpot of pork, mutton and beef baked with potato layers from Alsace

baguette stick of French bread

banane banana
  bananes flambées bananas flambéed in brandy

bar sea-bass

barbue brill

bardatte cabbage stuffed with rabbit or hare

barquette small boat-shaped flan

basilic basil

baudroie fish soup with vegetables, garlic and herbs, monkfish

bavarois moulded cream and custard pudding, usually served with fruit

Béarnaise, à la sauce similar to mayonnaise but flavoured with tarragon. Traditionally served with steak

bécasse woodcock

béchamel classic white sauce made with milk, butter and flour

beignets fritters, doughnuts

Bénédictine herb liqueur on a brandy base

betterave beetroot

beurre butter
  beurre blanc, ...à la sauce of white wine and shallots with butter

bien cuit well done

bière beer
  bière pression draught beer
  bière blonde lager
  bière brune bitter

bifteck steak

bigourneau periwinkle

biologique organic

bis wholemeal (of bread or flour)

biscuit de Savoie sponge cake

bisque smooth rich seafood soup
  bisque de homard lobster soup

blanquette white meat stew served with a creamy white sauce

blanquette de veau

blanquette de veau veal stew in white sauce
  blanquette de volaille chicken stew in white sauce

blé wheat

blette Swiss chard

bleu very rare

bœuf beef
  bœuf bourguignon beef in burgundy, onions and mushrooms
  bœuf en daube rich beef stew with wine, vegetables and herbs

bombe moulded ice cream dessert

bonite bonito, small tuna fish

bonne femme, ...à la cooked in white wine with mushrooms

bordelaise, ...à la cooked in a sauce of red wine, shallots and herbs

bouchée vol-au-vent
  bouchée à la reine vol-au-vent filled with chicken or veal in a white sauce

bœuf bourguignon

bouillabaisse

boudin pudding
boudin blanc white pudding
boudin noir black pudding

bouillabaisse rich seafood soup flavoured with saffron originally from Marseilles

bouilleture d'anguilles eels cooked with prunes and red wine

bouilli boiled

bouillon stock
bouillon de légumes vegetable stock
bouillon de poule chicken stock

boulangère, ...à la baked with potatoes and onions

boulettes meatballs

bourgeoise, ...à la with carrots, onions, bacon, celery and braised lettuce

bourguignonne, ...à la cooked in red wine, with onions, bacon and mushrooms

bouirride fish stew traditionally served with garlic mayonnaise (aïoli)

brandade de morue dried salt cod puréed with cream and olive oil

brème bream

brioche sweet bun
brioche aux fruits sweet bun soaked in liqueur and covered with fruit

brochet pike

brochette kebab

brocoli broccoli

brugnon nectarine
bulot whelk

C

cabillaud fresh cod

cacahuète peanut

café coffee
café au lait coffee with hot milk
café crème white coffee
café décaféiné decaffeinated coffee
café express espresso coffee
café glacé iced coffee
café irlandais Irish coffee
café noir black coffee

caille quail
caille sur canapé quail served on toast

caillettes rolled liver stuffed with spinach

calisson almond sweet

calmar (or **calamar**) squid

calvados apple brandy made from cider (Normandy)

canard duck
canard à l'orange roast duck with orange sauce
canard périgourdin roast duck with prunes, pâté de *foie gras* and truffles
canard Rouennais stuffed roast duck covered in red wine sauce

caneton duckling

cannelle cinnamon

câpres capers

carbonnade de bœuf braised beef

cardon cardoon

cari curry

carotte carrot
carottes Vichy carrots cooked in butter and sugar

carpe carp
carpe farcie carp stuffed with mushrooms or *foie gras*

carré persillé roast lamb Normandy style (with parsley)

carrelet plaice

carte des vins wine list

cassis blackcurrant, blackcurrant liqueur

cassoulet

cassoulet bean stew with pork or mutton and sausages. There are many regional variations

caviar caviar
  caviar blanc mullet roe
  caviar niçois a paste made with anchovies and olive oil

cédrat large citrus fruit, similar to a lemon

céleri celery
  céleri rémoulade celery in a mustard and herb dressing

céleri-rave celery root

cèpes boletus mushrooms, wild mushrooms
  cèpes marinés wild mushrooms marinated in oil, garlic, spices and herbs

cerfeuil chervil

cerise cherry

céleri

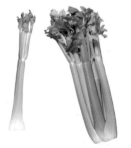

cervelas smoked pork sausages, saveloy

cervelle brains (usually lamb or calf)

champignon mushroom
  champignons à la grècque mushrooms cooked in wine, olive oil and herbs
  champignons de Paris button mushrooms
  champignons périgourdine mushrooms with truffles and *foie gras*

chanterelle chanterelle (wild golden-coloured mushroom)

chantilly whipped cream

charlotte custard and fruit in lining of almond fingers

Chartreuse aromatic herb liqueur made by Carthusian monks

chasseur literally hunter-style, cooked with white wine, shallots, mushrooms and herbs

châtaigne chestnut

châteaubriand thick fillet steak

châtelaine, ...à la with artichoke hearts and chestnut purée

chaud(e) hot

chaudrée rochelais a selection of fish stewed in red wine

chauffé heated

chausson a pasty filled with meat or seafood

cheval, à topped with a fried egg

chèvre goat

chevreuil venison

chichi doughnut shaped in a stick

chicorée chicory (for coffee), endive

chocolat chocolate
  chocolat chaud hot chocolate

chou cabbage

choucrote sauerkraut
  choucrote garnie sauerkraut with various types of sausages

chou-fleur cauliflower

choux brocolis broccoli

choux de Bruxelles Brussels sprouts

citron

cidre cider, sparkling (**bouché**) or still, quite strong
  cidre doux sweet cider
citron lemon
  citron pressé freshly squeezed lemon juice with water and sugar
citron vert lime
citrouille pumpkin
cives (or **ciboulettes**) chives
civet thick stew
  civet de langouste crayfish in wine sauce
  civet de lièvre hare stewed in wine, onions and mushrooms
clafoutis cherry pudding
claire type of oyster
clou de girofle clove
cochon pig
coco coconut
cocotte, en cooked in a small earthenware casserole
cœur heart
cœur d'artichauts artichoke hearts
cœurs de palmier palm hearts
cognac high quality white grape brandy
coing quince
Cointreau orange-flavoured liqueur
colbert,...à la fried, with a coating of egg and breadcrumbs
colin hake
compote de fruits mixed stewed fruit
concombre cucumber
condé rich rice pudding with fruits

confit pieces of meat preserved in fat
  confit d'oie goose pâté
  confit de canard duckmeat preserved in its own fat
confiture jam
  confiture d'oranges marmalade
congre conger eel
consommé clear soup, generally made from meat or fish stock
contre-filet sirloin fillet (beef)
coq au vin chicken cooked in red wine

coq au vin

coquelet cockerel
coques cockles
coquillages shellfish
coquilles scallops
  coquilles à la provençale scallops with garlic sauce
  coquilles Saint-Jacques scallops cooked in the shell with a breadcrumb and cheese topping
coquillettes pasta shells
cornichon gherkin
côtelette cutlet
  côtelettes de veau veal cutlets
côte rib, chop
  côtes de porc pork chops
cotriade fish stew (Brittany)
cou neck
coulibiac salmon cooked in puff pastry
coulis puréed fruit sauce
coupe goblet with ice cream

courge marrow

cousinat chestnut and cream soup

coussinet cranberry

crabe crab

craquelots smoked herring

crème cream
  crème anglaise fresh custard
  crème au beurre butter cream with egg yolks and sugar
  crème brûlée rich custard with caramelised sugar on top
  crème caramel baked custard with caramelised sugar sauce
  crème chantilly slightly sweetened whipped cream
  crème fraîche sour cream
  crème pâtisserie thick fresh custard used in tarts and desserts
  crème renversée (or **crème caramel**) custard with a caramelised top

crème de cream of… (soup)
  crème d'argenteuil white asparagus soup
  crème de cresson watercress soup
  crème de marrons chestnut purée
  crème de menthe peppermint-flavoured liqueur

crêpes sweet and savoury pancakes
  crêpes fourrées filled pancakes
  crêpes Suzette pancakes with Cointreau or Grand Marnier sauce usually flambéed

crépinette type of sausage

crevette prawn
  crevette grise shrimp
  crevette rouge large prawn
  crevettes en terrine potted prawns

croûte, en in pastry

croûtes, croûtons, …aux served with cubes of toasted or fried bread

cru raw

crudités assortment of raw vegetables (grated carrots, chopped tomatoes, etc) served as a starter

crustacés shellfish

cuisses de grenouille frogs' legs

cuit cooked

culotte rump steak

Curaçao orange-flavoured liqueur

D

darne fillet or steak

datte date

daube casserole with wine, herbs and garlic

dauphinoise, …à la cooked in milk

daurade sea bream

diable, …à la strong mustard seasoning

diabolo menthe mint cordial and lemonade

dinde turkey

diots au vin blanc pork sausages in white wine

duxelles fried mushrooms and shallots with cream

E

eau water
  eau de Seltz soda water
  eau-de-vie brandy (often made from plum, pear, etc)
  eau minérale mineral water
  eau minérale gazeuse sparkling mineral water
  eau nature tap water

échalote shallot

échine loin of pork

écrevisse freshwater crayfish

églefin haddock

crudités

emballé wrapped

en brochette cooked like a kebab (on a skewer)

encornet squid

endive chicory

entrecôte rib steak

entrées starters

entremets sweets (desserts)

épaule shoulder

éperlan whitebait

épice spice

épinards spinach

escalope escalope

escargots snails (generally cooked with strong seasonings)
  escargots à la bourguignonne snails with garlic butter

escargots

espadon swordfish

estouffade de boeuf beef stew cooked in red wine, herbs, onions, mushrooms and diced bacon

estragon tarragon

esturgeon sturgeon

F

faisan pheasant

farci(e) stuffed

faux-filet sirloin

faverolles haricot beans

favou(ille) tiny crab

fenouil fennel

férigoule thyme (in provençal dialect)

feuille leaf

figue

feuilleté aux fraises strawberry tart

fèves broad beans

figue fig

filet fillet steak
  filet de bœuf en croûte steak in pastry
  filet de bœuf tenderloin
  filet mignon small fillet steak

financière, ...à la rich sauce made with Madeira wine and truffles

fine de claire type of oyster

fines herbes mixed, chopped herbs

flageolet type of small green haricot bean

flamande, ...à la served with potatoes, cabbage, carrots and pork

flambé(e) doused with brandy or another spirit and set alight, usually cooked at your table

flétan halibut

flocons d'avoine rolled oats

florentine with spinach, usually served with mornay sauce

foie liver (usually calf's)
  foie de volailles chicken livers

foie gras goose liver pâté

fond d'artichaut artichoke heart

fondue a shared dish which is served in the middle of the table. Each person uses a long fork to dip their bread or meat into the pot
  fondue (au fromage) melted cheeses into which chunks of bread are dipped

fondue bourguignonne small chunks of meat dipped into boiling oil and eaten with different sauces. The meat equivalent to cheese fondue

fondue

forestière, ...à la with bacon and mushroom

fougasse type of bread

fourré(e) stuffed

frais (fraîche) fresh

fraise strawberry
　fraises des bois wild strawberries

framboise raspberry

frappé iced

fricassée a stew, usually chicken or veal, and vegetables

frisée curly endive

frit(e) fried

friture fried food, usually small fish

froid(e) cold

fromage cheese
　fromage blanc soft white cheese
　fromage frais creamy fresh cheese

fruit fruit
　fruit de la passion passion fruit
　fruits de mer shellfish, seafood

fumé(e) smoked

fumet fish stock

G

galantine meat in aspic

galette savoury buckwheat pancake

gambas large prawns

garbure thick vegetable and meat soup

gargouillau pear tart

garni(e) garnished i.e. served with something

garnitures side dishes

gâteau cake, gateau
　gâteau Saint-Honoré choux pastry cake filled with custard

gaufres waffles (often cream-filled)

gazeuse sparkling

gelée jelly, aspic

genièvre juniper berry

génoise sponge cake

gésier gizzard

gibier game

gigot d'agneau leg of lamb

gigot de mer large fish baked whole

gingembre ginger

glace ice cream

goyave guava

graines de soja soya beans

Grand Marnier tawny-coloured, orange-flavoured liqueur

gratin, au topped with cheese and breadcrumb and grilled

gratin dauphinois potatoes cooked in cream, garlic and Swiss cheese

fraise

grenade

gratinée Lyonnaise clear soup with eggs flavoured with Port wine and served with toasted french bread and grated cheese

grenade pomegranate

greque, ...à la cooked in olive oil, garlic and herbs, can be served hot or cold

grenouilles frogs legs
  grenouilles meunière frogs legs cooked in butter

grillade grilled meat

grillé(e) grilled

gros mollet lump fish

groseille redcurrant

groseille à maquereau gooseberry

H

hâchis mince hamburger

hareng herring

haricots beans
  haricots beurres butter beans
  haricots blancs haricot beans
  haricots rouges red kidney beans
  haricots verts green beans, French beans

herbes (fines herbes) herbs

hollandaise, sauce sauce made of butter, egg yolks and lemon juice, served warm

homard lobster
  homard à l'armoricaine lobster cooked with onions, tomatoes and wine
  homard thermidor lobster

served in cream sauce, topped with parmesan

hors d'œuvres variés varied appetizers

huile oil
  huile d'arachide groundnut oil
  huile de tournesol sunflower oil

huître oyster

I

îles flottantes soft meringues floating on fresh custard

Izarra vert green-coloured herb liqueur

J

jambon ham
  jambon de Bayonne cured raw ham from the Basque country
  jambon de Paris boiled ham

jardinière, ...à la with peas and carrots, or other fresh vegetables

julienne vegetables cut into fine strips

jus juice, meat-based glaze or sauce
  jus de pomme apple juice
  jus d'orange orange juice

K

kir white wine and *cassis* aperitif

kirsch a kind of *eau-de-vie* made from cherries (Alsace)

kugelhopf hat-shaped sugar-covered cake from Alsace

L

lait milk
  lait demi-écrémé semi-skimmed milk
  lait écrémé skimmed milk
  lait entier full-cream milk

laitue lettuce

lamproie à la bordelaise lamprey in red wine

langouste crayfish (saltwater)
  langouste froide crayfish served cold with mayonnaise and salad

langoustines scampi (large)

langue tongue

lapin rabbit

lard fat, streaky bacon
  lard fumé smoked bacon
lardon strip of fat, diced bacon
laurier bayleaf
légumes vegetables
lentilles lentils
levure yeast
lièvre hare
limande lemon sole
limousine, ...à la cooked with chestnuts and red cabbage
lotte de mer monkfish
loup de mer sea-bass
Lyonnaise, ...à la with onions

M

macaron macaroon
macédoine (de fruits) fresh fruit salad
macédoine de légumes mixed cooked vegetables
madeleine small sponge cake
magret de canard duck breast
maïs, maïs doux maize, sweet-corn
mange-tout sugar peas
mangue mango
maquereau mackerel
marcassin young wild boar
marinière, ...à la a sauce of white wine, onions and herbs (mussels or clams)
marmite casserole
marjolaine marjoram
marron chestnut
  marrons glacés candied chestnuts
  marrons Mont Blanc chestnut purée and cream on a rum-soaked sponge cake
matelote fresh-fish stew
  matelote à la normande sea-fish stew with cider, calvados and cream
médaillon thick, medal-sized slices of meat
melon melon
menthe mint, mint tea
merguez spicy, red sausage

meringues à la chantilly meringues filled with whipped cream
merlan whiting
merluche hake
merou grouper
merveilles fritters flavoured with brandy
mignonnette small fillet of lamb
mijoté stewed
mille-feuille thin layers of pastry filled with cream and jam
mirabelle small yellow plum, plum brandy from Alsace
mont-blanc pudding made with chestnuts and cream
Mornay, sauce cream and cheese sauce
morue dried salt cod

moules marinière

moules mussels
  moules marinière mussels cooked in white wine
  moules poulette mussels in wine, cream and mushroom sauce
mourtairol beef, chicken, ham and vegetable soup
mousse au chocolat chocolate mousse
mousseline mashed potatoes with cream and eggs
moutarde mustard
mouton mutton, sheep or lamb

mûre blackberry
muscade nutmeg
myrtille bilberry

N

navet turnip
nectarine nectarine
niçoise, ...à la with garlic and tomatoes
noisette hazelnut
noisettes d'agneau small round pieces of lamb
noix walnut, general term for a nut
nouilles noodles

O

œuf egg
  œufs à la causalade fried eggs with bacon
  œufs à la coque soft-boiled eggs
  œufs au plat fried eggs
  œufs à la tourangelle eggs served with red wine sauce
  œufs Bénédicte poached eggs on toast, with ham and hollandaise sauce
  œufs brouillés scrambled eggs
  œufs durs hard-boiled eggs
  œufs en cocotte eggs baked in individual containers
  œufs frits fried eggs
oie goose
  oie farci aux pruneaux goose stuffed with prunes

oignon

oignon onion
olive olive
omelette omelette
  omelette brayaude cheese and potato omelette
  omelette nature plain omelette

omelette norvégienne baked Alaska
onglet cut of beef
orange orange
orangeade orangeade
orge barley
os bone
oseille sorrel
oursin sea urchin

P

pain bread, loaf of bread
  pain au chocolat croissant with chocolate filling
  pain bagnat bread roll with egg, olives, salad, tuna, anchovies and olive oil
  pain bis brown bread
  pain complet wholemeal bread
  pain d'épice ginger cake
  pain de mie white sliced loaf
  pain de seigle rye bread
  pain grillé toast
palmier caramelized puff pastry
palombe wood pigeon
palourde clam
pamplemousse grapefruit
panais parsnip
pané(e) with breadcrumbs
panini toasted Italian sandwich
panisse thick chickpea flour pancake
papillote, en in filo pastry
parfait rich home-made ice cream
Paris Brest ring-shaped cake filled with praline-flavoured cream
parisienne, ...à la sautéed in butter with white wine, sauce and shallots
parmentier with potatoes
pastèque watermelon
pastis aniseed-based aperitif
patate douce sweet potato
pâté pâté
  pâté de foie de volailles chicken liver pâté
  pâté en croûte pâté encased in pastry
pâtes pasta
  pâtes fraîches fresh pasta

paupiettes meat slices stuffed and rolled

pavé thick slice

pays d'auge, ...à la cream and cider

paysanne, ...à la cooked with diced bacon and vegetables

pêche peach
  pêches melba poached peaches served with a raspberry sauce and vanilla ice cream or whipped cream

piment

pêche

pélandron type of string bean

perche perch (fish)
  perche du Menon perch cooked in champagne

perdreau (perdrix) partridge

Périgueux, sauce with truffles

Pernod aperitif with aniseed flavour (*pastis*)

persil parsley

persillé(e) with parsley

petit-beurre butter biscuit

petit farcis stuffed tomatoes, aubergines, courgettes and peppers

petit pain roll

petits fours bite-sized cakes and pastries

petits pois small peas

petit-suisse a smooth mixture of cream and curds

pieds et paques mutton or pork tripe and trotters

pigeon pigeon

pignons pine nuts

pilon drumstick (chicken)

piment red pepper
  piment doux sweet pepper
  piment fort chilli

pimenté peppery hot

pintade/pintadeau guinea fowl

pipérade tomato, pepper and onion omelette

piquant spicy

piquante, ...à la gherkins, vinegar and shallots

pissaladière a kind of flan made mainly in the Nice region, filled with onions, anchovies and black olives

pistache pistachio

pistou garlic, basil and olive oil sauce – similar to *pesto*.

plat dish
  plat principal main course

plate still

plie plaice

poché(e) poached

poêlé pan-fried

pimenté peppery hot

point, ...à medium rare

poire pear
  poires belle Hélène poached pears with vanilla ice cream and chocolate sauce

poireau leek

pois peas

pois cassés split peas

pois-chiches chickpeas

poisson fish

poitevin pork-stuffed cabbage

poitrine breast (lamb or veal)

poivre pepper

poivron sweet pepper
poivron rouge red pepper
poivron verde green pepper

pomme apple

pomme (de terre) potato
pommes à l'anglaise boiled potatoes
pommes à la vapeur steamed potatoes
pommes allumettes match-stick chips
pommes dauphine potato croquettes
pommes duchesse potato mashed then baked in the oven
pommes frites fried potatoes
pommes Lyonnaise potatoes fried with onions
pommes mousseline potatoes mashed with cream
pommes rissolées small potatoes deep-fried

pompe aux grattons pork flan

porc pork

pot au feu beef and vegetable stew

potage soup, generally creamed or thickened

poté auvergnate cabbage and meat soup

potiron type of pumpkin

poulet chicken
poulet basquaise chicken stew with wine, tomatoes, mushrooms and peppers

poulet céléstine chicken cooked in white wine with mushrooms and onion
poulet demi-deuil chicken breasts in a wine sauce
poulet Vallée d'Auge chicken cooked with cider, calvados, apples and cream

poulpe à la niçoise octopus in tomato sauce

pousses de soja bean sprouts

poussin baby chicken

poutargue mullet roe paste

praire clam

praliné hazelnut flavoured

primeurs spring vegetables

provençale, ...à la cooked with tomatoes, peppers, garlic and white wine

prune plum, plum brandy

pruneau prune, damson (Switz.)

purée mashed potatoes

Q

quatre-quarts cake made with equal parts of butter, flour, sugar and eggs

quenelles poached fish or meat mousse balls served in a sauce
quenelles de brochet pike mousse in cream sauce

quetsch type of plum

queue de bœuf oxtail

quiche Lorraine flan with egg, fresh cream and diced back bacon

R

râble saddle

radis radishes

ragoût stew, casserole

raie skate

raifort horseradish

raisin grape

raisin sec sultana, raisin

raïto red wine, olive, caper, garlic and shallot sauce

ramier wood pigeon

râpé(e) grated

rascasse scorpion fish

poires belle hélène

ratatouille

ratatouille tomatoes, aubergines, courgettes and garlic cooked in olive oil

rave turnip

raviolis pasta parcels of meat (in provençal dialect)

reine-claude greengage

rilettes coarse pork pâté
  rillettes de canard coarse duck pâté

ris de veau calf sweetbread

riz rice

rognon kidney
  rognons blancs testicles
  rognons sautés sauce madère sautéed kidneys served in Madeira sauce

romaine cos lettuce

romarin rosemary

romsteak rump steak

rond de gigot large slice of leg of lamb

rosbif roast beef

rôti roast

rouget red mullet

rouillé spicy version of garlic mayonnaise (aïoli) served with fish stew

roulade meat or fish, stuffed and rolled

roulé sweet or savoury roll

rutabaga swede

S

sabayon dessert made with egg yolks, sugar and Marsala wine

sablé shortbread

safran saffron

saignant rare

Saint-Hubert game consommé flavoured with wine

salade lettuce, salad
  salade aveyronnaise cheese salad (made with Roquefort)
  salade de fruits fruit salad
  salade de saison mixed salad and/or greens in season
  salade lyonnaise vegetable salad (cooked), dressed with anchovies and capers
  salade niçoise many variations on a famous theme: the basic ingredients are green beans, anchovies, black olives, green peppers

salade niçoise

salade russe mixed cooked vegetables in mayonnaise
  salade verte green salad

salé salted/spicy

salsifis salsify

sandwich sandwich
  sandwich croque-monsieur grilled gruyère cheese and ham sandwich
  sandwich croque-madame grilled cheese and bacon, sausage, chicken or egg sandwich

sanglier wild boar

sarrasin buckwheat

sarriette savoury (herb)

sauce sauce

saucisse/saucisson sausage

saumon salmon
  saumon fumé smoked salmon

saumon poché poached salmon

sauté(e) sautéed

sauté d'agneau lamb stew

savarin a filled ring-shaped cake

savoyarde, ...à la with gruyère cheese

scarole endive, escarole

sec dry or dried

seiche cuttlefish

sel salt

selle d'agneau saddle of lamb

semoule semolina

socca thin chickpea flour pancake

sole sole

sole Albert sole in cream sauce with mustard

sole cardinal sole cooked in wine, served with lobster sauce

sole Normande sole cooked in a cream, cider and shrimp sauce

sole Saint Germain grilled sole with butter and tarragon sauce

sole-limande lemon sole

soufflé light fluffy dish made wih egg yolks and stiffly beaten egg whites combined with cheese, ham, fish, etc

soufflé au Grand Marnier soufflé flavoured with Grand Marnier liqueur

soufflé au jambon ham soufflé

soupe hearty and chunky soup

soupe à l'oignon onion soup usually served with a crisp chunk of French bread in the dish with grated cheese piled on top

tarte tatin

soupe à la bière beer soup

soupe au pistou vegetable soup with garlic and basil

soupe aux choux cabbage soup with pork

soupe de poisson fish soup

soupe anglaise type of trifle

steak steak

steak au poivre steak with peppercorns

steak tartare minced raw steak mixed with raw egg, chopped onion, tartare or worcester sauce, parsley and capers

St Raphael aperitif (with quinine)

sucre sugar

sucré sweet

suprême de volaille breast of chicken in cream sauce

T

tagine North African casserole

tapendade olive paste

tarte open tart, generally sweet

tarte aux fraises strawberry tart

tarte aux pommes apple tart

tarte flambée thin pizza-like pastry topped with onion, cream and bacon

tarte Normande apple tart

tarte tatin upside down tart with caramelized apples or pears

tarte tropezienne sponge cake filled with custard cream topped with nuts

tartine open sandwich

terrine terrine, pâté

terrine de campagne pork and liver terrine

terrine de porc et gibier pork and game terrine

soupe à l'oignon

tête de veau calf's head

tétras grouse

thé tea
  thé au citron tea with lemon
  thé au lait tea with milk
  thé sans sucre tea without sugar

thermidor lobster grilled in its shell with cream sauce

thon tuna fish

tilleul lime tea

timbale round dish in which a mixture of usually meat or fish is cooked. Often lined with pastry and served with a rich sauce
  timbale d'écrevisses crayfish in a cream, wine and brandy sauce
  timbale de fruits pastry base covered with fruits

tiramisu mascarpone cheese, chocolate and cream

tisane herbal tea

tomate tomato
  tomates à la provençale grilled tomatoes steeped in garlic
  tomates farcies stuffed tomatoes

tomme type of cheese

tournedos thick fillet steak
  tournedos Rossini thick fillet steak on fried bread with goose liver and truffles on top

tourte à la viande meat pie usually made with veal and pork

tripe tripe
  tripes à la mode de Caen tripe cooked with vegetables, herbs, cider and calvados

tripoux mutton tripe

truffade potato pie with garlic and cheese originating in the Auvergne

tournedos rossini

truffe truffle

truffiat potato cake

truite trout
  truite aux amandes trout covered with almonds

turbot turbot

V

vacherin large meringue filled with cream, ice cream and fruit

vapeur, ...à la steamed

veau calf, veal
  veau sauté Marengo veal cooked in a casserole with white wine and garlic

velouté thick creamy white sauce made with fish, veal or chicken stock. Also used in soups

venaison venison

verdure, en garnished with green vegetables

verjus juice of unripe grapes

vermicelle vermicelli

véronique, ...à la grapes, wine and cheese

verveine herbal tea made with verbena

viande meat
  viande séchée thin slices of cured beef

vichyssoise leek and potato soup, served cold

viennoise fried in egg and breadcrumbs

vin wine
  vin blanc white wine
  vin de pays local regional wine
  vin de table table wine
  vin rosé rosé wine
  vin rouge red wine

vinaigrette French dressing of oil and vinegar

vinaigre vinegar

violet sea squirt

volaille poultry

Y

yaourt yoghurt

Z

zewelwai onion flan

DICTIONARY

english–french

french–english

A

a(n) un (m)/une (f)
abbey l'abbaye (f)
able: *to be able to* pouvoir
abortion l'avortement (m)
about (approximately) vers ; environ
  (concerning) au sujet de
  about 100 francs environ cent francs
  about 10 o'clock vers dix heures
above au-dessus (de)
  above the bed au-dessus du lit
  above the farm au-dessus de la
  ferme
abroad à l'étranger
abscess l'abcès (m)
accelerator l'accélérateur (m)
accent l'accent (m)
to accept accepter
  do you accept this card? vous
  acceptez cette carte?
access l'access (m)
accident l'accident (m)
accident & emergency department
  les urgences
accommodation le logement
to accompany accompagner
account le compte
account number le numéro de
  compte
to ache faire mal
  it aches ça fait mal
acid l'acide (m)
actor l'acteur (m), l'actrice (f)
adaptor (electrical) l'adaptateur (m)
address l'adresse (f)
  here's my address voici mon
  addresse
  what is the address? quelle est
  l'adresse?
address book le carnet d'adresse
admission charge l'entrée (f)
to admit (to hospital) hospitaliser
adult m/f l'adulte
  for adults pour adultes
advance: *in advance* à l'avance
advertisement (in paper) l'annonce (f)
  (on TV) la publicité
to advise conseiller
A&E les urgences
aeroplane l'avion (m)
aerosol l'aérosol (m)

afraid: *to be afraid of* avoir peur de 10
after après
afternoon l'après-midi (m)
  in the afternoon l'après-midi
  this afternoon cet après-midi
  tomorrow afternoon demain
  après-midi
aftershave l'après-rasage (m)
again encore
against contre
age l'âge (m)
agency l'agence (f)
ago: *a week ago* il y a une semaine
to agree être d'accord
agreement l'accord (m)
AIDS le SIDA
airbag (in car) l'airbag (m)
airbed le matelas pneumatique
air-conditioning la climatisation
air freshener le désodorisant
airline la ligne aérienne
air mail: *by airmail* par avion
airplane l'avion (m)
airport l'aéroport (m)
airport bus la navette pour
  l'aéroport
air ticket le billet d'avion
aisle le couloir
alarm l'alarme (f)
alarm clock le réveil
alcohol l'alcool (m)
alcohol-free sans alcool
alcoholic drink la boisson alcoolisée
all tout(e)/tous/toutes
allergic allergique
  I'm allergic to... je suis allergique à...
allergy l'allergie
to allow permettre
  it's not allowed c'est interdit
all right (agreed) d'accord
  are you all right? ça va?
almost presque
alone tout(e) seul(e)
Alps les Alpes
already déjà
also aussi
altar l'autel (m)
always toujours
a.m. du matin
am: *I am* je suis
amber (traffic light) orange
ambulance l'ambulance (f)
America l'Amérique (f)

American américain(e)
amount *(total)* le montant
anaesthetic l'anesthésique *(m)*
  a local anaesthetic une anesthésie locale
  a general anaesthetic une anesthésie générale
anchor l'ancre *(f)*
and et
angina l'angine de poitrine *(f)*
angry fâché(e)
animal l'animal *(m)*
aniseed l'anis *(m)*
ankle la cheville
anniversary l'anniversaire *(m)*
to announce annoncer
announcement l'annonce *(f)*
annual annuel(-elle)
another un(e) autre
  another beer une autre bière
answer la réponse
to answer répondre à
answerphone le répondeur
antacid le comprimé contre les brûlures d'estomac
antibiotic l'antibiotique *(m)*
antifreeze l'antigel *(m)*
antihistamine l'antihistaminique *(m)*
antiques les antiquités
antique shop le magasin d'antiquités
antiseptic l'antiseptique *(m)*
any de (du/de la/des)
  have you any apples? vous avez des pommes?
anyone quelqu'un/personne
anything quelque chose/rien
anywhere quelque part
apartment l'appartement *(m)*
appendicitis l'appendicite *(f)*
apple la pomme
application form le formulaire
appointment le rendez-vous
  I have an appointment j'ai rendez-vous
approximately environ
April avril
architect *m/f* l'architecte
architecture l'architecture *(f)*
are: *you are* vous êtes
  we are nous sommes
  they are ils/elles sont
arm le bras
armbands *(for swimming)* les bracelets gonflables

armchair le fauteuil
to arrange arranger
to arrest arrêter
arrival l'arrivée *(f)*
to arrive arriver
art l'art *(m)*
art gallery le musée
arthritis l'arthrite *(f)*
artificial artificiel
artist l'artiste *(m/f)*
ashtray le cendrier
to ask demander
  to ask a question poser une question
aspirin l'aspirine *(f)*
asthma l'asthme *(m)*
  I have asthma je suis asthmatique
at à
  at my/your home chez moi/vous
  at 8 o'clock à huit heures
  at once tout de suite
  at night la nuit
Atlantic Ocean l'Océan atlantique *(m)*
attack *(mugging)* l'agression *(f)*
  (medical) la crise
to attack agresser
attic le grenier
attractive séduisant(e)
auction la vente aux enchères
audience le public
August août *(m)*
aunt la tante
au pair la jeune fille au pair
Australia l'Australie *(f)*
Australian australien(ne)
author l'écrivain ; l'auteur *(m)*
automatic automatique
automatic car la voiture à boîte automatique
auto-teller le distributeur automatique (de billets)
autumn l'automne *(m)*
available disponible
avalanche l'avalanche *(f)*
avenue l'avenue *(f)*
average moyen(ne)
to avoid éviter
awake: *I was awake all night* je n'ai pas dormi(e) pendant toute la nuit
awful affreux(-euse)
axle *(car)* l'essieu *(m)*

B

baby le bébé
baby food les petits pots
baby milk *(formula)* le lait maternisé
baby's bottle le biberon
baby seat *(car)* le siège pour bébés
babysitter le/la babysitter
baby wipes les lingettes
back *(of body)* le dos
backpack le sac à dos
bacon le bacon ; le lard
bad *(food, weather)* mauvais(e)
badminton le badminton
bag le sac
  (suitcase) la valise
baggage les bagages
baggage allowance le poids (de bagages) autorisé
baggage reclaim la livraison des bagages
bait *(for fishing)* l'appât *(m)*
baked au four
baker's la boulangerie
balcony le balcon
bald *(person)* chauve
  (tyre) lisse
ball *(large: football, etc)* le ballon
  (small: golf, tennis, etc) la balle
ballet le ballet
balloon le ballon
banana la banane
band *(music)* le groupe
bandage le pansement
bank *(money)* la banque
  (river) la rive ; le bord
bank account le compte en banque
banknote le billet de banque
bar le bar
bar of chocolate la tablette de chocolat
barbecue le barbecue
  to have a barbecue faire un barbecue
barber's le coiffeur
to bark aboyer
barn la grange
barrel *(wine, beer)* le tonneau
basement le sous-sol
basil le basilic
basket le panier

basketball le basket-ball
bat *(baseball, cricket)* la batte
  (animal) la chauve-souris
bath le bain
  to have a bath prendre un bain
bathing cap le bonnet de bain
bathroom la salle de bains
  with bathroom avec salle de bains
battery *(for car)* la batterie
  (for radio, camera, etc) la pile
bay *(along coast)* la baie
B&B la chambre d'hôte
to be être
beach la plage
  private beach la plage privée
  sandy beach la plage de sable
  nudist beach la plage nudiste
beach hut la cabine
bean le haricot
beard la barbe
beautiful beau (belle)
beauty salon le salon de beauté
because parce que
to become devenir
bed le lit
  double bed le grand lit ; le lit de deux personnes
  single bed le lit d'une personne
  sofa bed le canapé-lit
  twin beds les lits jumeaux
bed clothes les couvertures
bedroom la chambre à coucher
bee l'abeille *(f)*
beef le bœuf
beer la bière
before avant
to begin commencer
behind derrière
beige beige
Belgian belge
Belgium la Belgique
to believe croire
bell *(church, school)* la cloche
  (doorbell) la sonnette
to belong to appartenir à
below sous
belt la ceinture
bend *(in road)* le virage
berth *(train, ship, etc)* la couchette
beside *(next to)* à côté de
  beside the bank à côté de la banque
best le/la meilleur(e)
bet le pari
to bet on faire un pari sur

1 **better** meilleur(e)
  better than meilleur que
between entre
bib *(baby's)* le bavoir
bicycle la bicyclette ; le vélo
bicycle repair kit la trousse de
  réparation (pour vélo)
bidet le bidet
big grand(e), gros(se)
bike *(pushbike)* le vélo
  (motorbike) la moto
bike lock l'antivol *(m)*
bikini le bikini
bill *(restaurant)* l'addition *(f)*
  (hotel) la note
  (for work done) la facture
bin *(dustbin)* la poubelle
bin liner le sac poubelle
binoculars les jumelles
bird l'oiseau *(m)*
biro le stylo
birth la naissance
birth certificate l'acte de naissance *(m)*
birthday l'anniversaire *(m)*
  happy birthday! bon anniversaire!
  my birthday is on... mon
  anniversaire c'est...
birthday card la carte d'anniversaire
birthday present le cadeau
  d'anniversaire
biscuits les biscuits
bit: *a bit (of)* un peu (de)
bite *(animal)* la morsure
  (insect) la piqûre
to bite *(animal)* mordre
  (insect) piquer
bitten *(by animal)* mordu(e)
  (by insect) piqué(e)
bitter amer(-ère)
black noir(e)
black ice le verglas
blanket la couverture
bleach l'eau de Javel *(f)*
to bleed saigner
blender *(for food)* le mixeur
blind *(person)* aveugle
blind *(for window)* le store
blister l'ampoule *(f)*
block of flats l'immeuble *(m)*
blocked bouché(e)
  the sink is blocked l'évier est
  bouché
blond *(person)* blond(e)
blood le sang
blood group le groupe sanguin

blood pressure la tension (artérielle)
blood test l'analyse de sang *(f)*
blouse le chemisier
blow-dry le brushing
blue bleu(e)
  dark blue bleu foncé
  light blue bleu clair
boar *(wild)* le sanglier
to board *(plane, train, etc)* embarquer
boarding card la carte
  d'embarquement
boarding house la pension (de
  famille)
boat le bateau
  (rowing) la barque
boat trip l'excursion en bateau *(f)*
body le corps
to boil faire bouillir
boiled bouilli(e)
boiler la chaudière
bomb la bombe
bone l'os *(m)*
  (fish) l'arête *(f)*
bonfire le feu
book le livre
to book *(reserve)* réserver
booking la réservation
booking office le bureau de location
bookshop la librairie
boots les bottes
  (short) les bottillons
border *(of country)* la frontière
boring ennuyeux(-euse)
born: *to be born* naître
to borrow emprunter
boss le chef
both les deux
bottle la bouteille
  a bottle of wine une bouteille
  de vin
  a bottle of water une bouteille
  d'eau
  a half-bottle une demi-bouteille
bottle opener l'ouvre-bouteilles *(m)*
bottom *(of pool, etc)* le fond
bowl *(for soup, etc)* le bol
bow tie le nœud papillon
box la boîte
box office le bureau de location
boxer shorts le boxer-short
boy le garçon
boyfriend le copain

bra le soutien-gorge
bracelet le bracelet
brain le cerveau
brake(s) le(s) frein(s)
to brake freiner
brake fluid le liquide de freins
brake lights les feux de stop
brake pads les plaquettes de frein
branch *(of tree)* la branche
  (of company, etc) la succursale
brand *(make)* la marque
brass le cuivre
brave courageux(-euse)
bread le pain
  (French stick) la baguette
  (thin French stick) la ficelle
  sliced bread le pain en tranches
bread roll le petit pain
to break casser
breakable fragile
breakdown *(car)* la panne
  (nervous) la dépression
breakdown van la dépanneuse
breakfast le petit déjeuner
breast le sein
to breast-feed allaiter
to breathe respirer
brick la brique
bride la mariée
bridegroom le marié
bridge le pont
briefcase la serviette
Brillo® pad le tampon Jex®
to bring apporter
Britain la Grande Bretagne
British britannique
brochure la brochure ; le dépliant
broken cassé(e)
  my leg is broken je me suis cassé
  la jambe
broken down *(car, etc)* en panne
bronchitis la bronchite
bronze le bronze
brooch la broche
broom *(brush)* le balai
brother le frère
brother-in-law le beau-frère
brown marron
bruise le bleu
brush la brosse
bubble bath le bain moussant

bucket le seau
buffet car *(train)* la voiture-buffet
to build construire
building l'immeuble *(m)*
bulb *(light)* l'ampoule *(f)*
bumbag la banane
bumper *(on car)* le pare-chocs
bunch *(of flowers)* le bouquet
  (of grapes) la grappe
bungee jumping le saut à l'élastique
bureau de change le bureau de
change
burger l'hamburger *(m)*
burglar le/la cambrioleur(-euse)
burglar alarm le système d'alarme
to burn brûler
bus le bus
  (coach) le car
bus pass la carte de bus
bus station la gare routière
bus stop l'arrêt de bus *(m)*
bus ticket le ticket de bus
business les affaires
  on business pour affaires
business card la carte de visite
business class la classe affaires
businessman/woman l'homme/la
femme d'affaires
business trip le voyage d'affaires
busy occupé(e)
but mais
butcher's la boucherie
butter le beurre
button le bouton
to buy acheter
by *(via)* par
  (beside) à côté de
  by bus en bus
  by car en voiture
  by ship en bateau
  by train en train
bypass *(road)* la rocade

C

cab *(taxi)* le taxi
cabaret le cabaret
cabin *(on boat)* la cabine
cabin crew l'équipage *(m)*
cablecar le téléphérique ; la benne
café le café
  internet café le cybercafé
cafetière la cafetière
cake *(large)* le gâteau
  (small) la pâtisserie

13 **cake shop** la pâtisserie
calculator la calculatrice
calendar le calendrier
call (telephone) l'appel (m)
to call (speak, phone) appeler
calm la calme
camcorder le caméscope
camera l'appareil photo (m)
camera case l'étui (m)
camera shop le magasin de photo
to camp camper
camping gas le butane
camping stove le réchaud de camping
campsite le camping
can (to be able to) pouvoir
  (to know how to) savoir
  I can je peux/sais
  we can nous pouvons/savons
can la boîte
can opener l'ouvre-boîtes (m)
Canada le Canada
Canadian canadien(ne)
canal le canal
to cancel annuler
cancellation l'annulation (f)
cancer le cancer
candle la bougie
canoe le kayak
canoeing: to go canoeing faire du canoë-kayak
cap (hat) la casquette
  (diaphragm) le diaphragme
capital (city) la capitale
car la voiture
car alarm l'alarme de voiture (f)
car ferry le ferry
car hire la location de voitures
car insurance l'assurance automobile (f)
car keys les clés de voiture
car phone le téléphone de voiture
car park le parking
car parts les pièces pour voiture
car radio l'autoradio (m)
car seat (for child) le siège pour enfant
carwash le lave-auto
carafe le pichet
caravan la caravane
carburettor le carburateur
card la carte
  birthday card la carte d'anniversaire
  business card la carte de visite
  playing cards les cartes à jouer

cardboard le carton
cardigan le cardigan
careful: *to be careful* faire attention
  careful! attention!
carpet (rug) le tapis
  (fitted) la moquette
carriage (railway) la voiture
carrot la carotte
to carry porter
carton (cigarettes) la cartouche
  (milk, juice) le brick
case (suitcase) la valise
cash l'argent liquide (m)
to cash (cheque) encaisser
cash desk la caisse
cash dispenser (ATM) le distributeur automatique (de billets)
cashier le/la caissier(-ière)
cashpoint le distributeur automatique (de billets)
casino le casino
casserole dish la cocotte
cassette la cassette
cassette player le magnétophone
castle le château
casualty department les urgences
cat le chat
cat food la nourriture pour chats
catalogue le catalogue
catch (bus, train) prendre
cathedral la cathédrale
Catholic catholique
cave la grotte
cavity (in tooth) la carie
CD le CD
CD player le lecteur de CD
ceiling le plafond
cellar la cave
cellphone le téléphone cellulaire
cemetery le cimetière
centimetre le centimètre
central central(e)
central heating le chauffage central
central locking le verrouillage central
centre le centre
century le siècle
ceramic la céramique
cereal la céréale
certain (sure) certain(e)
certificate le certificat
chain la chaîne

chair la chaise
chairlift le télésiège
chalet le chalet
chambermaid la femme de chambre
champagne le champagne
change *(small coins)* la monnaie
to change changer
  to change money changer de l'argent
  to change clothes se changer
  to change bus changer d'autobus
  to change train changer de train
changing room la cabine d'essayage
Channel *(English)* la Manche
chapel la chapelle
charcoal le charbon de bois
charge *(fee)* le prix
to charge prendre
charger *(battery)* le chargeur
charter flight le vol charter
cheap bon marché
cheaper moins cher
cheap rate *(phone)* le tarif réduit
to check vérifier
to check in enregistrer
check-in (desk) l'enregistrement des bagages *(m)*
  (at hotel) la réception
cheek la joue
cheers! santé!
cheese le fromage
chef le chef de cuisine
chemist's la pharmacie
cheque le chèque
cheque book le carnet de chèques
cheque card la carte d'identité bancaire
chest *(body)* la poitrine
chewing gum le chewing-gum
chicken le poulet
chickenpox la varicelle
child l'enfant *(m)*
child safety seat *(car)* le siège pour enfant
children les enfants
  for children pour enfants
chimney la cheminée
chin le menton
china la porcelaine
chips les frites
chocolate le chocolat

drinking-chocolate le chocolat (en poudre)   **11**
chocolates les chocolats
choir la chorale
to choose choisir
chop *(meat)* la côtelette
chopping board la planche à découper
christening le baptême
Christian name le prénom
Christmas Noël *(m)*
  merry Christmas! joyeux Noël!
Christmas card la carte de Noël
Christmas Eve la veille de Noël
church l'église *(f)*
cigar le cigare
cigarette la cigarette
cigarette lighter le briquet
cigarette paper le papier à cigarette
cinema le cinéma
circle *(theatre)* le balcon
circuit breaker le disjoncteur
circus le cirque
cistern *(toilet)* le réservoir de chasse d'eau
city la ville
city centre le centre-ville
class la classe
  first-class de première classe
  second-class de seconde classe
clean propre
to clean nettoyer
cleaner *(person)* la femme de ménage
cleanser *(for face)* le démaquillant
clear clair(e)
client le client/la cliente
cliff *(along coast)* la falaise
  (in mountains) l'escarpement
to climb *(mountain)* faire de la montagne
climbing boots les chaussures de montagne
Clingfilm® le Scellofrais®
clinic la clinique
cloakroom le vestiaire
clock l'horloge *(f)*
close by proche
to close fermer
closed *(shop, etc)* fermé(e)
cloth *(rag)* le chiffon
  (fabric) le tissu
clothes les vêtements
clothes line la corde à linge

5 **clothes pegs** les pinces à linge
clothes shop le magasin de confection
cloudy nuageux(-euse)
club le club
clutch (in car) l'embrayage (m)
coach (bus) le car ; l'autocar (m)
coach station la gare routière
coach trip l'excursion en car (f)
coal le charbon
coast la côte
coastguard le garde-côte
coat le manteau
coat hanger le cintre
cockroach le cafard
cocktail le cocktail
cocoa le cacao
code le code
coffee le café
  white coffee le café au lait
  black coffee le café noir
  cappuccino le cappuccino
  decaffeinated coffee le café décaféiné
coil (IUD) le stérilet
coin la pièce de monnaie
Coke® le Coca®
colander la passoire
cold froid
  I'm cold j'ai froid
  it's cold il fait froid
cold water l'eau froide (f)
cold (illness) le rhume
  I have a cold j'ai un rhume
cold sore le bouton de fièvre
collar le col
collar bone la clavicule
colleague le/la collègue
to collect (someone) aller chercher
collection la collection
colour la couleur
colour-blind daltonien(ne)
colour film (for camera) la pellicule couleur
comb le peigne
to come venir
  (to arrive) arriver
  to come back revenir
  to come in entrer
  come in! entrez!
comedy la comédie
comfortable confortable
company (firm) la compagnie ; la société
compartment le compartiment

compass la boussole
to complain faire un réclamation
complaint la plainte
to complete remplir
compulsory obligatoire
computer l'ordinateur (m)
computer disk (floppy) la disquette
computer game le jeu électronique
computer program le programme informatique
concert le concert
concert hall la salle de concert
concession la réduction
concussion la commotion (cérébrale)
conditioner l'après-shampooing (m)
condom le préservatif
conductor (on bus) le receveur
conference la conférence
to confirm confirmer
confirmation la confirmation
confused: I am confused je m'y perds
congratulations félicitations!
connection (bus, train, etc) la correspondance
constipated constipé(e)
consulate le consulat
to consult consulter
to contact contacter
contact lenses les verres de contact
contact lens cleaner le produit pour nettoyer les verres de contact
to continue continuer
contraceptive le contraceptif
contract le contrat
convenient: it's not convenient ça ne m'arrange pas
convulsions les convulsions
to cook (be cooking) cuisiner
  to cook a meal préparer un repas
cooked cuisiné
cooker la cuisinière
cookies les cookies
cool frais (fraîche)
cool-box (for picnic) la glacière
copper le cuivre
copy (duplicate) la copie
to copy copier
cork le bouchon
corkscrew le tire-bouchon
corner le coin

c/d   eng–french

cornflakes les corn-flakes
corridor le couloir
cortisone la cortisone
cosmetics les cosmétiques
cost le coût
to cost coûter
  how much does it cost? ça coûte combien?
costume *(swimming)* le maillot (de bain)
cot le lit d'enfant
cottage la maison de campagne
cotton le coton
cotton bud le coton-tige®
cotton wool le coton hydrophile
couchette la couchette
cough la toux
to cough tousser
cough mixture le sirop pour la toux
cough sweets les pastilles pour la toux
counter *(shop, bar, etc)* le comptoir
country *(not town)* la campagne
  (nation) le pays
countryside le paysage
couple *(two people)* le couple
  a couple of... deux ...
courgette la courgette
courier service le service de messageries
course *(syllabus)* le cours
  (of meal) le plat
cousin le/la cousin(e)
cover charge *(restaurant)* le couvert
cow la vache
crafts les objets artisanaux
craftsperson l'artisan(e)
cramps *(period pain)* les règles douloureuses
crash *(car)* l'accident *(m)* ; la collision
crash helmet le casque
cream *(food, lotion)* la crème
  soured cream la crème aigre
  whipped cream la crème fouettée
credit card la carte de crédit
crime le crime
crisps les chips
croissant le croissant
cross la croix
to cross *(road, sea, etc)* traverser
cross-country skiing le ski de fond
cross-channel ferry le ferry qui traverse la Manche

crossing *(by sea)* la traversée
crossroads le carrefour ; le croisement
crossword puzzle les mots croisés
crowd la foule
crowded bondé(e)
crown la couronne
cruise la croisière
crutches les béquilles
to cry *(weep)* pleurer
crystal le cristal
cucumber le concombre
cufflinks les boutons de manchette
cul-de-sac le cul-de-sac
cup la tasse
cupboard le placard
currant le raisin sec
currency la devise ; la monnaie
current *(air, water, etc)* le courant
curtain le rideau
cushion le coussin
custom *(tradition)* la tradition
customer le/la client(e)
customs la douane
  (duty) les droits de douane
customs declaration la déclaration de douane
to cut couper
cut la coupure
cutlery les couverts
to cycle faire du vélo
cycle track la piste cyclable
cycling le cyclisme
cyst le kyste
cystitis la cystite

D

daily *(each day)* tous les jours
dairy produce les produits laitiers
dam le barrage
damage les dégâts
damp humide
dance le bal
to dance danser
danger le danger
dangerous dangereux(-euse)
dark l'obscurité *(f)*
  after dark la nuit tombée
date la date
date of birth la date de naissance
daughter la fille
daughter-in-law la belle-fille ; la bru
dawn l'aube *(f)*

day le jour
  per day par jour
  every day tous les jours
dead mort(e)
deaf sourd(e)
dear *(expensive, in letter)* cher (chère)
debts les créances
decaffeinated décaféiné(e)
  decaffeinated coffee le café décaféiné
December décembre
deckchair la chaise longue
to declare déclarer
  nothing to declare rien à déclarer
deep profond(e)
deep freeze le congélateur
deer le cerf
to defrost décongeler
to de-ice *(windscreen)* dégivrer
delay le retard
  how long is the delay? il y a combien de retard?
delayed retardé(e)
delicatessen l'épicerie fine *(f)*
delicious délicieux(-euse)
demonstration la manifestation
dental floss le fil dentaire
dentist le/la dentiste
dentures le dentier
deodorant le déodorant
to depart partir
department le rayon
department store le grand magasin
departure le départ
departure lounge la salle d'embarquement
deposit les arrhes
to describe décrire
description la description
desk *(furniture)* le bureau
  (information) l'accueil *(m)*
dessert le dessert
details les détails
detergent le détergent
detour la déviation
to develop *(photos)* faire développer
diabetes le diabète
diabetic diabétique
  I'm diabetic je suis diabétique
to dial *(a number)* composer
dialling code l'indicatif *(m)*
dialling tone la tonalité
diamond le diamant
diapers les couches (pour bébé)

diaphragm le diaphragme
diarrhoea la diarrhée
diary l'agenda *(m)*
dice le dé
dictionary le dictionnaire
to die mourir
diesel le gas-oil
diet le régime
  I'm on a diet je suis au régime
  special diet le régime spécial
different différent(e)
difficult difficile
to dilute diluer ; ajouter de l'eau à
dinghy le youyou
dining room la salle à manger
dinner *(evening meal)* le dîner
  to have dinner dîner
diplomat le diplomate
direct *(train, etc)* direct(e)
directions les indications
  to ask for directions demander le chemin
directory *(telephone)* l'annuaire *(m)*
directory enquiries (le service des) renseignements
dirty sale
disability: *to have a disability* être handicapé(e)
disabled *(person)* handicapé(e)
to disagree ne pas être d'accord
to disappear disparaître
disaster la catastrophe
disco la discothèque
discount le rabais
to discover découvrir
disease la maladie
dish le plat
dishtowel le torchon à vaisselle
dishwasher le lave-vaisselle
disinfectant le désinfectant
disk *(floppy)* la disquette
to dislocate *(joint)* disloquer
disposable jetable
distant lointain(e)
distilled water l'eau distillée *(f)*
district *(of town)* le quartier
to disturb déranger
to dive plonger
diversion la déviation
divorced divorcé(e)
DIY shop le magasin de bricolage

dizzy pris(e) de vertige
to do faire
doctor le médecin
documents les papiers
dog le chien
dog food la nourriture pour chiens
dog lead la laisse
doll la poupée
dollar le dollar
domestic flight le vol intérieur
donor card la carte de doneur d'organes
door la porte
doorbell la sonnette
double double
double bed le grand lit
double room la chambre pour deux personnes
doughnut le beignet
down: *to go down* descendre
downstairs en bas
drain *(house)* le tuyau d'écoulement
draught *(of air)* le courant d'air
  there's a draught il y a un courant d'air
draught lager la bière pression
drawer le tiroir
drawing le dessin
dress la robe
to dress s'habiller
dressing *(for food)* la vinaigrette
  (for wound) le pansement
dressing gown le peignoir
drill *(tool)* la perceuse électrique
drink la boisson
to drink boire
drinking water l'eau potable *(f)*
to drive conduire
driver *(of car)* le conducteur/ la conductrice
driving licence le permis de conduire
drought la sécheresse
to drown se noyer
drug *(medicine)* le médicament
  (narcotics) la drogue
drunk ivre ; soûl(e)
dry sec (sèche)
to dry sécher
dry-cleaner's le pressing
dummy *(for baby)* la sucette ; la tétine

during pendant
dust la poussière
duster le chiffon
dustpan and brush la pelle et la balayette
duty-free hors taxe
duvet la couette
duvet cover la housse de couette
dye la teinture
dynamo la dynamo

E

each chacun/chacune
ear l'oreille *(f)*
earlier plus tôt
early tôt
to earn gagner
earphones le casque
earplugs les boules Quiès®
earrings les boucles d'oreille
earth la terre
earthquake le tremblement de terre
east l'est *(m)*
Easter Pâques
  happy Easter! joyeuses Pâques!
easy facile
to eat manger
economy *(class)* économique
egg l'œuf *(m)*
  fried eggs les œufs sur le plat
  hard-boiled egg l'œuf dur
  scrambled eggs les œufsbrouillés
  soft-boiled egg l'œuf à la coque
either ... or soit ... soit
elastic band l'élastique *(m)*
elastoplast® le sparadrap
elbow le coude
electric électrique
electric blanket la couverture chauffante
electric razor le rasoir électrique
electrician l'électricien *(m)*
electricity l'électricité *(f)*
electricity meter le compteur électrique
elevator l'ascenseur *(f)*
e-mail le e-mail
  to e-mail sb envoyer un e-mail à qn
e-mail address l'adresse éléctronique
embassy l'ambassade *(f)*
emergency l'urgence *(f)*

emergency exit la sortie de secours
empty vide
end la fin
engaged *(to be married)* fiancé(e)
(phone, toilet, etc) occupé(e)
engine le moteur
England l'Angleterre *(f)*
English anglais(e)
(language) l'anglais *(m)*
Englishman/-woman l'Anglais(e) *(m/f)*
to enjoy aimer
I enjoy swimming j'aime nager
I enjoy dancing j'aime danser
enjoy your meal! bon appétit!
enough assez
that's enough ça suffit
enquiry desk les renseignements
to enter entrer
entertainment les divertissements
entrance l'entrée *(f)*
entrance fee le prix d'entrée
envelope l'enveloppe *(f)*
epileptic épileptique
epileptic fit la crise d'épilepsie
equipment l'équipement *(m)*
equal égal
eraser la gomme
error l'erreur *(f)*
escalator l'escalator *(m)*
to escape s'échapper
essential indispensable
estate agency l'agence immobilière *(f)*
Euro *(unit of currency)* l'euro *(m)*
eurocheque l'eurochèque *(m)*
Europe l'Europe *(f)*
European européen(ne)
European Union l'Union européenne *(f)*
evening le soir
this evening ce soir
tomorrow evening demain soir
in the evening le soir
7 o'clock in the evening sept heures du soir
evening dress *(man)* la tenue de soirée
(woman) la robe du soir
evening meal le dîner
every chaque
everyone tout le monde
everything tout
everywhere partout
examination l'examen *(m)*
example: for example par example
excellent excellent(e)

eng-french   e/f

except sauf
excess baggage l'excédent de bagages *(m)*
exchange l'échange *(m)*
to exchange échanger
exchange rate le taux de change
exciting passionnant(e)
excursion l'excursion *(f)*
excuse: *excuse me!* excusez-moi!
(to get by) pardon!
exercise l'exercice *(m)*
exhaust pipe le pot d'échappement
exhibition l'exposition *(f)*
exit la sortie
expenses les frais
expensive cher (chère)
expert *m/f* l'expert(e)
to expire *(ticket, passport)* expirer
to explain expliquer
explosion l'explosion *(f)*
to export exporter
express *(train)* le rapide
express *(parcel, etc)* en exprès
extension *(electrical)* la rallonge
extra *(additional)* supplémentaire
(more) encore
eye l'œil *(m)*
eyes les yeux
eyebrows les sourcils
eye drops les gouttes pour les yeux
eyelashes les cils
eyeliner l'eye-liner *(m)*
eye shadow le fard à paupières

F

fabric le tissu
face le visage
face cloth/glove le gant de toilette
facial les soins du visage
facilities les installations
factory l'usine *(f)*
to faint s'évanouir
fainted évanoui(e)
fair *(hair)* blond(e)
(just) juste
fair *(funfair)* la fête foraine
fake faux (fausse)
fall *(autumn)* l'automne *(m)*
to fall tomber
he has fallen il est tombé

false teeth le dentier
family la famille
famous célèbre
fan (handheld) l'éventail (m)
 (electric) le ventilateur
 (sports) le supporter
fan belt la courroie de ventilateur
fancy dress le déguisement
far loin
 is it far? c'est loin?
fare (bus, metro, etc) le prix du billet
farm la ferme
farmer le fermier
farmhouse la ferme
fashionable à la mode
fast rapide
 too fast trop vite
to fasten (seatbelt) attacher
fat gros (grosse)
 (noun) la graisse
father le père
father-in-law le beau-père
fault (defect) un défaut
 it's not my fault ce n'est pas de
 ma faute
favour le service
favourite préféré(e)
fax le fax
 by fax par fax
fax number le numéro de fax
to fax (document) faxer
 (person) envoyer un fax à
February février
to feed nourrir
to feel sentir
 I feel sick j'ai la nausée
 I don't feel well je ne me sens
 pas bien
feet les pieds
felt-tip pen le feutre
female (animal) la femelle
ferry le ferry
festival le festival
to fetch aller chercher
fever la fièvre
few peu
 a few quelques-un(e)s
fiancé(e) le fiancé/la fiancée
field le champ
to fight se battre
file (computer) le fichier
 (for papers) le dossier

to fill remplir
to fill in (form) remplir
to fill up (with petrol) faire le plein
 fill it up! (car) le plein!
fillet le filet
filling (in tooth) le plombage
film le film
 (for camera) la pellicule
filter (on cigarette) le filtre
to find trouver
fine (penalty) la contravention
finger le doigt
to finish finir
finished fini(e)
fire le feu ; l'incendie (m)
fire alarm l'alarme d'incendie (f)
fire brigade les pompiers
fire engine la voiture de pompiers
fire escape (staircase) l'échelle de
 secours (f)
fire exit la sortie de secours
fire extinguisher l'extincteur (m)
fireplace la cheminée
fireworks les feux d'artifice
firm la compagnie
first premier(-ière)
first aid les premiers secours
first aid kit la trousse de secours
first-class de première classe
first name le prénom
fish le poisson
to fish pêcher
fisherman le pêcheur
fishing la pêche
 to go fishing aller à la pêche
fishing permit le permis de pêche
fishing rod la canne à pêche
fishmonger's le/la marchand(e) de
 poisson
fit (medical) l'attaque (f)
to fit: *it doesn't fit me* ça ne me va
 pas
to fix (repair) réparer
 can you fix it? vous pouvez le
 réparer?
fizzy gazeux(-euse)
flag le drapeau
flames les flammes
flash (for camera) le flash
flashlight la lampe de poche
flask (vacuum flask) le Thermos®
flat (appartment) l'appartement (m)
flat (level) plat
 (beer) éventé

flat tyre le pneu dégonflé
flavour le goût
(of ice cream) le parfum
flaw le défaut
fleas les puces
flesh la chair
flex *(electrical)* le fil
flight le vol
flip flops les tongs
flippers les palmes
flood l'inondation *(f)*
flash flood la crue subite
floor *(of room)* le plancher
(storey) l'étage
(on the) ground floor (au) rez-de-chaussée
(on the) first floor (au) premier étage
(on the) second floor (au) deuxième étage
which floor? quel étage?
floorcloth la serpillère
florist's shop le magasin de fleurs
flour la farine
flower la fleur
flu la grippe
fly la mouche
to fly *(person)* aller en avion
(bird) voler
fly sheet le double toit
fog le brouillard
foggy: *it was foggy* il y avait du brouillard
foil le papier alu(minium)
to fold plier
to follow suivre
food la nourriture
food poisoning l'intoxication alimentaire *(f)*
foot le pied
to go on foot aller à pied
football le football
football match le match de football
football pitch le terrain de football
football player le/la joueur(-euse) de football
footpath le sentier
for pour
for me/you/us pour moi/vous/nous
for him/her pour lui/elle
forbidden interdit(e)
forehead le front
foreign étranger(-ère)
foreign currency les devises étrangères
foreigner l'étranger(ère) *(m(f))*

forest la forêt
forever toujours
to forget oublier
fork *(for eating)* la fourchette
(in road) l'embranchement *(m)*
form *(document)* le formulaire
(shape, style) la forme
fortnight la quinzaine
forward en avant
foul *(football)* la faute
fountain la fontaine
four-wheel drive vehicle le quatre-quatre ; le 4 x 4
fox le renard
fracture la fracture
fragile fragile
fragrance le parfum
frame *(picture)* le cadre
France la France
in/to France en France
free *(not occupied)* libre
(costing nothing) gratis
freezer le congélateur
French français(e)
(language) le français
French fries les frites
French people les Français
frequent fréquent(e)
fresh frais (fraîche)
fresh water *(not salt)* l'eau douce *(f)*
Friday vendredi
fridge le frigo
fried frit(e)
friend *m/f* l'ami(e)
frog la grenouille
frogs' legs les cuisses de grenouille
from de
I'm from England je suis anglais(e)
I'm from Scotland je suis écossais(e)
front le devant
in front of... devant...
front door la porte d'entrée
frost le gel
frozen gelé(e)
(food) surgelé(e)
fruit le fruit
dried fruit les fruits secs
fruit juice le jus de fruit
fruit salad la salade de fruits
to fry frire
frying-pan la poêle
fuel le combustible

fuel gauge l'indicateur de niveau d'essence
fuel pump la pompe d'alimentation
fuel tank le réservoir d'essence
full plein(e)
  (occupied) occupé
full board la pension complète
fumes *(exhaust)* les gaz d'échappement
fun: *to have fun* s'amuser
funeral les obsèques
funfair la fête foraine
funny *(amusing)* amusant(e)
fur la fourrure
furnished meublé(e)
furniture les meubles
fuse le fusible
fuse box la boîte à fusibles
future l'avenir *(m)*

G

gallery la galerie
game le jeu
  (meat) le gibier
garage *(for petrol)* la station-service
  (for parking, repair) le garage
garden le jardin
garlic l'ail *(m)*
gas le gaz
gas cooker la gazinière
gas cylinder la bouteille de gaz
gastritis la gastrite
gate la porte
gay *(person)* homo
gear la vitesse
  in first gear en première
  in second gear en seconde
gearbox la boîte de vitesses
generous généreux(-euse)
gents *(toilet)* les toilettes
genuine authentique
German allemand(e)
  (language) l'allemand *(m)*
German measles la rubéole
Germany l'Allemagne *(f)*
to get *(obtain)* obtenir
  (to fetch) aller chercher
to get in *(vehicle)* monter
to get off *(bus, etc)* descendre
gift le cadeau
gift shop la boutique de souvenirs

girl la fille
girlfriend la copine
to give donner
to give back rendre
glacier le glacier
glass le verre
  a glass of water un verre d'eau
glasses *(spectacles)* les lunettes
glasses case l'étui à lunettes *(m)*
gloves les gants
glue la colle
to go aller
  I'm going to... je vais ...
  we're going to hire a car nous allons louer une voiture
to go back retourner
to go in entrer
to go out *(leave)* sortir
goat la chèvre
God Dieu *(m)*
goggles *(for swimming)* les lunettes de natation
gold l'or
  is it gold? c'est en or?
golf le golf
golf ball la balle de golf
golf clubs les clubs de golf
golf course le terrain de golf
good bon (bonne)
  (that's) good! (c'est) bien!
good afternoon bonjour
goodbye au revoir
good day bonjour
good evening bonsoir
good morning bonjour
good night bonne nuit
goose l'oie *(f)*
gram le gramme
grandchildren les petits-enfants
granddaughter la petite-fille
grandfather le grand-père
grandmother la grand-mère
grandparents les grands-parents
grandson le petit-fils
grapes le raisin
grass l'herbe *(f)*
grated *(cheese)* râpé(e)
grater la râpe
greasy gras (grasse)
great *(big)* grand(e)
  (wonderful) formidable
Great Britain la Grande-Bretagne
green vert(e)
green card *(insurance)* la carte verte

greengrocer's le magasin de fruits et légumes
greetings card la carte de vœux
grey gris(e)
grill *(part of cooker)* le gril
grilled grillé(e)
grocer's l'épicerie *(f)*
ground la terre ; le sol
ground floor le rez-de-chaussée
  on the ground floor au rez-de-chaussée
groundsheet le tapis de sol
group le groupe
guarantee la garantie
guard *(on train)* le chef de train
guest *m/f (house guest)* l'invité(e)
  (in hotel) le/la client(e)
guesthouse la pension
guide *(tourist guide)* le/la guide
guidebook le guide
guided tour la visite guidée
guitar la guitare
gun *(rifle)* le fusil
  (pistol) le pistolet
gym *(gymnasium)* le gymnase
gym shoes les chaussures de sport

H

haemorrhoids les hémorroïdes
hail la grêle
hair les cheveux
hairbrush la brosse à cheveux
haircut la coupe (de cheveux)
hairdresser le/la coiffeur(-euse)
hairdryer le sèche-cheveux
hair dye la teinture pour les cheveux
hair gel le gel pour cheveux
hairgrip la pince à cheveux
hair mousse la mousse coiffante
hair spray la laque
half la moitié
  half an hour une demi-heure
half board la demi-pension
half fare le demi-tarif
half-price à moitié prix
ham *(cooked)* le jambon
  (cured) le jambon cru
hamburger le hamburger
hammer le marteau
hand la main
handbag le sac à main
hand luggage les bagages à main
hand-made fait main

handicapped handicapé(e)
handkerchief le mouchoir
handle la poignée
handlebars le guidon
handsome beau (belle)
hanger *(coathanger)* le cintre
hangover la gueule de bois
to hang up *(telephone)* raccrocher
hang-gliding le deltaplane
  to go hang-gliding faire du deltaplane
to happen arriver ; se passer
  what happened? qu'est-ce qui s'est passé?
happy heureux(-euse)
  happy birthday! bon anniversaire!
harbour le port
hard *(not soft)* dur(e)
  (not easy) difficile
hard disk le disque dur
hardware shop la quincaillerie
to harm someone faire du mal à quelqu'un
harvest *(grape)* les vendanges
hat le chapeau
to have avoir
to have to devoir
hay fever le rhume des foins
he il
head la tête
headache le mal de tête
  I have a headache j'ai mal à la tête
headlights les phares
headphones les écouteurs
head waiter le maître d'hôtel
health la santé
health food shop la boutique de produits diététiques
healthy sain(e)
to hear entendre
hearing aid la prothèse auditive
heart le cœur
heart attack la crise cardiaque
heartburn les brûlures d'estomac
heater l'appareil de chauffage *(m)*
heating le chauffage
to heat up faire chauffer
heavy lourd(e)
heel le talon
heel bar le talon-minute
height la hauteur

helicopter l'hélicoptère *(m)*
hello bonjour!
  (on telephone) allô?
helmet le casque
help! au secours!
to help aider
  can you help me? vous pouvez m'aider?
hem l'ourlet *(m)*
hepatitis l'hépatite *(f)*
her son/sa/ses
  her passport son passeport
  her room sa chambre
  her suitcases ses valises
herb l'herbe *(f)*
herbal tea la tisane
here ici
  here is... voici...
hernia la hernie
hi! salut!
to hide *(something)* cacher
  (oneself) se cacher
high haut(e)
high blood pressure la tension
high chair la chaise haute
high tide la marée haute
hill la colline
hill-walking la randonnée (de basse montagne)
him il ; lui
hip la hanche
hip replacement la pose d'une prothèse de la hanche
hire la location
  car hire la location de voitures
  bike hire la location de bicyclettes
  boat hire la location de bateaux
  ski hire la location de skis
to hire louer
hired car la voiture de location
his son/sa/ses
  his passport son passeport
  his room sa chambre
  his suitcases ses valises
historic historique
history l'histoire *(f)*
to hit frapper
to hitchhike faire du stop
HIV le VIH
hobby le passe-temps
to hold tenir
  (contain) contenir

hold-up *(in traffic)* l'embouteillage *(m)*
hole le trou
holiday les vacances
  on holiday en vacances
home la maison
  at my/your/our home chez moi/vous/ nous
homesick: *to be homesick* avoir le mal du pays
  I'm homesick j'ai le mal du pays
homosexual homosexuel(le)
honest honnête
honey le miel
honeymoon la lune de miel
hood *(of car)* le capot
hook *(fishing)* l'hameçon *(m)*
to hope espérer
  I hope so/not j'espère que oui/non
horn *(of car)* le klaxon
hors d'œuvre le hors d'œuvre
horse le cheval
horse racing les courses de chevaux
horse-riding: *to go horse-riding* faire du cheval
hosepipe le tuyau d'arrosage
hospital l'hôpital *(m)*
hostel *(youth hostel)* l'auberge de jeunesse *(f)*
hot chaud(e)
  I'm hot j'ai chaud
  it's hot *(weather)* il fait chaud
hot-water bottle la bouillotte
hotel l'hôtel *(m)*
hour l'heure *(f)*
  half an hour une demi-heure
  1 hour une heure
  2 hours deux heures
house la maison
househusband l'homme au foyer *(m)*
housewife la femme au foyer
house wine le vin en pichet
housework: *to do the housework* faire le ménage
hovercraft l'aéroglisseur *(m)*
how? *(in what way)* comment?
  how much/many? combien?
  how are you? comment allez-vous?
hungry: *to be hungry* avoir faim
  I'm hungry j'ai faim
to hunt chasser
hunting permit le permis de chasse
hurry: *I'm in a hurry* je suis pressé
to hurt: *to hurt somebody* faire du mal à quelqu'un
  that hurts ça fait mal

husband le mari
hut *(bathing/beach)* la cabine
  (mountain) le refuge
hydrofoil l'hydrofoil *(m)*
hypodermic needle l'aiguille
hypodermique *(f)*

I

I je
ice la glace
  (cube) le glaçon
  with/without ice avec/sans glaçons
ice cream la glace
ice lolly l'esquimau *(m)*
ice rink la patinoire
to ice skate faire du patin (à glace)
ice skates les patins (à glace)
idea l'idée *(f)*
identity card la carte d'identité
if si
ignition l'allumage *(m)*
ignition key la clé de contact
ill malade
illness la maladie
immediately immédiatement
immersion heater le chauffe-eau
  électrique
immigration l'immigration *(f)*
immunisation l'immunisation *(f)*
to import importer
important important(e)
impossible impossible
to improve améliorer
in dans
  in 2 hours' time dans deux heures
  in France en France
  in Canada au Canada
  in London à Londres
in front of devant
included compris(e)
inconvenient gênant
to increase augmenter
indicator *(car)* le clignotant
indigestion l'indigestion *(f)*
indigestion tablets les comprimés
  contre les troubles digestifs
indoors à l'intérieur
infection l'infection *(f)*
infectious infectieux(-euse)
information les renseignements
information desk les renseignements
information office le bureau de
  renseignements
ingredients les ingrédients

inhaler l'inhalateur *(m)*
injection la piqûre
to injure blesser
injured blessé(e)
injury la blessure
inn l'auberge *(f)*
inner tube la chambre à air
inquiries les renseignements
inquiry desk le bureau de
  renseignements
insect l'insecte *(m)*
insect bite la piqûre (d'insecte)
insect repellent le produit pour
  éloigner les insectes
inside à l'intérieur
instant coffee le café instantané
instead of au lieu de
instructor le moniteur/la monitrice
insulin l'insuline *(f)*
insurance l'assurance *(f)*
insurance certificate l'attestation
  d'assurance *(f)*
to insure assurer
insured assuré(e)
to intend to avoir l'intention de
interesting intéressant(e)
international international(e)
internet l'internet *(m)*
  internet café le cybercafé
interpreter l'interprète *(m/f)*
interval *(theatre)* l'entracte *(m)*
interview l'entrevue *(f)*
  (TV, etc) l'interview *(f)*
into dans ; en
  into town en ville
to introduce présenter
invitation l'invitation *(f)*
to invite inviter
invoice la facture
Ireland l'Irlande *(f)*
Irish irlandais(e)
iron *(for clothes)* le fer à repasser
  (metal) le fer
to iron repasser
ironing board la planche à repasser
ironmonger's la quincaillerie
is est
island l'île *(f)*
it il ; elle
Italian italien(ne)
Italy l'Italie *(f)*

to itch démanger
  it itches ça me démange
item l'article *(m)*
itemized bill la facture détaillée

J

jack *(for car)* le cric
jacket la veste
  waterproof jacket l'anorak *(m)*
jam *(food)* la confiture
jammed *(stuck)* coincé(e)
January janvier
jar *(honey, jam, etc)* le pot
jaundice la jaunisse
jaw la mâchoire
jealous jaloux(-ouse)
jeans le jean
jellyfish la méduse
jet ski le jet-ski
jetty *(landing pier)* l'embarcadère *(m)*
Jew le Juif/la Juive
jeweller's la bijouterie
jewellery les bijoux
Jewish juif (juive)
job le travail ; l'emploi
to jog faire du jogging
to join *(become member)* s'inscrire
to join in participer
joint *(body)* l'articulation *(f)*
to joke plaisanter
joke la plaisanterie
journalist le/la journaliste
journey le voyage
judge le juge
jug le pichet
juice le jus
  fruit juice le jus de fruit
  orange juice le jus d'orange
  a carton of juice un brick de jus
July juillet
to jump sauter
jumper le pull
jump leads les câbles de
  raccordement pour batterie
junction *(road)* le croisement ; le
  carrefour
June juin
just: *just two* deux seulement
  I've just arrived je viens d'arriver

K

to keep *(retain)* garder
kennel la niche
kettle la bouilloire
key la clé
  the car key la clé de la voiture
keyboard le clavier
keyring le porte-clés
to kick donnre un coup de pied à
kid *(child)* le gosse
kidneys *(in body)* les reins
kill tuer
kilo(gram) le kilo
kilometre le kilomètre
kind *(person)* gentil(-ille)
kind *(sort)* la sorte
kiosk *(newsstand)* le kiosque
  (phone box) la cabine
kiss le baiser
to kiss embrasser
kitchen la cuisine
kitchen paper l'essuie-tout *(m)*
kite *(toy)* le cerf-volant
knee le genou
knickers la culotte
knife le couteau
to knit tricoter
to knock *(on door)* frapper
to knock down *(in car)* renverser
to knock over *(vase, glass, etc)* faire
  tomber
knot le nœud
to know *(be aware of)* savoir
  (person, place) connaître
  I don't know je ne sais pas
  I don't know Paris je ne connais
  pas Paris
to know how to do sth savoir faire
  quelque chose
  to know how to swim savoir nager
kosher kascher

L

label l'étiquette *(f)*
lace la dentelle
laces *(for shoes)* les lacets
ladder l'échelle *(f)*
ladies *(toilet)* les toilettes pour dames
lady la dame
lager la bière
  bottled lager la bière bouteille
  draught lager la bière pression

lake le lac
lamb l'agneau *(m)*
lamp la lampe
lamppost le réverbère
lampshade l'abat-jour *(m)*
to land atterrir
land la terre
landlady la propriétaire
landlord le propriétaire
landslide le glissement de terrain
lane la ruelle
  (of motorway) la voie
language la langue
language school l'école des langues *(f)*
laptop le portable
large grand(e)
last dernier(-ière)
  last month le mois dernier
  last night *(evening/night-time)* hier
  soir ; la nuit dernière
  last time la dernière fois
  last week la semaine dernière
  last year l'année dernière
  the last bus le dernier bus
  the last trian le dernier train
late tard
  the train is late le train a du retard
  sorry we are late excusez-nous
  d'arriver en retard
later plus tard
to laugh rire
launderette la laverie automatique
laundry service le service de
  blanchisserie
lavatory les toilettes
lavender la lavande
law la loi
lawn la pelouse
lawyer *m/f* l'avocat(e)
laxative le laxatif
layby l'aire de stationnement *(f)*
lead *(electric)* le fil
lead *(metal)* le plomb
lead-free petrol l'essence sans
  plomb *(m)*
leaf la feuille
leak la fuite
to leak: *it's leaking* il y a une fuite
to learn apprendre
lease *(rental)* le bail
leather le cuir
to leave *(depart for)* partir
  (depart from) quitter
  (to leave behind) laisser
  to leave for Paris partir pour Paris
  to leave London quitter Londres

left: *on/to the left* à gauche
left-handed *(person)* gaucher(-ère)
left-luggage *(office)* la consigne
left-luggage locker la consigne
  automatique
leg la jambe
legal légal(e)
leisure centre le centre de loisirs
lemon le citron
lemonade la limonade
to lend prêter
length la longueur
lens *(of camera, etc)* l'objectif *(m)*
  (contact lens) la lentille
lesbian la lesbienne
less moins
  less than moins de
lesson la leçon
to let *(allow)* permettre
  (to hire out) louer
letter la lettre
letterbox la boîte à lettres
lettuce la laitue
level crossing le passage à niveau
library la bibliothèque
licence le permis
lid le couvercle
to lie down s'allonger
life belt la bouée de sauvetage
lifeboat le canot de sauvetage
lifeguard le surveillant de plage
life insurance l'assurance-vie *(f)*
life jacket le gilet de sauvetage
life raft le radeau de sauvetage
lift *(elevator)* l'ascenseur *(m)*
lift pass *(on ski slopes)* le forfait
light *(not heavy)* léger(-ère)
light la lumière
  have you got a light? avez-vous
  du feu?
light bulb l'ampoule *(f)*
lighter le briquet
lighthouse le phare
lightning les éclairs
like *(preposition)* comme
  like this comme ça
to like aimer
  I like coffee j'aime le café
  I don't like coffee je n'aime pas
  le café
  I'd like… je voudrais…
  we'd like… nous voudrions…

lilo® le matelas pneumatique
lime *(fruit)* le citron vert
line *(mark)* la ligne
  (row) la file
  (telephone) la ligne
linen le lin
lingerie la lingerie
lip la lèvre
lip-reading lire sur les lèvres
lip salve le baume pour les lèvres
lipstick le rouge à lèvres
liqueur la liqueur
list la liste
to listen to écouter
litre le litre
litter *(rubbish)* les ordures
little petit(e)
  a little... un peu de...
to live *(in a place)* vivre ; habiter
  I live in London j'habite à Londres
  he lives in a flat il habite un
  appartement
liver le foie
living room le salon
loaf le pain
local local(e)
lock la serrure
  the lock is broken la serrure est
  cassée
to lock fermer à clé
locker *(for luggage)* le casier
locksmith le serrurier
log *(for fire)* la bûche
logbook *(of car)* la carte grise
lollipop la sucette
London Londres
  to/in London à Londres
long long(ue)
  for a long time longtemps
long-sighted hypermétrope
to look after garder
to look at regarder
to look for chercher
loose *(not fastened)* desserré(e)
  it's come loose *(unscrewed)* ça
  s'est déserré
  (detached) ça s'est détaché
lorry le camion
to lose perdre
lost *(object)* perdu(e)
  I've lost... j'ai perdu...
  I'm lost je suis perdu(e)

lost property office le bureau des
  objets trouvés
lot: *a lot of* beaucoup de
lotion la lotion
lottery la loterie
loud fort(e)
lounge *(in hotel, airport)* le salon
love l'amour
to love *(person)* aimer
  I love you je t'aime
  (food, activity, etc) adorer
  I love swimming j'adore nager
lovely beau (belle)
low bas (basse)
low-alcohol peu alcoolisé(e)
to lower baisser
low-fat allégé(e)
low tide la marée basse
luck la chance
lucky chanceux(-euse)
luggage les bagages
luggage allowance le poids
  maximum autorisé
luggage rack le porte-bagages
luggage tag l'étiquette à bagages *(f)*
luggage trolley le chariot (à bagages)
lump *(swelling)* la bosse
lunch le déjeuner
lunchbreak la pause de midi
lung le poumon
luxury le luxe

M

machine la machine
mad fou (folle)
magazine la revue
maggot l'asticot
magnet l'aimant *(m)*
magnifying glass la loupe
maid la domestique
maiden name le nom de jeune fille
mail le courrier
  by mail par la poste
main principal(e)
mains *(electricity, water)* le secteur
main course *(of meal)* le plat principal
main road la route principale
to make faire
make-up le maquillage
male *(person)* masculin
mallet le maillet
man l'homme *(m)*
to manage *(to be in charge of)* gérer

manager le/la directeur(-trice)
manual *(car)* manuel(le)
many beaucoup de
map la carte
  road map la carte routière
  street map le plan de la ville
March mars
margarine la margarine
marina la marina
mark *(stain)* la tache
market le marché
  where is the market? où est le marché?
  when is the market? le marché, c'est quel jour?
market place le marché
marmalade la marmelade d'oranges
married marié(e)
  I'm married je suis marié(e)
  are you married? vous êtes marié(e)?
marsh le marais
mascara le mascara
mass *(in church)* la messe
mast le mât
masterpiece le chef-d'œuvre
match *(game)* la partie
matches les allumettes
material *(cloth)* le tissu
to matter: *it doesn't matter* ça ne fait rien
  what's the matter? qu'est-ce qu'il y a?
mattress le matelas
May mai
mayonnaise la mayonnaise
mayor le maire
maximum le maximum
me moi
meal le repas
to mean vouloir dire
  what does this mean? qu'est-ce que ça veut dire?
measles la rougeole
to measure mesurer
meat la viande
mechanic le mécanicien
medical insurance l'assurance maladie *(f)*
medical treatment les soins médicaux
medicine le médicament
Mediterranean Sea la Méditérranée
medium rare *(meat)* à point
to meet rencontrer

meeting la réunion
meeting point le point de rencontre
to melt fondre
member *(of club, etc)* le membre
membership card la carte de membre
memory la mémoire
men les hommes
to mend réparer
meningitis la méningite
menu *(choices)* le menu
  (card) la carte
message le message
metal le métal
meter le compteur
metre le mètre
metro le métro
metro station la station de métro
microwave oven le four à micro-ondes
midday midi
  at midday à midi
middle le milieu
middle-aged d'un certain âge
midge le moucheron
midnight minuit
  at midnight à minuit
migraine la migraine
  I have a migraine j'ai la migraine
mild *(weather, cheese)* doux (douce)
  (curry) peu épicé(e)
  (tobacco) léger(-ère)
milk le lait
  baby milk (formula) le lait maternisé
  fresh milk le lait frais
  full cream milk le lait entier
  hot milk le lait chaud
  long-life milk le lait longue conservation
  powdered milk le lait en poudre
  semi-skimmed milk le lait demi-écrémé
  skimmed milk le lait écrémé
  soya milk le lait de soja
  UHT milk le lait UHT
  with/without milk avec/sans lait
milkshake le milk-shake
millimetre le millimètre
mince *(meat)* la viande hachée
to mind: *do you mind if I...?* ça vous gêne si je...?
  I don't mind ça m'est égal
  do you mind? vous permettez?
mineral water l'eau minérale *(f)*

m/n/o eng–french

minibar le minibar
minimum le minimum
minister (church) le pasteur
minor road la route secondaire
mint (herb) la menthe
  (sweet) le bonbon à la menthe
minute la minute
mirror la glace
  (in car) le rétroviseur
miscarriage la fausse couche
to miss (train, flight, etc) rater
Miss Mademoiselle
missing (disappeared) disparu(e)
mistake l'erreur (f)
misty brumeux(-euse)
misunderstanding le malentendu
to mix mélanger
mobile phone le portable
modem le modem
modern moderne
moisturizer la crème hydratante
mole (on skin) le grain de beauté
moment: at the moment en ce
  moment
monastery le monastère
Monday lundi
money l'argent (m)
  I have no money je n'ai pas
  d'argent
moneybelt la ceinture porte-
  monnaie
money order le mandat
month le mois
  this month ce mois-ci
  last month le mois dernier
  next month le mois prochain
monthly mensuel(-elle)
monument le monument
moon la lune
mooring (place) le mouillage (m)
mop (for floor) le balai à laver
moped le vélomoteur (m)
more encore
  more wine plus de vin
more than plus de
  more than 3 plus de trois
morning le matin
  in the morning le matin
  this morning ce matin
  tomorrow morning demain matin
morning-after pill la pilule du
  lendemain

mosque la mosquée
mosquito le moustique
mosquito bite la piqûre de moustique
mosquito coil la spirale anti-
  moustiques
mosquito net la moustiquaire
mosquito repellent le produit pour
  éloigner les moustiques
most (of the) la plupart (de)
moth (clothes) la mite
mother la mère
mother-in-law la belle-mère
motor le moteur
motorbike la moto
motorboat le bateau à moteur
motorway l'autoroute (f)
mountain la montagne
mountain bike le VTT (vélo tout-
  terrain)
mountain rescue le sauvetage en
  montagne
mountaineering l'alpinisme (m)
mouse (animal, computer) la souris
moustache la moustache
mouth la bouche
mouthwash l'eau dentifrice (f)
to move bouger
  it's moving ça bouge
movie le film
Mr Monsieur
Mrs Madame
Ms Madame
much beaucoup
  too much trop
muddy boueux(-euse)
mug: I've been mugged je me suis
  fait agresser
mugging l'agression (f)
mumps les oreillons
muscle le muscle
museum le musée
mushrooms les champignons
music la musique
musical (show) la comédie musicale
mussels les moules
must devoir
  I/we must go il faut que j'aille/que
  nous allions
  you must be there il faut que vous
  soyez là
mustard la moutarde
my mon/ma/mes
  my passport mon passeport
  my room ma chambre
  my suitcases mes valises

N

nail *(metal)* le clou
(finger) l'ongle *(m)*
nailbrush la brosse à ongles
nail clippers le coupe-ongles
nail file la lime à ongles
nail polish le vernis à ongles
nail polish remover le dissolvant
nail scissors les ciseaux à ongles
name le nom
my name is… je m'appelle…
what is your name? comment vous appelez-vous?
nanny le/la baby-sitter
napkin la serviette de table
nappy la couche
narrow étroit(e)
national national(e)
nationality la nationalité
national park le parc national
natural naturel(le)
nature reserve la réserve naturelle
nature trail le sentier de grande randonnée
navy blue bleu marine
near près de
near the bank près de la banque
is it near? c'est près d'ici?
necessary nécessaire
neck le cou
necklace le collier
nectarine le brugnon
to need (to) avoir besoin de
I need… j'ai besoin de…
we need… nous avons besoin de…
I need to phone j'ai besoin de téléphoner
needle l'aiguille *(f)*
a needle and thread du fil et une aiguille
negative *(photography)* le négatif
neighbour le/la voisin(e)
nephew le neveu
net le filet
the Net le net ; l'internet *(m)*
never jamais
I never drink wine je ne bois jamais de vin
new nouveau(-elle)
news *(TV, radio, etc)* les informations
newsagent's le magasin de journaux
newspaper le journal
news stand le kiosque

New Year le Nouvel An
happy New Year! bonne année!
New Year's Eve la Saint-Sylvestre
New Zealand la Nouvelle-Zélande
next prochain(e)
(after) ensuite
the next train le prochain train
next month le mois prochain
next week la semaine prochaine
next Monday lundi prochain
next to à côté de
we're going to Paris next ensuite nous allons à Paris
nice beau (belle)
(enjoyable) bon (bonne)
(person) sympathique
niece la nièce
night *(night-time)* la nuit
(evening) le soir
at night la nuit/le soir
last night hier soir
tomorrow night (evening) demain soir
tonight ce soir
nightclub la boîte de nuit
nightdress la chemise de nuit
night porter le gardien de nuit
no non
(without) sans
no problem pas de problème
no thanks non merci
no ice sans glaçons
no sugar sans sucre
nobody personne
noise le bruit
it's very noisy il y a beaucoup de bruit
non-alcoholic sans alcool
none aucun(e)
non-smoker: *I'm a non-smoker* je ne fume pas
non-smoking *(seat, compartment)* non-fumeurs
north le nord
Northern Ireland l'Irlande du Nord *(f)*
North Sea la mer du Nord
nose le nez
not pas
I am not… je ne suis pas…
note *(banknote)* le billet
(letter) la note
note pad le bloc-notes
nothing rien
nothing else rien d'autre

notice *(warning)* l'avis *(m)*
  (sign) le panneau
notice board le panneau d'affichage
novel le roman
November novembre
now maintenant
nowhere nulle part
nuclear nucléaire
number *(quantity)* le nombre
  (of room, house) le numéro
  phone number le numéro de
  téléphone
numberplate *(of car)* la plaque
  d'immatriculation
nurse *m/f* l'infirmier/l'infirmière
nursery la garderie
nursery slope la piste pour
  débutants
nut *(to eat)* la noix
  (for bolt) l'écrou *(m)*

oar l'aviron *(m)* ; la rame
oats l'avoine *(f)*
to obtain obtenir
occupation *(work)* l'emploi *(m)*
ocean l'océan *(m)*
October octobre
odd *(strange)* bizarre
of de
  a glass of... un verre de...
  made of... en...
off *(light)* éteint(e)
  (rotten) mauvais(e) ; pourri(e)
office le bureau
often souvent
oil *(for car, food)* l'huile *(f)*
oil filter le filtre à huile
oil gauge la jauge de niveau d'huile
ointment la pommade
OK! *(agreed)* d'accord!
old vieux (vieille)
  how old are you? quel âge avez-
  vous?
  I'm... years old j'ai... ans
old-age pensioner le/la retraité(e)
olive l'olive *(f)*
olive oil l'huile d'olive *(f)*
on *(light)* allumé(e)
  (engine, etc) en marche
  on the table sur la table

on time à l'heure
once une fois
  at once tout de suite
one-way *(street)* à sens unique
onion l'oignon *(m)*
only seulement
open ouvert(e)
to open ouvrir
opera l'opéra *(m)*
operation *(surgical)* l'opération *(f)*
operator *(phone)* le/la standardiste
opposite en face de
  opposite the bank en face de la
  banque
  quite the opposite bien au contraire
optician l'opticien/l'opticienne
or ou
orange *(fruit)* l'orange
  (colour) orange
orange juice le jus d'orange
orchestra l'orchestre *(m)*
order *(in restaurant)* la commande
  out of order en panne
to order *(in restaurant)* commander
organic biologique
to organize organiser
ornament le bibelot
other autre
  have you any others? vous en avez
  d'autres?
our *(sing)* notre
  (plural) nos
  our room notre chambre
  our passports nos passeports
  our baggage nos bagages
out *(light)* éteint(e)
  he's/she's out il/elle est sorti(e)
outdoor *(pool, etc)* en plein air
outside dehors
oven le four
ovenproof dish le plat qui va au four
over *(on top of)* au-dessus de
to overbook faire du surbooking
to overcharge faire payer trop cher
overdone *(food)* trop cuit(e)
overdose la surdose
to overheat surchauffer
to overload surcharger
to oversleep se réveiller en retard
to overtake *(in car)* doubler ; dépasser
to owe devoir
  you owe me... vous me devez...
to own posséder
owner le/la propriétaire
oyster l'huître *(f)*

P

pace le pas
pacemaker le stimulateur (cardiaque)
to pack *(luggage)* faire les bagages
package le paquet
package tour le voyage organisé
packet le paquet
padded envelope l'enveloppe matelassée
paddling pool la pataugeoire
padlock le cadenas
page la page
paid payé(e)
  I've paid j'ai payé
pain la douleur
painful douloureux(-euse)
painkiller l'analgésique *(m)*
to paint peindre
painting *(picture)* le tableau
pair la paire
palace le palais
pale pâle
pan *(saucepan)* la casserole
  (frying pan) la poêle
pancake la crêpe
panniers *(for bike)* les sacoches
panties la culotte
pants *(underwear)* le slip
panty liner le protège-slip
paper le papier
paper hankies les mouchoirs en papier
paper napkins les serviettes en papier
paragliding le parapente
paralysed paralysé(e)
parcel le colis
pardon? comment?
  I beg your pardon! pardon!
parents les parents
Paris Paris
park le parc
to park garer (la voiture)
parking disk le disque de stationnement
parking meter le parcmètre
parking ticket le p.-v.
part: *spare parts* les pièces de rechange
partner *(business)* m/f l'associé(e)
  (boy/girlfriend) le compagnon/la compagne
party *(group)* le groupe

(celebration) la fête ; la soirée
(political) le parti
pass *(bus, train)* la carte
  (mountain) le col
passenger le passager/la passagère
passport le passeport
passport control le contrôle des passeports
pasta les pâtes
pastry la pâte
  (cake) la pâtisserie
path le chemin
patient *(in hospital)* le/la patient(e)
pavement le trottoir
to pay payer
  I'd like to pay je voudrais payer
  where do I pay? où est-ce qu'il faut payer?
payment le paiement
payphone le téléphone public
peace *(after war)* la paix
peach la pêche
peak rate le plein tarif
peanut allergy l'allergie aux cacahuètes *(f)*
pear la poire
peas les petits pois
pedal la pédale
pedalo le pédalo®
pedestrian le/la piéton(ne)
pedestrian crossing le passage clouté
to pee faire pipi
to peel *(fruit)* peler
peg *(for clothes)* la pince à linge
  (for tent) le piquet
pen le stylo
pencil le crayon
penfriend le/la correspondant(e)
penicillin la pénicilline
penis le pénis
penknife le canif
pensioner le/la retraité(e)
people les gens
pepper *(spice)* le poivre
  (vegetable) le poivron
per par
  per day par jour
  per hour à l'heure
  per person par personne
  per week par semaine
  100 km per hour 100 km à l'heure
perfect parfait(e)

performance *(show)* le spectacle
perfume le parfum
perhaps peut-être
period *(menstruation)* les règles
perm la permanente
permit le permis
person la personne
personal organizer l'agenda *(m)*
personal stereo le baladeur
pet l'animal de compagnie
pet food les aliments pour animaux
pet shop la boutique d'animaux
petrol l'essence *(f)*
  4-star le super
  unleaded l'essence sans plomb
petrol cap le bouchon de réservoir
petrol pump la pompe à essence
petrol station la station-service
petrol tank le réservoir
pharmacy la pharmacie
phone le téléphone
  by phone par téléphone
to phone téléphoner
phonebook l'annuaire *(m)*
phonebox la cabine *(téléphonique)*
phone call l'appel *(m)*
phonecard la télécarte
photocopy la photocopie
to photocopy photocopier
photograph la photo
  to take a photograph prendre une
  photo
phrase book le guide de conversation
piano le piano
to pick *(choose)* choisir
  (pluck) cueillir
pickpocket le pickpocket
picnic le pique-nique
  to have a picnic pique-niquer
picnic hamper le panier à pique-nique
picnic rug le plaid
picture *(painting)* le tableau
  (photo) la photo
pie *(savoury)* la tourte
piece le morceau
pier la jetée
pig le cochon
pill la pilule
  I'm on the pill je prends la pilule
pillow l'oreiller *(m)*
pillowcase la taie d'oreiller

pilot le pilote
pin l'épingle *(f)*
pink rose
pint: a pint of... un demi-litre de...
pipe *(for water, gas)* le tuyau
  (smoking) la pipe
pity: what a pity quelle dommage
pizza la pizza
place l'endroit *(m)*
place of birth le lieu de naissance
plain *(unflavoured)* ordinaire
plait la natte
to plan prévoir
plan *(map)* le plan
plane *(aircraft)* l'avion *(m)*
plant *(in garden)* la plante
plaster *(sticking plaster)* le sparadrap
  (for broken limb, on wall) le plâtre
plastic *(made of)* en plastique
plastic bag le sac en plastique
plate l'assiette *(f)*
platform *(railway)* le quai
  which platform? quel quai?
play *(at theatre)* la pièce
to play *(games)* jouer
play park l'aire de jeux *(f)*
playroom la salle de jeux
pleasant agréable
please s'il vous plaît
pleased content(e)
  pleased to meet you! enchanté(e)!
plenty of beaucoup de
pliers la pince
plug *(electrical)* la prise
  (for sink) la bonde
to plug in brancher
plum la prune
plumber le plombier
plumbing la tuyauterie
plunger *(to clear sink)* le débouchoir à
  ventouse
p.m. de l'après-midi
poached poché(e)
pocket la poche
points *(in car)* les vis platinées
poison le poison
poisonous vénéneux
police *(force)* la police
policeman le policier
  (police woman) la femme policier
police station le commissariat ; la
  gendarmerie
polish *(for shoes)* le cirage
pollen le pollen

polluted pollué(e)
pony le poney
pony-trekking la randonnée à cheval
pool *(swimming)* la piscine
pool attendant le/la surveillant(e) de baignade
poor pauvre
popcorn le pop-corn
pop socks les mi-bas
popular populaire
pork le porc
port *(seaport)* le port
(wine) le porto
porter *(for luggage)* le porteur
portion la portion
Portugal le Portugal
possible possible
post *(letters)* le courrier
by post par courrier
to post poster
postbox la boîte aux lettres
postcard la carte postale
postcode le code postal
poster l'affiche *(f)*
postman/woman le facteur/la factrice
post office la poste
to postpone remettre à plus tard
pot *(for cooking)* la casserole
potato la pomme de terre
baked potato la pomme de terre cuite au four
boiled potatoes les pommes vapeur
fried potatoes les pommes frites
mashed potatoes la purée
roast potatoes les pommes de terre rôties
potato salad la salade de pommes de terre
pothole le nid de poule
pottery la poterie
pound *(money)* la livre
to pour verser
powder la poudre
powdered milk le lait en poudre
power *(electricity)* le courant
power cut la coupure de courant
pram le landau
to pray prier
to prefer préférer
pregnant enceinte
I'm pregnant je suis enceinte
to prepare préparer
to prescribe prescrire

prescription l'ordonnance *(f)*
present *(gift)* le cadeau
preservative conservateur *(m)*
president le président
pressure la pression
tyre pressure la pression des pneus
pretty joli(e)
price le prix
price list le tarif
priest le prêtre
print *(photo)* la photo
printer l'imprimante *(f)*
prison la prison
private privé(e)
prize le prix
probably probablement
problem le problème
professor le professeur d'université
programme *(TV, etc)* l'émission *(f)*
prohibited interdit(e)
promise la promesse
to promise promettre
to pronounce prononcer
how's it pronounced? comment ça se prononce?
Protestant protestant(e)
to provide fournir
public public(-que)
public holiday le jour férié
pudding le dessert
to pull tirer
to pull a muscle se faire une élongation
to pull over *(car)* s'arrêter
pullover le pull
pump la pompe
puncture la crevaison
puncture repair kit la boîte de rustines®
puppet la marionnette
puppet show le spectacle de marionnettes
purple violet(-ette)
purpose le but
on purpose exprès
purse le porte-monnaie
to push pousser
pushchair la poussette
to put *(place)* mettre
pyjamas le pyjama
Pyrenees les Pyrénées

Q

quality la qualité
quantity la quantité
quarantine la quarantaine
to quarrel se disputer
quarter le quart
quay le quai
queen la reine
query la question
question la question
queue la queue
to queue faire la queue
quick rapide
quickly vite
quiet *(place)* tranquille
quilt la couette
quite *(rather)* assez
  (completely) complètement
  quite good pas mal
  it's quite expensive c'est assez cher
quiz le jeu-concours

R

rabbit le lapin
rabies la rage
race *(people)* la race
  (sport) la course
race course le champ de courses
racket la raquette
radiator le radiateur
radio la radio
railcard la carte d'abonnement (de chemin de fer)
railway le chemin de fer
railway station la gare
rain la pluie
to rain: *it's raining* il pleut
raincoat l'imperméable *(m)*
rake le râteau
rape le viol
to rape violer
raped: *to be raped* être violé(e)
rare *(uncommon)* rare
  (steak) saignant(e)
rash *(skin)* la rougeur
rat le rat
rate *(price)* le tarif
rate of exchange le taux de change

raw cru(e)
razor le rasoir
razor blades les lames de rasoir
to read lire
ready prêt(e)
real vrai(e)
to realize (that ...) se rendre compte (que ...)
rearview mirror le rétroviseur
receipt le reçu
receiver *(of phone)* le récepteur
reception *(desk)* la réception
receptionist le/la réceptionniste
to recharge *(battery, etc)* recharger
recipe la recette
to recognize reconnaître
to recommend recommander
to record enregistrer
to recover *(from illness)* se remettre
to recycle recycler
red rouge
to reduce réduire
reduction la réduction
to refer to parler de
refill la recharge
to refund rembourser
to refuse refuser
regarding concernant
region la région
register le registre
to register *(at hotel)* se présenter
registered *(letter)* recommandé(e)
registration form la fiche
to reimburse rembourser
relation *(family)* le/la parent(e)
relationship les rapports
to remain rester
remember se rappeler
  I don't remember je ne m'en souviens pas
remote control la télécommande
removal firm les déménageurs
to remove enlever
rent le loyer
to rent louer
rental la location
repair la réparation
to repair réparer
to repeat répéter
to reply répondre
report *(of theft, etc)* la déclaration
to report *(theft, etc)* déclarer
request la demande

to request demander
to require avoir besoin de
to rescue sauver
reservation la réservation
to reserve réserver
reserved réservé(e)
resident *m/f* l'habitant(e)
resort *(seaside)* la station balnéaire
  ski resort la station de ski
rest *(relaxation)* le repos
  (remainder) le reste
to rest se reposer
restaurant le restaurant
restaurant car le wagon-restaurant
retired retraité(e)
to return *(to a place)* retourner
  (to return something) rendre
return ticket le billet aller-retour
to reverse faire marche arrière
to reverse the charges appeler
  en PCV
reverse-charge call l'appel
  en PCV *(m)*
reverse gear la marche arrière
rheumatism le rhumatisme
rib la côte
ribbon le ruban
rice le riz
rich *(person, food)* riche
to ride *(horse)* faire du cheval
right *(correct)* exact(e)
right la droite
  on/to the right à droite
right of way la priorité
ring *(on finger)* la bague
to ring *(bell)* sonner
  it's ringing *(phone)* ça sonne
  to ring sb *(phone)* téléphoner à
  quelqu'un
ring road le périphérique
ripe mûr(e)
river la rivière
Riviera *(French)* la Côte d'Azur
road la route
road map la carte routière
road sign le panneau
roadworks les travaux
roast rôti(e)
roll *(bread)* le petit pain
roller blades les patins en ligne
romantic romantique
roof le toit
roof-rack la galerie
room *(in house)* la pièce

  (in hotel) la chambre
  (space) la place
  double room la chambre pour
  deux personnes
  family room la chambre pour une
  famille
  single room la chambre pour une
  personne
room number le numéro de chambre
room service le service des chambres
root la racine
rope la corde
rose la rose
rosé wine le rosé
rotten *(fruit, etc)* pourri(e)
rough: *rough sea* la mer agitée
round rond(e)
roundabout *(traffic)* le rond-point
route la route ; l'itinéraire *(m)*
row *(theatre, etc)* la rangée
rowing *(sport)* l'aviron *(m)*
rowing boat la barque
rubber *(material)* le caoutchouc
  (eraser) la gomme
rubber band l'élastique *(m)*
rubber gloves les gants en
  caoutchouc
rubbish les ordures
rubella la rubéole
rucksack le sac à dos
rug *(carpet)* le tapis
ruins les ruines
ruler *(for measuring)* la règle
to run courir
rush hour l'heure de pointe *(f)*
rusty rouillé(e)

S

sad triste
saddle la selle
safe *(for valuables)* le coffre-fort
safe sûr ; sans danger
  is it safe? ce n'est pas dangereux?
safety belt la ceinture de sécurité
safety pin l'épingle de sûreté *(f)*
sail la voile
sailboard la planche à voile
sailing *(sport)* la voile
sailing boat le voilier
saint le/la saint(e)

salad la salade
  green salad la salade verte
  mixed salad la salade composée
  potato salad la salade de pommes
  de terre
  tomato salad la salade de tomates
salad dressing la vinaigrette
salami le salami
salary le salaire
sale la vente
sales (reductions) les soldes
salesman/woman le vendeur/la
  vendeuse
sales rep le/la représentant(e)
salt le sel
salt water l'eau salée
salty salé(e)
same même
sample l'échantillon (m)
sand le sable
sandals les sandales
sandwich le sandwich
  toasted sandwich le croque-
  monsieur
sanitary towel la serviette
  hygiénique
satellite dish l'antenne parabolique (f)
satellite TV la télévision par satellite
Saturday samedi
sauce la sauce
saucepan la casserole
saucer la soucoupe
sauna le sauna
sausage la saucisse
to save (life) sauver
  (money) épargner ; économiser
savoury salé(e)
saw la scie
to say dire
scales (for weighing) la balance
scarf (headscarf) le foulard
  (woollen) l'écharpe (f)
scenery le paysage
schedule le programme
school l'école (f)
  primary school l'école primaire
  secondary school (11-15) le collège
  (15-18) le lycée
scissors les ciseaux
score (of match) le score
to score (goal, point) marquer
Scot m/f l'Écossais(e)

Scotland l'Écosse (f)
Scottish écossais(e)
scouring pad le tampon à récurer
screen (computer, TV) l'écran (m)
screen wash le lave-glace
screw la vis
screwdriver le tournevis
  phillips screwdriver le tournevis
  cruciforme
scuba diving la plongée sous-marine
sculpture la sculpture
sea la mer
seafood les fruits de mer
seam (of dress) la couture
to search fouiller
seasickness le mal de mer
seaside le bord de la mer
  at the seaside au bord de la mer
season (of year, holiday time) la saison
  in season de saison
seasonal saisonnier
season ticket la carte
  d'abonnement
seat (chair) le siège
  (in train) la place
  (cinema, theatre) le fauteuil
seatbelt la ceinture de sécurité
second second(e)
second (time) la seconde
second class seconde classe
second-hand d'occasion
secretary la secrétaire
security guard le/la vigile
sedative le calmant
to see voir
to seize saisir
self-catering flat l'appartement
  indépendant (avec cuisine)
self-employed: *to be self employed*
  travailler à son compte
self-service le libre-service
to sell vendre
  do you sell…? vous vendez…?
sell-by date la date limite de vente
Sellotape® le Scotch®
to send envoyer
senior citizen la personne du
  troisième âge
sensible raisonnable
separated séparé(e)
separately: *to pay separately* payer
  séparément
September septembre
serious grave
to serve servir

service *(church)* l'office *(m)*
(in restaurant, shop, etc) le service
   is service included? le service est
compris?
service charge le service
service station la station-service
set menu le menu à prix fixe
settee le canapé
several plusieurs
to sew coudre
sex le sexe
shade l'ombre *(f)*
   in the shade à l'ombre
to shake *(bottle, etc)* agiter
shallow peu profond(e)
shampoo le shampooing
shampoo and set le shampooing et
la mise en plis
to share partager
sharp *(razor, knife)* tranchant
to shave se raser
shaving cream la crème à raser
shawl le châle
she elle
sheep le mouton
sheet *(for bed)* le drap
shelf le rayon
shell *(seashell)* le coquillage
sheltered abrité(e)
to shine briller
shingles *(illness)* le zona
ship le navire
shirt la chemise
shock le choc
shock absorber l'amortisseur *(m)*
shoe la chaussure
shoelaces les lacets
shoe polish le cirage
shoeshop le magasin de chaussures
shop le magasin
to shop faire du shopping
shop assistant le vendeur/la
vendeuse
shop window la vitrine
shopping centre le centre
commercial
shore le rivage
short court(e)
shortage le manque
short circuit le court-circuit
short cut le raccourci
shortly bientôt
shorts le short
short-sighted myope

shoulder l'épaule *(f)*
to shout crier
show le spectacle
to show montrer
shower *(wash)* la douche
   to take a shower prendre une
douche
shower cap le bonnet de douche
shower gel le gel de douche
to shrink *(clothes)* rétrécir
shut *(closed)* fermé(e)
to shut fermer
shutter *(on window)* le volet
shuttle service la navette
sick *(ill)* malade
   I feel sick j'ai envie de vomir
side le côté
side dish la garniture
sidelight le feu de position
sidewalk le trottoir
sieve la passoire
sightseeing le tourisme
   to go sightseeing faire du tourisme
sightseeing tour l'excursion
touristique *(f)*
sign *(notice)* le panneau
to sign signer
signature la signature
signpost le poteau indicateur
silk la soie
silver l'argent *(m)*
similar (to) semblable (à)
since depuis
to sing chanter
single *(unmarried)* célibataire
   (bed, room) pour une personne
single ticket l'aller simple *(m)*
sink *(washbasin)* l'évier *(m)*
sir Monsieur
sister la sœur
sister-in-law la belle-sœur
to sit s'asseoir
   sit down! asseyez-vous!
size *(clothes)* la taille
   (shoe) la pointure
skates *(ice)* les patins à glace
   (roller) les patins à roulettes
to skate *(on ice)* patiner
   (roller) faire du patin à roulettes
skateboard le skate-board
   to go skateboarding faire du
skate-board

ski le ski
to ski faire du ski
ski boots les chaussures de ski
skiing le ski
ski instructor le/la moniteur(-trice) de ski
ski jump *(place)* le tremplin de ski
ski lift le remonte-pente
ski pants le fuseau
ski pass le forfait
ski pole le bâton (de ski)
ski run la piste
ski suit la combinaison de ski
skilled adroit(e) ; qualifié(e)
skin la peau
skirt la jupe
sky le ciel
slate l'ardoise *(f)*
sledge la luge
to sleep dormir
sleeper *(couchette)* la couchette
 (carriage) la voiture-lit
 (train) le train-couchettes
to sleep in faire la grasse matinée
sleeping bag le sac de couchage
sleeping car la voiture-lit
sleeping pill le somnifère
slice *(bread, cake, etc)* la tranche
sliced bread le pain en tranches
slide *(photograph)* la diapositive
to slip glisser
slippers les pantoufles
slow lent(e)
to slow down ralentir
slowly lentement
small petit(e)
 smaller than plus petit(e) que
smell l'odeur *(f)*
 a bad smell une mauvaise odeur
smile le sourire
to smile sourire
smoke la fumée
to smoke fumer
 I don't smoke je ne fume pas
 can I smoke? est-ce qu'on peut fumer?
smoke alarm le détecteur de fumée
smoked fumé(e)
smokers *(sign)* fumeurs
smooth lisse
snack le casse-croûte

to have a snack casser la croûte
snack bar le snack-bar
snail l'escargot *(m)*
snake le serpent
snake bite la morsure de serpent
to sneeze éternuer
snorkel le tuba
snow la neige
to snow: *it's snowing* il neige
snowboard le snowboard
snowboarding le surf des neiges
 to go snowboarding faire du snowboard
snow chains les chaînes
snowed up enneigé(e)
snow tyres les pneus cloutés
soap le savon
soap powder *(detergent)* la lessive
sober: *to be sober* ne pas avoir bu
socket *(for plug)* la prise de courant
socks les chaussettes
soda water l'eau de Seltz
sofa le canapé
sofa bed le canapé-lit
soft doux (douce)
soft drink le soda
software le logiciel
soldier le soldat
sole *(shoe)* la semelle
soluble soluble
some de (du/de la/des)
someone quelqu'un
something quelque chose
sometimes quelquefois
son le fils
son-in-law le gendre
song la chanson
soon bientôt
 as soon as possible dès que possible
sore douloureux(-euse)
sore throat: *to have a sore throat* avoir mal à la gorge
sorry: *I'm sorry!* excusez-moi!
sort la sorte
 what sort de quelle sorte?
soup le potage ; la soupe
sour aigre
soured cream la crème aigre
south le sud
souvenir le souvenir
spa la station thermale
space la place
spade la pelle

41 **Spain** l'Espagne (f)
Spanish espagnol(e)
spanner la clé plate
spare parts les pièces de rechange
spare room la chambre d'amis
spare tyre le pneu de rechange
spare wheel la roue de secours
sparkling (wine) mousseux(-euse)
   (water) gazeux(-euse)
spark plug la bougie
to speak parler
   do you speak English? vous parlez anglais?
special spécial(e)
specialist (medical) le/la spécialiste
speciality la spécialité
speeding l'excès de vitesse (m)
   a speeding ticket un p.-v. pour excès de vitesse
speed limit la limitation de vitesse
   to exceed speed limit dépasser la vitesse permise
speedboat le hors-bord
speedometer le compteur
to spell: *how is it spelt?* comment ça s'écrit?
to spend (money) dépenser
   (time) passer
spice l'épice (f)
spicy épicé(e)
spider l'araignée (f)
to spill renverser
spine la colonne vertébrale
spin dryer le sèche-linge
spirits (alcohol) les spiritueux
splinter (in finger) l'écharde (f)
spoke (of wheel) le rayon
sponge l'éponge (f)
spoon la cuiller
sport le sport
sports centre le centre sportif
sports shop le magasin de sports
spot (pimple) le bouton
sprain l'entorse (f)
spring (season) le printemps
   (metal) le ressort
square (in town) la place
squeeze presser
squid le calmar
stadium le stade
stage la scène
staff le personnel
stain la tache
stained glass window le vitrail

stairs l'escalier (m)
stale (bread) rassis(e)
stalls (in theatre) l'orchestre (m)
stamp le timbre
to stand (get up) se lever
   (be standing) être debout
star l'étoile (f)
   (celebrity) la vedette
to start commencer
starter (in meal) le hors d'œuvre
   (in car) le démarreur
station la gare
stationer's la papeterie
statue la statue
stay le séjour
   enjoy your stay! bon séjour!
to stay (remain) rester
   (reside for while) loger
   I'm staying at... je loge à...
steak le bifteck
to steal voler
steam la vapeur
steamed cuit(e) au vapeur
steel l'acier (m)
steep raide
steeple le clocher
steering wheel le volant
step le pas
stepdaughter la belle-fille
stepfather le beau-père
stepmother la belle-mère
stepson le beau-fils
stereo la chaîne (stéréo)
sterling la livre sterling
steward le steward
stewardess l'hôtesse (f)
sticking-plaster le sparadrap
still: *still water* l'eau plate (f)
still (yet) encore
sting la piqûre
to sting piquer
stitches (surgical) les points de suture
stockings les bas
stolen volé(e)
stomach l'estomac (m)
stomachache: *to have a stomach-ache* avoir mal au ventre
stomach upset l'estomac dérangé
stone la pierre
to stop arrêter

store *(shop)* le magasin
storey l'étage *(m)*
storm l'orage *(m)*
story l'histoire *(f)*
straightaway tout de suite
straight on tout droit
strange bizarre
straw *(for drinking)* la paille
strawberries les fraises
stream le ruisseau
street la rue
street map le plan des rues
strength la force
stress le stress
strike *(of workers)* la grève
string la ficelle
striped rayé(e)
stroke *(haemorrhage)* l'attaque (d'apoplexie)
  to have a stroke avoir une attaque
strong fort(e)
stuck bloqué(e)
student *(male)* l'étudiant
  (female) l'étudiante
student discount le tarif étudiant
stuffed farci(e)
stung piqué(e)
stupid stupide
subscription l'abonnement *(m)*
subtitles les sous-titres
subway le passage souterrain
suddenly soudain
suede le daim
sugar le sucre
sugar-free sans sucre
to suggest suggérer
suit *(man's)* le costume
  (woman's) le tailleur
suitcase la valise
sum la somme
summer l'été *(m)*
summer holidays les vacances d'été
summit le sommet
sun le soleil
to sunbathe prendre un bain de soleil
sunblock l'écran total *(m)*
sunburn le coup de soleil
Sunday le dimanche
sunflower le tournesol
sunglasses les lunettes de soleil

sunny: *it's sunny* il fait beau
sunrise le lever du soleil
sunroof le toit ouvrant
sunscreen *(lotion)* l'écran solaire *(m)*
sunset le coucher du soleil
sunshade le parasol
sunstroke l'insolation *(f)*
suntan le bronzage
suntan lotion le lait solaire
supermarket le supermarché
supper *(dinner)* le souper
supplement le supplément
to supply fournir
to surf faire du surf
  to surf the Net surfer sur Internet
surfboard la planche de surf
surfing le surf
surgery *(operation)* l'opération chirurgicale *(f)*
surname le nom de famille
surprise la surprise
to survive survivre
to swallow avaler
to sweat transpirer
sweater le pull
sweatshirt le sweat-shirt
sweet sucré(e)
sweetener l'édulcorant *(m)*
sweets les bonbons
to swell *(bump, eye, etc)* enfler
to swim nager
swimming pool la piscine
swimsuit le maillot de bain
swing *(for children)* la balançoire
Swiss suisse
switch le bouton
to switch off éteindre
to switch on allumer
Switzerland la Suisse
swollen enflé(e)
synagogue la synagogue
syringe la seringue

T

table la table
tablecloth la nappe
table tennis le tennis de table
table wine le vin de table
tablet le comprimé
to take *(something)* prendre
to take away *(something)* emporter
to take off *(clothes)* enlever

143

talc le talc
to talk (to) parler (à)
tall grand(e)
tampons les tampons hygiéniques
tangerine la mandarine
tank (petrol) le réservoir
  (fish) l'aquarium (m)
tap le robinet
tap water l'eau du robinet (f)
tape le ruban
  (cassette) la cassette
  adhesive tape le Scotch®
  video tape la cassette vidéo
tape measure le mètre à ruban
tape recorder le magnétophone
tart la tarte
taste le goût
to taste goûter
  can I taste some? je peux goûter?
tax l'impôt (m)
taxi le taxi
taxi driver le chauffeur de taxi
taxi rank la station de taxis
tea le thé
  herbal tea la tisane
  lemon tea le thé au citron
  tea with milk le thé au lait
teabag le sachet de thé
teapot la théière
teaspoon la cuiller à café
tea towel le torchon
to teach enseigner
teacher le professeur
team l'équipe (f)
tear (in material) la déchirure
teat (on bottle) le téton
teenager l'adolescent(e)
teeth les dents
telegram le télégramme
telephone le téléphone
to telephone téléphoner
telephone box la cabine téléphonique
telephone call le coup de téléphone
telephone card la télécarte
telephone directory l'annuaire (m)
telephone number le numéro de
  téléphone
television la télévision
to tell dire
temperature la température
  to have a temperature avoir de la
  fièvre
temporary temporaire
tenant le/la locataire

tendon le tendon
tennis le tennis
tennis ball la balle de tennis
tennis court le court de tennis
tennis racket la raquette de tennis
tent la tente
tent peg le piquet de tente
terminal (airport) l'aérogare (f)
terrace la terrasse
terracotta la terre cuite
to test (try out) tester
testicles les testicules
tetanus injection la piqûre
  antitétanique
than que
to thank remercier
thank you merci
  thank you very much merci
  beaucoup
that cela
  that one celui-là/celle-là
the le/la/l'/les
theatre le théâtre
theft le vol
their (sing) leur
  (plural) leurs
them eux
there là
there is/are... il y a...
thermometer le thermomètre
these ces
  these ones ceux-ci/celles-ci
they ils/elles
thick (not thin) épais(se)
thief le voleur/la voleuse
thigh la cuisse
thin (person) mince
thing la chose
  my things mes affaires
to think penser
thirsty: I'm thirsty j'ai soif
this ceci
  this one celui-ci/celle-ci
thorn l'épine (f)
those ces
  those ones ceux-là/celles-là
thread le fil
throat la gorge
throat lozenges les pastilles pour la
  gorge
through à travers

thumb le pouce
thunder le tonnerre
thunderstorm l'orage (m)
Thursday jeudi
thyme le thym
ticket le billet ; le ticket
  a single ticket un aller simple
  a return ticket un aller-retour
  book of tickets le carnet de tickets
ticket inspector le contrôleur/la
  contrôleuse
ticket office le guichet
tide la marée
  low tide la marée basse
  high tide la marée haute
tidy bien rangé(e)
to tidy up tout ranger
tie la cravate
tight (fitting) serré(e)
tights le collant
tile (on roof) la tuile
  (on wall, floor) le carreau
till (cash desk) la caisse
till (until) jusqu'à
  till 2 o'clock jusqu'à deux heures
time le temps
  (of day) l'heure (f)
  this time cette fois
  what time is it? quelle heure est-il?
timer le minuteur
timetable l'horaire (m)
tin (can) la boîte
tinfoil le papier d'alu(minium)
tin-opener l'ouvre-boîtes (m)
tip (to waiter, etc) le pourboire
to tip (waiter, etc) donner un
  pourboire à
tipped (cigarette) à bout filtre
tired fatigué(e)
tissue (Kleenex®) le kleenex®
to à
  (with name of country) en/au
  to London à Londres
  to the airport à l'aéroport
  to France en France
  to Canada au Canada
toadstool le champignon vénéneux
toast (to eat) le pain grillé ; le toast
tobacco le tabac
tobacconist's le bureau de tabac
today aujourd'hui
toddler le bambin

toe le doigt de pied
together ensemble
toilet les toilettes
  toilet for disabled les toilettes
  pour handicapés
toilet brush la balayette pour les WC
toilet paper le papier hygiénique
toiletries les articles de toilette
token le jeton
toll (motorway) le péage
tomato la tomate
  tomato soup la soupe de tomates
  tinned tomatoes les tomates en
  boîte
tomorrow demain
  tomorrow morning demain matin
  tomorrow afternoon demain
  après-midi
  tomorrow evening demain soir
tongue la langue
tonic water le tonic
tonight ce soir
tonsillitis l'angine (f)
too (also) aussi
  it's too big c'est trop grand
  it's too hot il fait trop chaud
  too noisy il y a trop de bruit
toolkit la trousse à outils
tools les outils
tooth la dent
toothache le mal de dents
  I have toothache j'ai mal aux dents
toothbrush la brosse à dents
toothpaste le dentifrice
toothpick le cure-dent
top: *the top floor* le dernier étage
top (of jar, bottle) le bouchon
  (of pen) le capuchon
  (of pyjamas, bikini, etc) le haut
  (of hill, mountain) le sommet
  on top of sur
topless: *to go topless* enlever le haut
torch la lampe de poche
torn déchiré(e)
total (amount) le total
to touch toucher
tough (meat) dur(e)
tour l'excursion (f)
  guided tour la visite guidée
tour guide le/la guide
tour operator le tour-opérateur ; le
  voyagiste
tourist le/la touriste
tourist (information) office le syndicat
  d'initiative
tourist route l'itinéraire touristique (m)

145

tourist ticket le billet touristique
to tow remorquer
towbar (on car) le crochet d'attelage
tow rope le câble de remorquage
towel la serviette
tower la tour
town la ville
town centre le centre-ville
town hall la mairie
town plan le plan de la ville
toxic toxique
toy le jouet
toyshop le magasin de jouets
tracksuit le survêtement
traditional traditionnel(-elle)
traffic la circulation
traffic jam l'embouteillage (m)
traffic lights les feux
traffic warden le/la contractuel(le)
trailer la remorque
train le train
  by train par le train
  the next train le prochain train
  the first train le premier train
  the last train le dernier train
trainers les baskets
tram le tramway
tranquillizer le tranquillisant
to translate traduire
translation la traduction
to travel voyager
travel agent's l'agence de voyages (f)
travel guide le guide
travel insurance l'assrance voyage (f)
travel pass la carte de transport
travel sickness le mal des transports
traveller's cheques les chèques de voyage
tray le plateau
tree l'arbre (m)
trip l'excursion (f)
trolley le chariot
trouble les ennuis
  to be in trouble avoir des ennuis
trousers le pantalon
truck le camion
true vrai(e)
trunk (luggage) la malle
trunks (swimming) le maillot (de bain)
to try essayer
to try on (clothes, shoes) essayer
t-shirt le tee-shirt
Tuesday mardi
tumble dryer le sèche-linge

tunnel le tunnel
to turn tourner
  to turn round faire demi-tour
to turn off (light, etc) éteindre
  (to turn off engine) couper le moteur
to turn on (light, etc) allumer
  (engine) mettre en marche
turquoise (colour) turquoise
tweezers la pince à épiler
twice deux fois
twin-bedded room la chambre à deux lits
twins (male) les jumeaux
  (female) les jumelles
to type taper à la machine
typical typique
tyre le pneu
tyre pressure la pression des pneus

U

ugly laid(e)
ulcer l'ulcère (m)
  mouth ulcer l'aphte (m)
umbrella le parapluie
  (sunshade) le parasol
uncle l'oncle (m)
uncomfortable inconfortable
unconscious sans connaissance
under sous
undercooked pas assez cuit(e)
underground le métro
underpants (man's) le caleçon
underpass le passage souterrain
to understand comprendre
  I don't understand je ne comprends pas
  do you understand? vous comprenez?
underwear les sous-vêtements
to undress se déshabiller
unemployed au chômage
to unfasten (clothes, etc) défaire
  (door) ouvrir
United Kingdom le Royaume-Uni
United States les États Unis
university l'université (f)
unkind pas gentil(-ille)
unleaded petrol l'essence sans plomb (f)
unlikely peu probable
to unlock ouvrir

to unpack *(suitcase)* défaire
unpleasant désagréable
to unplug débrancher
to unscrew dévisser
up: *to get up (out of bed)* se lever
upside down à l'envers
upstairs en haut
urgent urgent(e)
urine l'urine *(f)*
us nous
to use utiliser
useful utile
usual habituel(-elle)
usually d'habitude
U-turn le demi-tour

V

vacancy *(in hotel)* la chambre
vacant libre
vacation les vacances
vaccination le vaccin
vacuum cleaner l'aspirateur *(m)*
vagina le vagin
valid *(ticket, driving licence, etc)* valable
valley la vallée
valuable d'une grande valeur
valuables les objets de valeur
value la valeur
valve la soupape
van la camionnette
vase le vase
VAT la TVA
vegan végétalien(ne)
  I'm a vegan je suis végétalien(ne)
vegetables les légumes
vegetarian végétarien(ne)
  I'm vegetarian je suis végétarien(ne)
vehicle le véhicule
vein la veine
velvet le velours
vending machine le distributeur automatique
venereal disease la maladie vénérienne
ventilator le ventilateur
very très
vest le maillot de corps
vet le/la vétérinaire
via par

to video *(from TV)* enregistrer
video *(machine)* le magnétoscope
  (cassette) la (cassette) vidéo
video camera la caméra vidéo
video cassette la cassette vidéo
video game le jeu vidéo
video recorder le magnétoscope
video tape la cassette vidéo
view la vue
  a room with a sea view une chambre avec vue sur la mer
villa la maison de campagne
village le village
vinegar le vinaigre
vineyard le vignoble
viper la vipère
virus le virus
visa le visa
visit le séjour
to visit visiter
visiting hours les heures de visite
visitor le/la visiteur(-euse)
vitamin la vitamine
voice la voix
volcano le volcan
volleyball le volley-ball
voltage le voltage
to vomit vomir
voucher le bon

W

wage le salaire
waist la taille
waistcoat le gilet
to wait for attendre
waiter le/la serveur(-euse)
waiting room la salle d'attente
waitress la serveuse
to wake up se réveiller
Wales le pays de Galles
walk la promenade
  to go for a walk faire une promenade
to walk aller à pied ; marcher
walking boots les chaussures de marche
walking stick la canne
Walkman® le walkman®
wall le mur
wallet le portefeuille
to want vouloir
  I want… je veux…
  we want… nous voulons…

war la guerre
ward *(hospital)* la salle
wardrobe l'armoire *(f)*
warehouse l'entrepôt *(m)*
warm chaud(e)
  it's warm (weather) il fait bon
  it's too warm il fait trop chaud
to warm up *(milk, etc)* faire chauffer
warning triangle le triangle de présignalisation
to wash laver
  to wash oneself se laver
washbasin le lavabo
washing machine la machine à laver
washing powder la lessive
washing-up bowl la cuvette
washing-up liquid le produit pour la vaisselle
wasp la guêpe
wasp sting la piqûre de guêpe
waste bin la poubelle
watch la montre
to watch *(look at)* regarder
watchstrap le bracelet de montre
water l'eau *(f)*
  bottled water l'eau en bouteille
  cold water l'eau froide
  drinking water (fit to drink) l'eau potable
  hot water l'eau chaude
  sparkling mineral water l'eau minérale gazeuse
  still mineral water l'eau minérale plate
waterfall la cascade
water heater le chauffe-eau
watermelon la pastèque
waterproof imperméable
water-skiing le ski nautique
water sports les sports nautiques
waterwings les bracelets gonflables
waves *(on sea)* les vagues
waxing *(hair removal)* l'épilation à la cire *(f)*
way *(manner)* la manière
  (route) le chemin
way in *(entrance)* l'entrée *(f)*
way out *(exit)* la sortie
we nous *see*
weak faible
  (coffee, etc) léger(-ère)
to wear porter
weather le temps
weather forecast la météo
web *(internet)* le Web
website le site web

wedding le mariage
wedding anniversary l'anniversaire de mariage *(m)*
wedding present le cadeau de mariage
Wednesday mercredi
week la semaine
  last week la semaine dernière
  next week la semaine prochaine
  per week par semaine
  this week cette semaine
weekday le jour de semaine
weekend le week-end
  next weekend le week-end prochain
  this weekend ce week-end
weekly par semaine ; hebdomadaire
  (pass, ticket) valable pendant une semaine
to weigh peser
weight le poids
welcome! bienvenu(e)!
well *(for water)* le puits
well *(healthy)* en bonne santé
  I'm very well je vais très bien
  he's not well il est souffrant
well done *(steak)* bien cuit(e)
wellingtons les bottes en caout-chouc
Welsh gallois(e)
west l'ouest *(m)*
wet mouillé(e)
wetsuit la combinaison de plongée
what que ; quel/quelle ; quoi
  what is it? qu'est-ce que c'est?
wheel la roue
wheelchair le fauteuil roulant
wheel clamp le sabot de Denver
when quand
  (at what time?) à quelle heure?
  when is it? c'est quand? ; à quelle heure?
where où
  where is it? c'est où?
  where is the hotel? où est l'hôtel?
which quel/quelle
  which (one)? lequel/laquelle?
  which (ones)? lesquels/lesquelles?
while pendant que
  in a while bientôt ; tout à l'heure
white blanc (blanche)
who qui
  who is it? qui c'est?
whole entier(-ière)

wholemeal bread le pain complet
whose: *whose is it?* c'est à qui?
why pourquoi
wide large
widow la veuve
widower le veuf
width la largeur
wife la femme
wig la perruque
to win gagner
wind le vent
windbreak *(camping, etc)* le pare-vent
windmill le moulin à vent
window la fenêtre
  (shop) la vitrine
windscreen le pare-brise
windscreen wipers les essuie-glaces
windsurfing la planche à voile
  to go windsurfing faire de la
  planche à voile
windy: *it's windy* il y a du vent
wine le vin
  dry wine le vin sec
  house wine le vin en pichet
  red wine le vin rouge
  rosé wine le rosé
  sparkling wine le vin mousseux
  sweet wine le vin doux
  white wine le vin blanc
wine list la carte des vins
wing *(bird, aircraft)* l'aile *(f)*
wing mirror le rétroviseur latéral
winter l'hiver *(m)*
wire le fil
with avec
  with ice avec des glaçons
  with milk/sugar avec du lait/sucre
without sans
  without ice sans glaçons
  without milk/sugar sans lait/sucre
witness le témoin
woman la femme
wonderful merveilleux(-euse)
wood le bois
wooden en bois
wool la laine
word le mot
work le travail
to work *(person)* travailler
  (machine, car) fonctionner ; marcher
  it doesn't work ça ne marche pas
work permit le permis de travail

world le monde
worried inquiet(-iète)
worse pire
worth: *it's worth…* ça vaut…
to wrap (up) emballer
wrapping paper le papier d'emballage
wrinkles les rides
wrist le poignet
to write écrire
  please write it down vous me
  l'écrivez, s'il vous plaît?
writing paper le papier à lettres
wrong faux (fausse)
wrought iron le fer forgé

X

X-ray la radiographie
to x-ray radiographier

Y

yacht le yacht
year l'an *(m)* ; l'année *(f)*
  this year cette année
  next year l'année prochaine
  last year l'année dernière
yearly annuel(le)
yellow jaune
Yellow Pages les pages jaunes
yes oui
  yes please oui, merci
yesterday hier
yet: *not yet* pas encore
yoghurt le yaourt
  plain yoghurt le yaourt nature
yolk le jaune d'œuf
you *(familiar)* tu
  (polite) vous
young jeune
your *(familiar sing)* ton/ta
  (familiar plural) tes
  (polite singular) votre
  (polite plural) vos
youth hostel l'auberge de jeunesse *(f)*

Z

zebra crossing le passage pour
  piétons
zero le zéro
zip la fermeture éclair
zone la zone
zoo le zoo
zoom lens le zoom

A

à to ; at

abbaye f abbey

abcès m abscess

abeille f bee

abîmer to damage

abonné(e) m/f subscriber ; season ticket holder

abonnement m subscription ; season ticket

abri m shelter

abrité(e) sheltered

accélérateur m accelerator

accepter to accept

accès m access
  accès aux trains to the trains
  accès aux quais to the trains
  accès interdit no entry
  accès réservé authorized entry only

accident m accident

accompagner to accompany

accord m agreement

accotement m verge

accueil m reception

accueillir to greet ; to welcome

ACF m Automobile Club de France

achat m purchase

acheter to buy

acier m steel

acte de naissance m birth certificate

activité f activity

adaptateur m adaptor (electrical)

addition f bill

adhérent(e) m/f member

adolescent(e) m/f teenager

adresse f address

adresse électronique e-mail address

adresser to address
  adressez-vous à enquire at (office)

adroit(e) skilful

adulte m/f adult

aérogare f terminal

aéroglisseur m hovercraft

aéroport m airport

affaires fpl business ; belongings
  bonne affaire bargain

affiche f poster ; notice

affreux(-euse) awful

âge m age

d'un certain âge middle-aged
du troisième âge senior citizen

âgé(e) elderly
  âgé de ... ans aged ... years

agence f agency ; branch
  agence de voyages travel agency
  agence immobilière estate agent's

agenda m diary
  agenda électronique m personal organizer (electronic)

agent m agent
  agent de police police officer

agiter to shake
  agiter avant emploi shake before use

agneau m lamb

agrandissement m enlargement

agréable pleasant ; nice

agréé(e) registered ; authorized

agression f attack (mugging)

aider to help

aigre sour

aiguille f needle

ail m garlic

aimer to enjoy ; to love (person)

air: en plein air in the open air

aire: *aire de jeux* play area
  aire de repos rest area
  aire de service service area
  aire de stationnement layby

airelles fpl bilberries ; cranberries

alarme f alarm

alcool m alcohol ; fruit brandy

alcoolisé(e) alcoholic

alentours mpl surroundings

algues fpl seaweed

alimentation f food

allée f driveway ; path

allégé(e) low- fat

Allemagne f Germany

allemand(e) German

aller to go

aller (simple) m single ticket

aller-retour m return ticket

allergie f allergy

allô? hello? (on telephone)

allumage m ignition

allumé(e) on (light)

allume-feu m fire lighter

allumer to turn on ; to light
  allumez vos phares switch on headlights

allumette f match

Alpes Alps

alpinisme m mountaineering

alsacien(ne) Alsatian

ambassade f embassy
ambulance f ambulance
améliorer to improve
amende f fine
amer(-ère) bitter
américain(e) American
Amérique f America
ameublement m furniture
ami(e) m/f friend
 petit(e) ami(e) boyfriend/girlfriend
amortisseur m shock absorber
amour m love
 faire l'amour to make love
ampoule f blister ; light bulb
amusant(e) funny (amusing)
amuser to entertain
 s'amuser (bien) to enjoy oneself
an m year
 Nouvel An m New Year
analgésique m painkiller
ananas m pineapple
ancien(ne) old ; former
ancre f anchor
anesthésique m anaesthetic
ange m angel
angine f tonsillitis
 angine de poitrine angina
Anglais m Englishman
anglais m English (language)
anglais(e) English
Angleterre f England
animal m animal
 animal de compagnie pet
animations fpl entertainment ; activities
anis m aniseed
anisette f aniseed liqueur
année f year ; vintage
 bonne année! happy New Year!
anniversaire m anniversary ;
 birthday
annonce f advertisement
annuaire m directory
annulation f cancellation
annuler to cancel
antenne f aerial
 antenne parabolique f satellite dish
anti-insecte m insect repellent
antibiotique m antibiotic
antigel m antifreeze
antihistaminique m antihistamine
antimoustique m mosquito
 repellent
antiquaire m/f antique dealer
antiquités mpl antiques

antiseptique m antiseptic
antivol m bike lock
août August
apéritif m apéritif
aphte m mouth ulcer
appareil m appliance ; camera
 appareil acoustique hearing aid
 appareil photo camera
appartement m apartment ; flat
appât m bait (for fishing)
appel m phone call
appeler to call (speak, phone)
 appeler en PCV to reverse the
 charges
appendicite f appendicitis
apporter to bring
apprendre to learn
appuyer to press
après after
après-midi m afternoon
après-rasage m after-shave
après-shampooing m conditioner
aquarium m fish tank
arachide f groundnut
araignée f spider
arbre m tree
arête f fishbone
argent m money ; silver (metal)
 argent de poche pocket money
 argent liquide cash
argot m slang
armoire f wardrobe
arranger to arrange
arrêt m stop
 arrêt d'autobus bus stop
 arrêt facultatif request stop
arrêter to arrest ; to stop
 arrêter le moteur to turn off the engine
arrêtez! stop!
arrhes fpl deposit (part payment)
arrière m rear ; back
arrivées fpl arrivals
arriver to arrive ; to happen
arrondissement m district (in large city)
art m art
arthrite f arthritis
article m item ; article
 articles de toilette toiletries
articulation f joint (body)
artificiel artificial
artisan(e) m/f craftsman/woman

artisanat m arts and crafts
artiste m/f artist
ascenseur m lift
aspirateur m vacuum cleaner
aspirine f aspirin
assaisonnement m seasoning ; dressing
asseoir to sit (someone) down
  s'asseoir to sit down
assez enough ; quite *(rather)*
assiette f plate
associé(e) m/f partner *(business)*
assorti(e) assorted ; matching
assurance f insurance
assuré(e) insured
assurer to assure ; to insure
asthme m asthma
atelier m workshop ; artist's studio
attacher to fasten *(seatbelt)*
attaque f fit *(medical)*
  attaque (d'apoplexie) stroke
attendre to wait (for)
attention! look out!
  attention au feu danger of fire
  faire attention to be careful
atterrissage m landing *(aircraft)*
attestation f certificate
  l'attestation d'assurance green card
attrayant(e) attractive
au-delà de beyond
au-dessus de above ; on top of
au lieu de instead of
au revoir goodbye
au secours! help!
aube f dawn
auberge f inn
  auberge de jeunesse youth hostel
aubergine f aubergine
aucun(e) none ; no ; not any
audiophone m hearing aid
augmenter to increase
aujourd'hui today
aussi also
aussitôt immediately
  aussitôt que possible as soon as possible
Australie f Australia
australien(ne) Australian
autel m altar
auteur m author
authentique genuine

auto-école f driving school
auto-stop m hitch-hiking
autobus m bus
autocar m coach
automatique automatic
automne m autumn
automobiliste m/f motorist
autoradio m car radio
autorisé(e) permitted ; authorized
autoroute f motorway
autre other
  autres directions other routes
avalanche f avalanche
avaler to swallow
  ne pas avaler not to be taken internally
avance f advance
  à l'avance in advance
avant before ; front
  à l'avant at the front
  en avant forward
avec with
avenir m future
avenue f avenue
avertir to inform ; to warn
avion m aeroplane
aviron m oar ; rowing *(sport)*
avis m notice ; warning
aviser to advise
avocat m avocado ; lawyer
avoine f oats
avoir to have
avortement m abortion
avril April

B

bacon m bacon
bagages mpl luggage
  bagages à main hand luggage
  faire les bagages to pack
bague f ring *(on finger)*
baguette f stick of French bread
baie f bay *(along coast)*
baignade f bathing
  baignade interdite no bathing
bain m bath
  bain moussant bubble bath
baiser kiss
baisser to lower
bal m ball ; dance
balade f walk ; drive ; trek
balai m broom *(brush)*
  balai à laver mop *(for floor)*
balance f scales *(for weighing)*

balançoire f swing (for children)
balcon m circle (theatre) ; balcony
ball-trap m clay pigeon shooting
balle f ball (small: golf, tennis, etc)
ballet m ballet
ballon m balloon ; ball (large) ; brandy glass
bambin m toddler
banane f banana ; bumbag
banc m seat ; bench
banlieue f suburbs
banque f bank
bar m bar
barbe f beard
barbecue m barbecue
barque f rowing boat
barrage m dam
 barrage routier road block
barré: *route barrée* road closed
barrer to cross out
barrière f barrier
bas m bottom (of page, etc) ; stocking
 en bas below ; downstairs
bas(se) low
baskets fpl trainers
bassin m pond ; washing-up bowl
bateau m boat ; ship
 bateau à rames rowing boat
 bateau-mouche river boat
bâtiment m building
bâton (de ski) m ski pole
batte f bat (baseball, cricket)
batterie f battery (for car)
 batterie à plat flat battery
baume pour les lèvres m lip salve
bavoir m bib (baby's)
beau (belle) lovely ; handsome ; beautiful ; nice (enjoyable)
beau-frère m brother-in-law
beau-père m father-in-law ; stepfather
beaucoup (de) much/many ; a lot of
bébé m baby
beignet m fritter ; doughnut
belge Belgian
Belgique f Belgium
belle-fille f daughter-in-law
belle-mère f mother-in-law ; step-mother
béquilles fpl crutches
berger m shepherd
berlingots mpl boiled sweets
besoin: *avoir besoin de* to need
beurre m butter
 beurre doux unsalted butter

biberon m baby's bottle
bibliothèque f library
bicyclette f bicycle
bien well ; right ; good
 bien cuit(e) well done (steak)
bientôt soon ; shortly
bienvenu(e) welcome!
bière f beer
 bière (à la) pression draught beer
 bière blonde lager
 bière bouteille bottled lager
 bière brune bitter
bifteck m steak
bijouterie f jeweller's ; jewellery
bijoux mpl jewellery
bikini m bikini
billet m note ; ticket
 billet aller-retour return ticket
 billet d'avion plane ticket
 billet de banque banknote
 billet simple one-way ticket
biologique organic
biscotte f breakfast biscuit ; rusk
biscuit m biscuit
bisque f thick seafood soup
blanc (blanche) white ; blank
 en blanc blank (on form)
blanc d'œuf m egg white
blanchisserie f laundry
blé m wheat
blessé(e) injured
blesser to injure
bleu m bruise
bleu(e) blue ; very rare (steak)
 bleu marine navy blue
bloc-notes m note pad
blond(e) fair (hair)
bloqué(e) stuck
body m body (clothing)
bœuf m beef
boire to drink
bois m wood
boisson f drink
 boisson non alcoolisée soft drink
boîte f can ; box
 boîte à fusibles fuse box
 boîte à lettres post box
 boîte de nuit night club
 boîte de vitesses gearbox
bol m bowl (for soup, etc)
bombe f aerosol ; bomb
bon m token ; voucher

bon (bonne) good ; right ; nice
bon anniversaire happy birthday
bon marché inexpensive

bonbon m sweet

bondé(e) crowded

bonhomme m chap
bonhomme de neige snowman

bonjour hello ; good morning/afternoon

bonnet m hat
bonnet de bain bathing cap

bonneterie f hosiery

bonsoir good evening

bord m border ; edge ; verge
à bord on board
au bord de la mer at the seaside

bosse f lump *(swelling)*

botte f boot ; bunch

bottillons mpl ankle boots

bouche f mouth
bouche d'incendie fire hydrant

bouché(e) blocked

bouchée f mouthful ; chocolate

boucherie f butcher's shop

bouchon m cork ; plug *(for sink)* ;
top *(of jar, bottle)*

boucle d'oreille f earring

bouée de sauvetage f life belt

bougie f candle ; spark plug

bouillabaisse f rich fish soup/stew

bouilli(e) boiled

bouillir to boil

bouilloire f kettle

bouillon m stock

bouillotte f hot-water bottle

boulangerie f bakery

boule f ball

boules fpl game similar to bowls

bouquet m bunch *(of flowers)*

Bourgogne Burgundy

boussole f compass

bout m end
à bout filtre filter-tipped

bouteille f bottle

boutique f shop

bouton m button ; switch ; spot
bouton d'or buttercup
bouton de fièvre cold sore
boutons de manchette cufflinks

boxe f boxing

bracelet m bracelet
bracelet de montre watchstrap

braisé(e) braised

bras m arm

brasserie f café ; brewery

Bretagne f Brittany

breton(ne) from Brittany

bricolage m do-it-yourself

briquet m cigarette lighter

briser to break ; to smash

britannique British

brocante f second-hand goods ; flea
market

broche f brooch ; spit

brochette f skewer ; kebab

brocoli m broccoli

brodé main hand-embroidered

bronzage m suntan

bronze bronze

brosse f brush
brosse à cheveux hairbrush
brosse à dents toothbrush

brouillard m fog

bru f daughter-in-law

bruit m noise

brûlé(e) burnt

brûler to burn

brûlures d'estomac fpl heartburn

brun(e) brown ; dark

brushing m blow-dry

brut(e) gross ; raw

Bruxelles Brussels

bûche f log *(for fire)*

buisson m bush

bulletin de consigne m left-
luggage ticket

bureau m desk ; office
bureau de change foreign exchange
office
bureau de location booking office
bureau de poste post office
bureau de renseignements information office
bureau des objets trouvés lost
property office

bus m bus

butane m camping gas

C

ça va it's OK

cabaret m cabaret

cabine f beach hut ; cubicle ; cabin
cabine d'essayage changing room

cabinet m office

câble de remorquage m tow rope

cacahuète f peanut

5

cacao *m* cocoa
cacher to hide
cadeau *m* gift
cadenas *m* padlock
cadre *m* picture frame
cafard *m* cockroach
café *m* coffee ; café
  café au lait white coffee
  café crème white coffee
  café décaféiné decaff coffee
  café instantané instant coffee
  café noir black coffee
cafetière *f* coffee pot
cahier *m* exercise book
caisse *f* cash desk ; case
  caisse d'épargne savings bank
caissier(ière) *m/f* cashier ; teller
calculatrice *f* calculator
caleçon *m* boxer shorts
calendrier *m* calendar ; timetable
calmant *m* sedative
cambriolage *m* break-in
cambrioleur(-euse) *m/f* burglar
caméra vidéo *f* video camera
caméscope *m* camcorder
camion *m* lorry ; truck
camionnette *f* van
camomille *f* camomile
campagne *f* countryside ; campaign
camper to camp
camping *m* camping ; camp-site
  camping sauvage camping on
  unofficial sites
  camping-gaz® camping stove
Canada *m* Canada
canadien(ne) Canadian
canal *m* canal
canapé *m* sofa ; open sandwich
  canapé-lit sofa bed
canard *m* duck
caneau de sauvetage *m* life raft
canif *m* penknife
canne *f* walking stick
  canne à pêche fishing rod
cannelle *f* cinnamon
canoë *m* canoe
canot *m* boat
  canot de sauvetage lifeboat
canotage *m* boating
caoutchouc *m* rubber *(material)*
capable efficient
capitale *f* capital *(city)*
capot *m* bonnet ; hood *(of car)*
câpres *fpl* capers
capuchon *m* hood ; top *(of pen)*

car *m* coach
carabine de chasse *f* hunting rifle
carafe *f* carafe ; decanter
caravane *f* caravan
carburateur *m* carburettor
Carême *m* Lent
carnet *m* notebook ; book
  carnet de billets book of tickets
  carnet de chèques cheque book
carotte *f* carrot
carré *m* square
carreau *m* tile *(on wall, floor)*
carrefour *m* crossroads
carte *f* map ; card ; menu ;
  pass *(bus, train)*
  carte bleue credit card
  carte d'abonnement season ticket
  carte d'embarquement boarding
  card/pass
  carte d'identité identity card
  carte de crédit credit card
  carte des vins wine list
  carte du jour menu of the day
  carte grise log book *(car)*
  carte orange monthly or yearly
  season ticket
  carte postale postcard
  carte routière road map
  carte vermeille senior citizen's rail pass
cartes (à jouer) *fpl* playing cards
carton *m* cardboard
cartouche *f* carton *(of cigarettes)*
cas *m* case
cascade *f* waterfall
caserne *f* barracks
casier *m* rack ; locker
casino *m* casino
casque *m* helmet
  casque (à écouteurs) headphones
casquette *f* cap *(hat)*
cassé(e) broken
casse-croûte *m* snacks
casser to break
  casser la croûte to have a snack
casserole *f* saucepan
cassette *f* cassette
catch *m* wrestling
cathédrale *f* cathedral
catholique Catholic
cause *f* cause
  pour cause de on account of
caution *f* security *(for loan)* ; deposit
  caution à verser deposit required

cave f cellar
caveau m cellar
caviar m caviar(e)
CD m CD
ceci this
cédez le passage give way
CE f EC (European Community)
ceinture f belt
  ceinture de sécurité seatbelt
  ceinture porte-monnaie moneybelt
cela that
célèbre famous
célibataire single (unmarried)
cendrier m ashtray
cent m hundred
centimètre m centimetre
central(e) central
centre m centre
  centre commercial shopping centre
  centre de loisirs leisure centre
  centre équestre riding school
  centre ville city centre
céramique f ceramics
cercle m circle ; ring
céréales fpl cereal (for breakfast)
cerise f cherry
certain(e) certain (sure)
certificat m certificate
cerveau m brain
cervelle f brains (as food)
cesser to stop
cette this ; that
ceux-ci/celles-ci these ones
ceux-là/celles-là those ones
CFF mpl Swiss Railways
chacun/chacune each
chaîne f chain ; channel ;
  (mountain) range
  chaîne (stéréo) stereo
  chaînes obligatoires snow chains
  compulsory
chair f flesh
chaise f chair
  chaise haute high chair
  chaise longue deckchair
châle m shawl
chalet m chalet
chambre f bedroom ; room
  chambre à air inner tube
  chambre à coucher bedroom
  chambre à deux lits twin-bedded
  room
  chambre d'hôte bed and breakfast

  chambre individuelle single room
  chambre pour deux personnes
  double room
  chambres rooms to let
champ m field
  champ de courses racecourse
champagne m champagne
champignon m mushroom
  champignon vénéneux toadstool
chance f luck
change m exchange
changement m change
changer to change
  changer de l'argent to change
  money
  changer de train to change train
  se changer to change clothes
chanson f song
chanter to sing
chanterelle f chanterelle
chantier m building site ; roadworks
chapeau m hat
chapelle f chapel
chaque each ; every
charbon m coal
  charbon de bois charcoal
charcuterie f pork butcher's ;
  delicatessen ; cooked meat
chariot m trolley
charter m charter flight
chasse f hunting ; shooting
  chasse gardée private hunting
  chasse-neige m snowplough
chasser to hunt
chasseur m hunter
chat m cat
châtaigne f chestnut
château m castle ; mansion
chaud(e) hot
chauffage m heating
chauffer to heat up (milk, water)
chauffeur m driver
chaussée f carriageway
  chaussée déformée uneven road
  surface
  chaussée rétrécie road narrows
  chaussée verglacée icy road
chaussette f sock
chaussure f shoe ; boot
chauve bald (person)
chauve-souris f bat (creature)
chef m chef ; chief ; head ; leader
  chef de train guard (on train)
chef-d'œuvre m masterpiece
chef-lieu m county town
chemin m path ; lane ; track ; way

7 *chemin de fer* railway
cheminée f chimney ; fireplace
chemise f shirt
  chemise de nuit nightdress
chemisier m blouse
chèque m cheque
  chèque de voyage traveller's cheque
cher (chère) dear ; expensive
chercher to look for
  aller chercher to fetch ; to collect
cheval m horse
  faire du cheval to ride *(horse)*
cheveux mpl hair
cheville f ankle
chèvre f goat
chevreau m kid *(goat, leather)*
chez at the house of
  chez moi at my home
chien m dog
chiffon m duster ; rag
chips fpl crisps
chirurgien m surgeon
chocolat m chocolate ; hot chocolate
  chocolat à croquer plain chocolate
  chocolat au lait milk chocolate
choisir to choose
choix m range ; choice ; selection
chômage: au chômage unemployed
chope f tankard
chorale f choir
chose f thing
chou m cabbage
chou-fleur m cauliflower
chute f fall
cidre m cider
ciel m sky
cigare m cigar
cigarette f cigarette
cil m eyelash
cimetière m cemetery ; graveyard
cinéma m cinema
cintre m coat hanger
cirage m shoe polish
circuit m round trip ; circuit
circulation f traffic
cire f wax ; polish
cirque m circus
ciseaux mpl scissors
cité f city ; housing estate
citron m lemon
  citron vert lime
citronnade f still lemonade

french–eng C

clair(e) clear ; light
classe f grade ; class
clavicule f collar bone
clavier m keyboard
clé f key ; spanner
  clé de contact ignition key
  clé minute keys cut while you wait
clef f key
client(e) m/f client ; customer
clignotant m indicator *(on car)*
climatisation f air-conditioning
climatisé(e) air-conditioned
clinique f clinic *(private)*
cloche f bell *(church, school)*
clocher m steeple
clou m nail *(metal)*
  clou de girofle clove
club m club
cocher to tick *(on form)*
cochon m pig
cocktail m cocktail
cocotte f casserole dish
cocotte-minute f pressure cooker
code barres m barcode
code postal m postcode
cœur m heart
coffre-fort m strongbox ; safe
cognac m brandy
coiffeur m hairdresser ; barber
coiffeuse f hairdresser
coin m corner
coincé(e) jammed ; stuck
col m collar ; pass *(in mountains)*
colis m parcel
collant m pair of tights
colle f glue
collège m secondary school
collègue m/f colleague
coller to stick ; to glue
collier m necklace ; dog collar
colline f hill
collision f crash *(car)*
colonne f column
  colonne vertébrale spine
combien how much/many
combinaison de plongée f wetsuit
combinaison de ski ski suit
combustible m fuel
comédie f comedy
  comédie musicale musical (show)*

commande f order (in restaurant)
commander to order
comme like
  comme ça like this ; like that
commencer to begin
comment? pardon? ; how?
commerçant(e) m/f trader
commerce m commerce ; business ; trade
commissariat (de police) m police station
commode f chest of drawers
commotion f shock
  commotion (cérébrale) concussion
communication f communication ; call (on telephone)
communion f communion
compagne f girlfriend
compagnie f firm ; company
compagnon m boyfriend
compartiment m compartment (train)
complet(-ète) full (up)
complètement completely
comporter to consist of
  se comporter to behave
composer to dial (a number)
composter to date-stamp/punch (ticket)
  composter votre bille validate your ticket
comprenant including
comprendre to understand
comprimé m tablet
compris(e) included
  non compris not included
comptant m cash
compte m number ; account
  compte en banque bank account
compter to count (add up)
compteur m speedometer ; meter
comptoir m counter (in shop, etc)
comte m count ; earl
concert m concert
concierge m/f caretaker ; janitor
concours m contest ; aid
concurrent(e) m/f competitor
conducteur(-trice) m/f driver
conduire to drive
conduite f driving ; behaviour
confection f ready-to-wear clothes
conférence f conference
confession f confession

confirmer to confirm
confiserie f sweetshop
confiture f jam ; preserve
congélateur m freezer
congelé(e) frozen
connaître to know
conseil m advice ; council
conseiller to advise
conserver to keep
consigne f deposit ; left luggage
consommation f drink
consommé m clear soup
constat m report
constipé(e) constipated
construire to build
consulat m consulate
contacter to contact
contenir to contain
content(e) pleased
contenu m contents
continuer to continue
contraceptif m contraceptive
contrat m contract
  contrat de location lease
contravention f fine (penalty)
contre against ; versus
contre-filet m sirloin
contrôle m check
  contrôle des passeports passport control
  contrôle radar speed trap
contrôler to check
contrôleur(-euse) m/f ticket inspector
convenu(e) agreed
convoi exceptionnel m large load
copie f copy (duplicate)
copier to copy
coque f shell ; cockle
coquelicot m poppy
coquet(te) pretty (place, etc)
coquillages mpl shellfish
coquille f shell
  coquille Saint-Jacques scallop
corail m coral ; type of train
corde f rope
  corde à linge clothes line
cordonnerie f shoe repair shop
cornet m cone
corniche f coast road
corps m body
correspondance f connection (transport)
correspondant(e) m/f penfriend
corrida f bull-fight

Corse f Corsica

costume m suit (man's)

côte f coast ; hill ; rib
  Côte d'Azur French Riviera

côté m side
  à côté de beside ; next to

côtelette f cutlet

coton m cotton
  coton hydrophile cotton wool
  coton-tige® cotton bud

cou m neck

couche (de bébé) f nappy

coucher du soleil m sunset

couchette f bunk ; berth

coude m elbow

coudre to sew

couette f continental quilt ; duvet

couler to run (water)

couleur f colour

coulis m purée

couloir m corridor ; aisle

coup m stroke ; shot ; blow
  coup de pied kick
  coup de soleil sunburn
  coup de téléphone phone call

coupe f goblet (ice cream)
  coupe (de cheveux) haircut

couper to cut

couple m couple (two people)

coupure f cut
  coupure de courant power cut

cour f court ; courtyard

courant m power ; current

courant(e) common ; current

courir to run

couronne f crown

courrier m mail ; post
  courrier électronique e-mail

courroie de ventilateur f fan belt

cours m lesson ; course ; rate

course f race (sport) ; errand
  course hippique horse race
  faire des courses to go shopping

court de tennis m tennis court

court(e) short

cousin(e) m/f cousin

coussin m cushion

coût m cost

couteau m knife

coûter to cost

coûteux(-euse) expensive

couture f sewing ; seam

couvent m convent ; monastery

couvercle m lid

couvert m cover charge ; place setting

couverts cutlery

couvert(e) covered

couverture f blanket ; cover

crabe m crab

crapaud m toad

cravate f tie

crayon m pencil

crème f cream (food, lotion)
  crème à raser shaving cream
  crème aigre soured cream
  crème anglaise custard
  crème Chantilly whipped cream
  crème hydratante moisturizer
  crème pâtissière confectioner's custard

crémerie f dairy

crêpe f pancake

crêperie f pancake shop/restaurant

cresson m watercress

crevaison f puncture

crevette f shrimp ; prawn

cric m jack (for car)

crier to shout

crime m crime ; offence ; murder

crise f crisis ; attack (medical)
  crise cardiaque heart attack

cristal m crystal

crochet d'attelage m towbar

croire to believe

croisement m junction (road)

croisière f cruise

croix f cross

croquant(e) crisp ; crunchy

croque-madame m toasted cheese sandwich with ham and fried egg

croque-monsieur m toasted ham and cheese sandwich

croustade f pastry shell with filling

croûte f crust

cru(e) raw

crudités fpl raw vegetables

crue subite f flash flood

crustacés mpl shellfish

cube de bouillon m stock cube

cuiller f spoon
  cuiller à café teaspoon

cuir m leather

cuisiné(e) cooked

cuisine f cooking ; cuisine ; kitchen
  cuisine familiale home cooking
  faire la cuisine to cook

cuisiner to cook

cuisinier m cook
cuisinière f cook ; cooker
cuisse f thigh
  cuisses de grenouille frogs' legs
cuit(e) cooked ; well done (steak)
cuivre m copper
  cuivre jaune brass
culotte f panties
curieux(-euse) strange
curseur m cursor (computer)
cuvée f vintage
cuvette f washing up bowl
cyclisme m cycling
cystite f cystitis

D

daltonien(ne) colour-blind
dame f lady
  dames ladies
danger m danger
dangereux(-euse) dangerous
dans into ; in ; on
danser to dance
date f date (day)
  date de naissance date of birth
  date limite de vente sell-by date
daube f stew
de from ; of ; some
dé m dice
début m beginning
débutant(e) m/f beginner
décaféiné(e) decaffeinated
décembre December
décès m death
décharge f electric shock
  décharge publique rubbish dump
déchargement m unloading
déchirer to rip
déclaration f statement ; report
  déclaration de douane customs
  declaration
décollage m takeoff
décoller to take off (plane)
décolleté m low neck
décongeler to defrost
découvrir to discover
décrire to describe
décrocher to lift the receiver
dedans inside
défaire to unfasten ; to unpack

défaut m fault ; defect
défectueux(-euse) faulty
défense de... no.../... forbidden
  défense de fumer no smoking
  défense de stationner no parking
dégâts mpl damage
dégeler to thaw
dégivrer to de-ice (windscreen)
dégustation f tasting
  dégustation de vins wine tasting
dehors outside ; outdoors
déjeuner m lunch
délicieux(-euse) delicious
délit m offence
deltaplane m hang-glider
demain tomorrow
demande f application ; request
  demandes d'emploi situations
  wanted
demander to ask (for)
démaquillant m make-up remover
démarqué(e) reduced (goods)
démarreur m starter (in car)
demi(e) half
demi-pension f half board
demi-sec medium-dry
demi-tarif m half fare
demi-tour m U-turn
dent f tooth
dentelle f lace
dentier m dentures
dentifrice m toothpaste
dentiste m/f dentist
déodorant m deodorant
dépannage m breakdown service
dépanneuse f breakdown van
départ m departure
département m county
dépasser to exceed ; to overtake
dépenses fpl expenditure
dépliant m brochure
dépôt m deposit ; depot
  dépôt d'ordures rubbish dump
dépression f depression ; nervous
  breakdown
depuis since
déranger to disturb
dernier(-ère) last ; latest
derrière at the back ; behind
derrière m bottom (buttocks)
dès from ; since
  dès votre arrivée as soon as you
  arrive
désagréable unpleasant

descendre to go down ; to get off
description f description
déshabiller to undress
  se déshabiller to get undressed
désirer to want
désodorisant m air freshener
désolé(e) sorry
dessein m design ; plan
desserré(e) loose *(not fastened)*
dessert m pudding
dessous (de) underneath (of)
dessus (de) on top (of)
destinataire m/f addressee
destination f destination
  à destination de bound for
détail m detail
  au détail retail
détergent m detergent
détourner to divert
deux two
  deux fois twice
  les deux both
deuxième second
devant in front (of)
développer to develop
devenir to become
déviationdéviation f diversion
devis m quotation *(price)*
devises fpl currency
dévisser to unscrew
devoir to have to; to owe
diabète m diabetes
diabétique diabetic
diamant m diamond
diaphragme m cap *(contraceptive)*
diapositive f slide *(photograph)*
diarrhée f diarrhoea
dictionnaire m dictionary
diététique f dietary ; health foods
différent(e) different
difficile difficult
digue f dyke ; jetty
dimanche m Sunday
dinde f turkey
dîner to have dinner
dîner m dinner
  dîner spectacle cabaret dinner
dire to say ; to tell
direct: train direct through train
directeur m manager ; headmaster
direction f management ; direction
directrice f manageress ; headmistress
discothèque f disco
discussion f argument

disjoncteur m circuit breaker
disloquer to dislocate
disparaître to disappear
disparu(e) missing *(disappeared)*
disponible available
disque m record ; disk *(computer)*
  disque de stationnement parking disk
  disque dur hard disk
disquette f floppy disk
dissolvant m nail polish remover
distractions fpl entertainment
distributeur m dispenser
  distributeur automatique vending machine ; cash machine
divers(e) various
divertissements mpl entertainment
divorcé(e) divorced
docteur m doctor
doigt m finger
  doigt de pied toe
domestique m/f servant ; maid
domicile m home ; address
donner to give ; to give away
doré(e) golden
dormir to sleep
dos m back *(of body)*
dossier m file
douane f customs
double double
doubler to overtake
douche f shower
douleur f pain
douloureux(-euse) painful
doux (douce) mild ; gentle ; soft ; sweet
douzaine f dozen
dragée f sugared almond
drap m sheet
drapeau m flag
drogue f drug
droguerie f hardware shop
droit m right *(entitlement)*
droit(e) right *(not left)* ; straight
droite f right-hand side
  à droite on/to the right
  tenez votre droite keep to right
dur(e) hard ; hard-boiled ; tough
durée f duration

E

eau f water
 eau de Javel bleach
 eau dentifrice mouthwash
 eau douce fresh water *(not salt)*
 eau du robinet tap-water
 eau minérale mineral water
 eau potable drinking water
 eau salée salt water
 eau-de-vie brandy
ébène f ebony
échanger to exchange
échantillon m sample
échapper to escape
écharpe f scarf *(woollen)*
échelle f ladder
 échelle de secours fire escape
éclairage m lighting
éclairs mpl lightning
écluse f lock *(in canal)*
école f school
 école maternelle nursery school
écorce f peel *(of orange, lemon)*
écossais(e) Scottish
Écosse f Scotland
écouter to listen to
écran m screen
 écran solaire sunscreen *(lotion)*
 écran total sunblock
écrire to write
écrivain m author
écrou m nut *(for bolt)*
écurie f stable
édulcorant m sweetener
église f church
élastique m elastic band
électricien m electrician
électricité f electricity
électrique electric
élément m unit ; element
emballer to wrap (up)
embarcadère m jetty *(landing pier)*
embarquement m boarding
embouteillage m traffic jam
embrayage m clutch *(in car)*
émission f programme ; broadcast
emploi m use ; job
emporter to take away
 à emporter take-away
emprunter to borrow

en some ; any ; in ; to ; made of
 en cas de in case of
 en face de opposite
 en gros in bulk ; wholesale
 en panne out of order
 en retard late
 en train/voiture by train/car
encaisser to cash *(cheque)*
enceinte pregnant
enchanté(e)! pleased to meet you!
encore still ; yet ; again
encre f ink
endommager to damage
endroit m place ; spot
enfant m/f child
enfler to swell *(bump, eye, etc)*
enlever to take away ; to take off
 (clothes)
 enlever le haut to go topless
enneigé(e) snowed up
ennui m boredom ; nuisance ; trouble
ennuyeux boring
enregistrement m check-in desk
enregistrer to record ; to check in ; to
 video
enseignement m education
enseigner to teach
ensemble together
ensuite next ; after that
entendre to hear
entier(-ère) whole
entorse f sprain
entracte m interval
entre between
entrecôte f rib steak
entrée f entrance ; admission ; starter
 (food)
 entrée gratuite admission free
 entrée interdite no entry
entreprise f firm ; company
entrer to come in ; to go in
entretien m maintenance ; interview
entrez! come in!
enveloppe f envelope
 enveloppe matelassée padded
 envelope
envers: *l'envers* wrong side
 à l'envers upside down ; back to
 front
environ around ; about
environs mpl surroundings
envoyer to send
épais(se) thick
épargner to save *(money)*
épaule f shoulder

63 **épi** m ear (of corn)
  épi de maïs corn-on-the-cob
épice f spice
épicerie f grocer's shop
  épicerie fine delicatessen
épilation f hair removal
  épilation à la cire f waxing
épileptique epileptic
épinards mpl spinach
épine f thorn
épingle f pin
  épingle de sûreté safety pin
éponge f sponge
époque f age
  d'époque period (furniture)
épuisé(e) sold out ; used up
épuiser to use up ; to run out of
équipage m crew
équipe f team ; shift
équipement m equipment
équitation f horse-riding
erreur f mistake
escalade f climbing
escalator m escalator
escalier m stairs
  escalier de secours fire escape
  escalier mécanique escalator
escargot m snail
escarpement m cliff (in mountains)
Espagne f Spain
espagnol(e) Spanish
espèce f sort
espérer to hope
esquimau m ice lolly
essai m trial ; test
essayer to try ; to try on
essence f petrol
  essence sans plomb unleaded petrol
essorer to spin(-dry) ; to wring
essoreuse f spin dryer
essuie-glace m windscreen wipers
essuie-tout m kitchen paper
esthétique f beauty salon
estivants mpl summer holiday-makers
estomac m stomach
estragon m tarragon
et and
étage m storey
  le dernier étage the top floor
étain m tin ; pewter
étang m pond
étape f stage
état m state
  États Unis United States

été m summer
éteindre to turn off
éteint(e) out (light)
étiquette f label
  étiquette à bagages luggage tag
étoile f star
étranger(-ère) m/f foreigner
  à l'étranger overseas ; abroad
être see (to be) **GRAMMAR**
étroit(e) narrow ; tight
étudiant(e) m/f student
étudier to study
étui m case (camera, glasses)
étuvée: à l'étuvée braised
eurochèque m eurocheque
Europe f Europe
européen(ne) European
eux them
évanoui(e) fainted
événement m occasion ; event
éventail m fan (handheld)
éventé(e) flat (beer)
évêque m bishop
évier m sink (washbasin)
éviter to avoid
exact(e) right (correct)
examen m examination
excédent de bagages m excess baggage
excellent(e) excellent
excès de vitesse m speeding
exclu(e) excluded
exclure to expel
exclusif (-ive) exclusive
excursion f trip ; outing ; excursion
excuses fpl apologies
excusez-moi! excuse me!
exemplaire m copy
exercice m exercise
expéditeur m sender
expert(e) m/f expert
expirer to expire (ticket, passport)
expliquer to explain
exporter to export
exposition f exhibition
exprès on purpose ; deliberately
  en exprès express (parcel, etc)
extérieur(e) outside
extincteur m fire extinguisher
extra top-quality ; first-rate

F

fabrication f manufacturing
fabriquer to manufacture
  fabriqué en... made in...
face: en face (de) opposite
fâché(e) angry
facile easy
façon f way ; manner
facteur(-trice) m/f postman
facture f invoice
  facture détaillée itemized bill
faible weak
faïence f earthenware
faim f hunger
  avoir faim to be hungry
faire to make ; to do
  faire du stop to hitchhike
faisan m pheasant
fait main handmade
falaise f cliff
famille f family
farci(e) stuffed
fard à paupières m eye shadow
farine f flour
fatigué(e) tired
fausse couche f miscarriage
faute f mistake ; foul *(football)*
fauteuil m armchair ; seat
  fauteuil roulant wheelchair
faux (fausse) fake ; false ; wrong
fax m fax
faxer to fax
félicitations fpl congratulations
femme f woman ; wife
  femme au foyer housewife
  femme d'affaires businesswoman
  femme de chambre chambermaid
  femme de ménage cleaner
  femme policier policewoman
fenêtre f window
fenouil m fennel
fente f crack ; slot
fer m iron *(material, golf club)*
  fer à repasser iron *(for clothes)*
férié(e): jour férié public holiday
ferme f farmhouse ; farm
fermé(e) closed
fermer to close/shut ; to turn off
  fermer à clé to lock
fermeture f closing

fermeture Éclair® zip
ferroviaire railway ; rail
ferry m car ferry
fête f holiday ; fête ; party
  fête des rois Epiphany
  fête foraine funfair
feu m fire ; traffic lights
  feu (de joie) bonfire *(celebration)*
  feu d'artifice fireworks
  feu de position sidelight
  feu rouge red light
feuille f leaf ; sheet *(of paper)*
feuilleton m soap opera
feutre m felt ; felt-tip pen
février February
fiancé(e) engaged *(to be married)*
ficelle f string ; thin French stick
fiche f token ; form ; slip *(of paper)*
fichier m file *(computer)*
fièvre f fever
  avoir de la fièvre to have a
  temperature
figue f fig
fil m thread ; lead *(electrical)*
  fil dentaire dental floss
file f lane ; row
filet m net ; fillet *(of meat, fish)*
  filet à bagages luggage rack
fille f daughter ; girl
film m film
fils m son
filtre m filter *(on cigarette)*
  filtre à huile oil filter
fin f end
fin(e) thin *(material)* ; fine *(delicate)*
fini(e) finished
finir to end ; to finish
fixer to fix
flacon m bottle *(small)*
flamand(e) Flemish
flan m sweet tart
flash m flash *(for camera)*
fleur f flower
fleuriste m/f florist
fleuve m river
flipper m pinball
flûte f long, thin loaf
foie m liver
  foie gras goose liver
foire f fair
  foire à/aux... special offer on...
fois f time
  cette fois this time
  une fois once
folle mad

5 **foncé(e)** dark *(colour)*
fonctionner to work *(machine)*
fond *m* back *(of hall, room)* ; bottom
fondre to melt
force *f* strength
forêt *f* forest
forfait *m* fixed price ; ski pass
forme *f* shape ; style
formidable great *(wonderful)*
formulaire *m* form *(document)*
fort(e) loud; strong
forteresse *f* fort
fosse *f* pit ; grave
   fosse septique septic tank
fou (folle) mad
fouetté(e) whipped *(cream, eggs)*
foulard *m* scarf *(headscarf)*
foule *f* crowd
four *m* oven
   four à micro-ondes microwave
fourchette *f* fork
fournir to supply
fourré(e) filled ; fur-lined
fourrure *f* fur
fraîche fresh ; cool ; wet *(paint)*
frais fresh ; cool
frais *mpl* costs ; expenses
fraise *f* strawberry
framboise *f* raspberry
français(e) French
Français(e) Frenchman/woman
frapper to hit; to knock *(on door)*
frein *m* brake
freiner to brake
fréquent(e) frequent
frère *m* brother
fret *m* freight *(goods)*
frigo *m* fridge
frit(e) fried
friterie *f* chip shop
frites *fpl* french fries ; chips
friture *f* small fried fish
froid(e) cold
fromage *m* cheese
froment *m* wheat
front *m* forehead
frontière *f* border ; boundary
frotter to rub
fruit *m* fruit
   fruits de mer seafood
   fruits secs dried fruit
fuite *f* leak
fumé(e) smoked
fumée *f* smoke

fumer to smoke
fumeurs smokers
fumier *m* manure
funiculaire *m* funicular railway
fuseau *m* ski pants
fusible *m* fuse
fusil *m* gun

G

gagner to earn ; to win
galerie *f* art gallery ; arcade ; roof-rack
gallois(e) Welsh
gambas *fpl* large prawns
gant *m* glove
   gant de toilette face cloth
   gants de ménage rubber gloves
garage *m* garage
garantie *f* guarantee
garçon *m* boy ; waiter
garde *f* custody ; guard
   garde-côte coastguard
garder to keep ; to look after
gardien(ne) *m/f* caretaker ; warden
gare *f* railway station
   gare routière bus terminal
garer to park
garni(e) served with vegetables or chips
gas-oil *m* diesel fuel
gâteau *m* cake ; gateau
gauche left
   à gauche to/on the left
gaucher(-ère) left-handed
gaz *m* gas
   gaz d'échappement exhaust fumes
gaz-oil *m* diesel fuel
gazeux(-euse) fizzy
gel *m* frost
   gel pour cheveux hair gel
gelé(e) frozen
gelée *f* jelly ; aspic
gênant inconvenient
gendarme *m* policeman *(in rural areas)*
gendarmerie *f* police station
gendre *m* son-in-law
généreux(-euse) generous
genou *m* knee
gentil(-ille) kind *(person)*
gérant(e) *m/f* manager/manageress
gérer to manage *(be in charge of)*

gibier m game (hunting)
gilet m waistcoat
  gilet de sauvetage life jacket
gingembre m ginger
gîte m self-catering house/flat
glace f ice ; ice cream ; mirror
glacé(e) chilled ; iced
glacier m glacier ; ice-cream maker
glacière f cool-box (for picnic)
glaçon m ice cube
glissant(e) slippery
glisser to slip
gomme f rubber (eraser)
gorge f throat ; gorge
gosse m/f kid (child)
gothique Gothic
goût m flavour ; taste
goûter to taste
graine f seed
gramme m gram
grand(e) great ; high (speed, number) ; big ; tall
grand-mère f grandmother
grand-père m grandfather
Grande-Bretagne f Great Britain
grands-parents mpl grandparents
grange f barn
granité m flavoured crushed ice
grappe f bunch (of grapes)
gras(se) fat ; greasy
gratis free
gratuit(e) free of charge
grave serious
gravure f print (picture)
grêle f hail
grenier m attic
grenouille f frog
grève f strike
grillé(e) grilled
grille-pain m toaster
Grèce f Greece
grippe f flu
gris(e) grey
gros(se) big ; large ; fat
gros lot m jackpot
grotte f cave
groupe m group ; party ; band
  groupe sanguin blood group
guêpe f wasp
guerre f war

gueule de bois f hangover
guichet m ticket office
guide m guide ; guidebook
  guide de conversation phrase book
guidon m handlebars
guitare f guitar

H

habillé(e) dressed
habiller to dress
  s'habiller to get dressed
habitant(e) m/f inhabitant
habiter to live (in)
habituel(le) usual ; regular
haché(e) minced
  steak haché m hamburger
hachis m minced meat
halles fpl central food market
hamburger m burger
hameçon m hook (fishing)
hanche f hip
handicapé(e) disabled (person)
haricot m bean
haut m top (of ladder, bikini, etc)
  en haut upstairs
haut(e) high ; tall
hauteur f height
hebdomadaire weekly
hébergement m lodging
hépatite f hepatitis
herbe f grass
  fines herbes herbs
hernie f hernia
heure f hour ; time of day
  à l'heure on time
  heure de pointe rush hour
heureux(-euse) happy
hibou m owl
hier yesterday
hippisme m horse riding
hippodrome m racecourse
historique historic
hiver m winter
hollandais(e) Dutch
homard m lobster
homéopathie f homeopathy
homme m man
  homme au foyer house-husband
  homme d'affaires businessman
  hommes gents
homo m gay (person)
honnête honest
honoraires mpl fee
hôpital m hospital

horaire m timetable ; schedule
horloge f clock
hors: hors de out of
  hors service out of order
  hors-taxe duty-free
  hors-saison off-season
hôte m host ; guest
hôtel m hotel
  hôtel de ville town hall
hôtesse f stewardess
huile f oil
  huile d'olive olive oil
  huile d'arachide peanut oil
  huile de tournesol sunflower oil
huître f oyster
hypermarché m hypermarket
hypermétrope long-sighted
hypertension f high blood pressure

I

ici here
idée f idea
il y a... there is/are...
  il y a un défaut there's a fault
  il y a une semaine a week ago
île f island
illimité(e) unlimited
immédiatement immediately
immeuble m building (offices, flats)
immunisation f immunisation
impair(e) odd (number)
impasse f dead end
imperméable waterproof
important(e) important
importer to import
impossible impossible
impôt m tax
imprimer to print
incendie m fire
inclus(e) included ; inclusive
inconfortable uncomfortable
incorrect(e) wrong
indicateur m guide ; timetable
indicatif m dialling code
indications fpl instructions ; directions
indigestion f indigestion
indispensable essential
infectieux(-euse) infectious
infection f infection
inférieur(e) inferior ; lower
infirmerie f infirmary
infirmier(-ière) m/f nurse
informations fpl news ; information

infusion f herbal tea
ingénieur m/f engineer
ingrédient m ingredient
inhalateur m inhaler
inondation f flood
inquiet(-iète) worried
inscrire to write (down) ; to enrol
insecte m insect
insolation f sunstroke
installations fpl facilities
instant m moment
  un instant! just a minute!
institut m institute
  institut de beauté beauty salon
insuline f insulin
intelligent(e) intelligent
interdit forbidden
intéressant(e) interesting
intérieur: à l'intérieur indoors
international(e) international
interprète m/f interpreter
intervention f operation (surgical)
intoxication alimentaire f food poisoning
introduire to introduce ; to insert
inutile useless ; unnecessary
invalide m/f disabled person
invité(e) m/f guest (house guest)
inviter to invite
irlandais(e) Irish
Irlande f Ireland
Irlande du Nord f Northern Ireland
issue de secours f emergency exit
Italie f Italy
italien(ne) Italian
itinéraire m route
  itinéraire touristique scenic route
ivoire m ivory
ivre drunk

J

jaloux(-ouse) jealous
jamais never
jambe f leg
jambon m ham
janvier January
Japon m Japan
jardin m garden
jauge (de niveau d'huile) f dipstick
jaune yellow

jaune d'œuf m egg yolk
jaunisse f jaundice
jetable disposable
jetée f pier
jeter to throw
jeton m token
jeu m game ; set *(of tools, etc)* ; gambling
  jeu électronique computer game
  jeu vidéo video game
  jeu-concours quiz
jeudi m Thursday
jeune young
jeunesse f youth
joindre to join ; to enclose
joli(e) pretty
jonquille f daffodil
joue f cheek
jouer to play *(games)*
jouet m toy
jour m day
  jour férié public holiday
journal m newspaper
journaliste m/f journalist
journée f day *(length of time)*
juge m judge
juif (juive) Jewish
juillet July
juin June
jumeaux mpl twins
jumelles fpl twins ; binoculars
jupe f skirt
jus m juice
  jus d'orange orange juice
  jus de fruit fruit juice
  jus de viande gravy
jusqu'à (au) until ; till
juste fair ; reasonable

K

kart m go-cart
kas(c)her kosher
kayak m canoe
kilo m kilo
kilométrage m mileage
  kilométrage illimité unlimited
  mileage
kilomètre m kilometre
kiosque m kiosk ; newsstand
klaxonner to sound one's horn
kyste m cyst

L

là there
lac m lake
lacets mpl shoelaces
laid(e) ugly
laine f wool
  laine polaire fleece *(top/jacket)*
laisse f leash
laisser to leave
  laissez en blanc leave blank
lait m milk
  lait démaquillant cleansing milk
  lait demi-écrémé semi-skimmed milk
  lait écrémé skim(med) milk
  lait entier full-cream milk
  lait longue conservation long-life
  milk
  lait maternisé baby milk *(formula)*
  lait solaire suntan lotion
laiterie f dairy
laitue f lettuce
lame f blade
  lames de rasoir razor blades
lampe f light ; lamp
  lampe de poche torch
landau m pram ; baby carriage
langue f tongue ; language
lapin m rabbit
laque f hair spray
lard m fat ; *(streaky)* bacon
large wide ; broad
largeur f width
laurier m sweet bay ; bay leaves
lavable washable
lavabo m washbasin
  lavabos toilets
lavage m washing
lavande f lavender
lave-auto m car wash
lave-glace m screen wash
lave-linge m washing machine
laver to wash
  se laver to wash oneself
laverie automatique f launderette
lave-vaisselle m dishwasher
laxatif m laxative
layette f baby clothes
leçon f lesson
  leçons particulières private lessons
lecture f reading
légal(e) legal
léger(-ère) light ; weak *(tea, etc)*
légume m vegetable
lendemain m next day

lent(e) slow

lentement slowly

lentille *f* lentil ; lens *(of glasses)*
  lentille de contact contact lens

lesbienne *f* lesbian

lessive *f* soap powder ; washing

lettre *f* letter
  lettre recommandée registered letter

leur(s) their

levée *f* collection *(of mail)*

lever to lift
  se lever to get up *(out of bed)*

lever du soleil *m* sunrise

lèvre *f* lip

levure *f* yeast

libellule *f* dragonfly

librairie *f* bookshop

libre free ; vacant

libre-service self-service

lieu *m* place *(location)*

lièvre *m* hare

ligne *f* line ; service ; route

lime à ongles *f* nail file

limitation de vitesse *f* speed limit

limonade *f* lemonade

lin *m* linen *(cloth)*

linge *m* linen *(bed, table)* ; laundry

lingerie *f* lingerie

lingettes *fpl* baby wipes

lion *m* lion

liquide *f* liquid
  liquide de freins brake fluid

lire to read

liste *f* list

lit *m* bed
  lit d'enfant cot
  lit simple single bed
  lits jumeaux twin beds
  grand lit double bed

litre *m* litre

livraison *f* delivery *(of goods)*
  livraison des bagages baggage reclaim

livre *f* pound

livre *m* book

local(e) local

locataire *m/f* tenant ; lodger

location *f* hiring (out) ; letting

logement *m* accommodation

loger to stay *(reside for while)*

logiciel *m* computer software

loi *f* law

loin far

lointain(e) distant

loisir *m* leisure

Londres London

long(ue) long
  le long de along

longe *f* loin *(of meat)*

longtemps for a long time

longueur *f* length

lot *m* prize ; lot *(at auction)*

loterie *f* lottery

lotion *f* lotion

loto *m* numerical lottery

lotte *f* monkfish ; angler fish

louer to let ; to hire ; to rent
  à louer for hire/to rent

loup *m* wolf ; sea perch

loupe *f* magnifying glass

lourd(e) heavy

loyer *m* rent

luge *f* sledge ; toboggan

lumière *f* light

lundi *m* Monday

lune *f* moon
  lune de miel honeymoon

lunettes *fpl* glasses
  lunettes de soleil sunglasses
  lunettes protectrices goggles

luxe *m* luxury

lycée *m* secondary school

M

M sign for the Paris metro

machine *f* machine
  machine à laver washing machine

mâchoire *f* jaw

Madame *f* Mrs ; Ms ; Madam

madeleine *f* small sponge cake

Mademoiselle *f* Miss

madère *m* Madeira *(wine)*

magasin *m* shop
  grand magasin department store

magnétophone *m* tape recorder

magnétoscope *m* video-cassette recorder

magret de canard *m* breast fillet of duck

mai May

maigre lean *(meat)*

maigrir to slim

maillet *m* mallet

maillot *m* vest
  maillot de bain swimsuit

m   french–eng

main f hand
maintenant now
maire m mayor
mairie f town hall
mais but
maison f house ; home
  maison de campagne villa
maître d'hôtel m head waiter
majuscule f capital letter
mal badly
mal m harm ; pain
  mal de dents toothache
  mal de mer seasickness
  mal de tête headache
  faire du mal à quelqu'un to harm
  someone
malade sick (ill)
malade m/f sick person ; patient
maladie f disease
malentendu m misunderstanding
malle f trunk (luggage)
maman f mummy
manche f sleeve
Manche f the Channel
mandat m money order
manger to eat
manière f way (manner)
manifestation f demonstration
manque m shortage ; lack
manteau m coat
maquereau m mackerel
maquillage m make-up
marais m marsh
marbre m marble (material)
marc m white grape spirit
marchand m dealer ; merchant
  marchand de poisson
  fishmonger
  marchand de vin wine merchant
marche f step ; march; walking
  marche arrière reverse gear
marché m market
  marché aux puces flea market
marcher to walk; to work (machine, car)
  en marche on (machine)
mardi m Tuesday
  mardi gras Shrove Tuesday
marée f tide
  marée basse low tide
  marée haute high tide
margarine f margarine
mari m husband

mariage m wedding
marié m bridegroom
marié(e) married
mariée f bride
marier to marry
  se marier to get married
mariné(e) marinated
marionnette f puppet
marque f make ; brand (name)
marquer to score (goal, point)
marron brown
marron m chestnut
mars March
marteau m hammer
masculin male (person, on forms)
mât m mast
match de football m football match
match en nocturne m floodlit fixture
matelas m mattress
  matelas pneumatique lilo®
matériel m equipment ; kit
matin m morning
mauvais(e) bad ; wrong ; off (food)
maximum m maximum
mazout m oil (for heating)
mécanicien m mechanic
méchant(e) naughty ; wicked
médecin m doctor
médicament m medicine ; drug ;
  medication
médiéval(e) medieval
Méditerranée f Mediterranean Sea
méduse f jellyfish
meilleur(e) best ; better
  meilleurs vœux best wishes
membre m member (of club, etc)
même same
mémoire f memory
ménage m housework
méningite f meningitis
mensuel(le) monthly
menthe f mint ; mint tea
menton m chin
menu m menu (set)
  menu à prix fixe set price menu
mer f sea
  mer du Nord North Sea
mercerie f haberdasher's
merci thank you
mercredi m Wednesday
mère f mother
merlan m whiting
merlu m hake
mérou m grouper

merveilleux(-euse) wonderful

message m message

messe f mass *(church)*

messieurs mpl men

messieurs gents

mesure f measurement

mesurer to measure

métal m metal

météo f weather forecast

métier m trade ; occupation ; craft

mètre m metre
  mètre à ruban tape measure

métro m underground railway

mettre to put ; to put on
  mettre au point focus *(camera)*
  mettre en marche to turn on

meublé(e) furnished

meubles mpl furniture
  meubles de style period furniture

mi-bas mpl pop-socks ; knee-highs

midi m midday ; noon

Midi m the south of France

miel m honey

mieux better ; best

migraine f headache ; migraine

milieu m middle

mille m thousand

millimètre m millimetre

million m million

mince slim ; thin

mine f expression ; mine *(coal, etc)*

mineur m miner

mineur(e) under age ; minor

minimum m minimum

minuit m midnight

minuscule tiny

minute f minute

minuteur m timer

mirabelle f plum ; plum brandy

miroir m mirror

mise en plis f set *(for hair)*

mistral m strong cold dry wind

mite f moth *(clothes)*

mixte mixed

mobilier m furniture

mode f fashion
  à la mode fashionable
  mode d'emploi instructions for use

modem m modem

moderne modern

moelle f marrow *(beef, etc)*

moi me

moineau m sparrow

moins less ; minus

moins (de) less (than)
  moins cher cheaper

moins m the least

mois m month

moississure f mould *(fungus)*

moitié f half
  à moitié prix half-price

moka m coffee cream cake ; mocha coffee

molle soft

moment m moment
  en ce moment at the moment

mon/ma/mes my

monastère m monastery

monde m world
  il y a du monde there's a lot of people

moniteur m instructor ; coach

monitrice f instructress ; coach

monnaie f currency ; change

monnayeur m automatic change machine

monsieur m gentleman

Monsieur m Mr ; Sir

montagne f mountain

montant m amount *(total)*

monter to take up ; to go up ; to rise ; to get in *(car)*
  monter à cheval to horse-ride

montre f watch

montrer to show

monument m monument

moquette f fitted carpet

morceau m piece ; bit ; cut *(of meat)*

mordu(e) bitten

morsure f bite
  morsure de serpent snake bite

mort(e) dead

mosquée f mosque

mot m word ; note *(letter)*
  mot de passe password
  mots croisés crossword puzzle

motel m motel

moteur m engine ; motor

motif m pattern

moto f motorbike

mou (molle) soft

mouche f fly

moucheron m midge

mouchoir m handkerchief

mouette f seagull

mouillé(e) wet

moule f mussel
moulin m mill
  moulin à vent windmill
moulinet m reel *(fishing)*
mourir to die
mousse f foam ; mousse
  mousse à raser shaving foam
  mousse coiffante hair mousse
mousseux(-euse) sparkling *(wine)*
moustache f moustache
moustique m mosquito
moutarde f mustard
mouton m sheep ; lamb ; mutton
moyen(ne) average
moyenne f average
muguet m lily of the valley ; thrush
  (candida)
muni(e) de supplied with ; in
  possession of
mur m wall
mûr(e) mature ; ripe
mûre f blackberry
muscade f nutmeg
musée m museum
  musée d'art art gallery
musique f music
myope short-sighted

N

nager to swim
naissance f birth
nappe f tablecloth
nappé(e) coated *(with chocolate, etc)*
natation f swimming
national(e) national
nationalité f nationality
natte f plait
nature f wildlife
naturel(le) natural
nautique nautical ; water
navette f shuttle *(bus service)*
navigation f sailing
navire m ship
né(e) born
négatif m negative *(photography)*
neige f snow
neiger to snow
nettoyage m cleaning
  nettoyage à sec dry-cleaning
nettoyer to clean

neuf (neuve) new
neveu m nephew
névralgie f headache
nez m nose
niche f kennel
nid m nest
  nid de poule pothole
nièce f niece
niveau m level ; standard
noce f wedding
nocturne m late opening
Noël m Christmas
  joyeux Noël! merry Christmas!
noir(e) black
noisette f hazelnut
noix f nut ; walnut
nom m name ; noun
  nom de famille family name
  nom de jeune fille maiden name
nombre m number
nombreux(-euse) numerous
non no ; not
non alcoolisé(e) non-alcoholic
non-fumeur non-smoking
nord m north
normal(e) normal ; standard *(size)*
nos our
notaire m solicitor
note f note ; bill ; memo
notre our
nœud m knot
nourrir to feed
nourriture f food
nouveau (nouvelle) new
  de nouveau again
nouvelles fpl news
novembre November
noyer m walnut tree
nu(e) naked ; bare
nuage m cloud
nuageux(-euse) cloudy
nucléaire nuclear
nuit f night
  bonne nuit good night
numéro m number ; act ; issue

O

objectif m objective ; lens *(of camera)*
objet m object
  objets de valeur valuable items
  objets trouvés lost property
obligatoire compulsory
obsèques fpl funeral

3

obtenir to get ; to obtain
occasion f occasion ; bargain
occupé(e) busy ; hired *(taxi)*
occupé(e) engaged
océan m ocean
octobre October
odeur f smell
œuf m egg
 œuf de Pâques Easter egg
office m service *(church)* ; office
 office du tourisme tourist office
offre f offer
oie f goose
oignon m onion
œil m eye
œillet m carnation
oiseau m bird
olive f olive
ombre f shade/shadow
 à l'ombre in the shade
oncle m uncle
onde f wave
ongle m nail *(finger)*
opéra m opera
or m gold
orage m storm
orange orange ; amber *(traffic light)*
orange f orange
orangeade f orange squash
orchestre m orchestra ; stalls *(in theatre)*
ordinaire ordinary
ordinateur m computer
ordonnance f prescription
ordre m order
 à l'ordre de payable to
ordures fpl litter *(rubbish)*
oreille f ear
oreiller m pillow
oreillons mpl mumps
organiser to organize
orge f barley
origan m oregano
os m bone
oseille f sorrel
osier m wicker
ou or
où where
oublier to forget
ouest m west
oui yes
ours(e) m/f bear *(animal)*
oursin m sea urchin
outils mpl tools
ouvert(e) open ; on *(tap, gas, etc)*

ouvert(e) open
ouverture f overture ; opening
ouvrable working *(day)*
ouvre-boîtes m tin-opener
ouvre-bouteilles m bottle-opener
ouvrir to open

P

page f page
 pages jaunes Yellow Pages
paiement m payment
paille f straw
pain m bread ; loaf of bread
 pain bis brown bread
 pain complet wholemeal bread
 pain grillé toast
pair(e) even
paire f pair
paix f peace
palais m palace
pâle pale
palmes fpl flippers
palourde f clam
pamplemousse m grapefruit
panaché m shandy
pané(e) in breadcrumbs
panier m basket
 panier repas packed lunch
panne f breakdown
panneau m sign
pansement m bandage
pantalon m trousers
pantoufles fpl slippers
pape m pope
papeterie f stationer's shop
papier m paper
 papier à lettres writing paper
 papier alu(minium) foil
 papier cadeau gift-wrap
 papier hygiénique toilet paper
 papiers identity papers ; driving licence
papillon m butterfly
pâquerette f daisy
Pâques m or fpl Easter
paquet m package ; pack ; packet
par by ; through ; per
 par exemple for example
 par jour per day
 par téléphone by phone
 par voie orale take by mouth *(medicine)*

paradis m heaven
paralysé(e) paralysed
parapluie m umbrella
parasol m sunshade
parc m park
　parc d'attractions funfair
parce que because
parcmètre m parking meter
parcours m route
pardon! sorry! ; excuse me!
parer to ward off
pare-brise m windscreen
pare-chocs m bumper
parent(e) m/f relative
parents mpl parents
paresseux(-euse) lazy
parfait(e) perfect
parfum m perfume ; flavour
parfumerie f perfume shop
pari m bet
parier sur to bet on
parking m car park
　parking assuré parking facilities
　parking souterrain underground car park
　parking surveillé attended car park
parler (à) to speak (to) ;
　to talk (to)
paroisse f parish
partager to share
parterre m flowerbed
parti m political party
partie f part ; match (game)
partir to leave ; to go
　à partir de from
partout everywhere
pas not
　pas encore not yet
pas m step ; pace
passage m passage
　passage à niveau level crossing
　passage clouté pedestrian crossing
　passage interdit no through way
　passage souterrain underpass
passager(-ère) m/f passenger
passé(e) past
passe-temps m hobby
passeport m passport
passer to pass ; to spend (time)
　se passer to happen
passerelle f gangway (bridge)
passionnant(e) exciting

passoire f sieve ; colander
pastèque f watermelon
pasteur m minister (of religion)
pastille f lozenge
pastis m aniseed-flavoured apéritif
pataugeoire f paddling pool
pâte f pastry ; dough ; paste
pâté m pâté
pâtes fpl pasta
patient(e) m/f patient (in hospital)
patin m skate
　patins à glace ice skates
　patins à roulettes roller skates
patinoire f skating rink
pâtisserie f cake shop ; little cake
patron m boss ; pattern (knitting, dress, etc)
patronne f boss
pauvre poor
payer to pay (for)
　payé(e) paid
　payé(e) d'avance prepaid
pays m land ; country
　du pays local
Pays-Bas mpl Netherlands
paysage countryside ; scenery
péage m toll (motorway, etc)
peau f hide (leather) ; skin
pêche f peach ; fishing
pêcher to fish
pêcheur m angler
pédale f pedal
pédalo m pedal boat/pedalo
pédicure m/f chiropodist
peigne m comb
peignoir m dressing gown ; bath-robe
peindre to paint ; to decorate
peinture f painting ; paintwork
peler to peel (fruit)
pèlerinage m pilgrimage
pelle f spade
　pelle à poussière dustpan
pellicule f film (for camera)
　pellicule couleur colour film
　pellicule noir et blanc black and white film
pelote f ball (of string, wool)
　pelote basque pelota (ball game for 2 players)
pelouse f lawn
pencher to lean
pendant during
pendant que while
pénicilline f penicillin
péninsule f peninsula

pénis m penis
penser to think
pension f guesthouse
  pension complète full board
pente f slope
Pentecôte f Whitsun
pépin m pip
perceuse électrique f electric drill
perdre to lose
perdu(e) lost *(object)*
père m father
périmé(e) out of date
périphérique m ring road
perle f bead ; pearl
permanente f perm
permettre to permit
permis m permit ; licence
  permis de chasse hunting permit
  permis de conduire driving licence
  permis de pêche fishing permit
perruque f wig
persil m parsley
personne f person
peser to weigh
pétanque f type of bowls
pétillant(e) fizzy
petit(e) small ; slight
  petit déjeuner breakfast
  petit pain roll
petit-fils m grandson
petite-fille f granddaughter
pétrole m oil *(petroleum)* ; paraffin
peu little ; few
  à peu près approximately
  un peu (de) a bit (of)
peur f fear
  avoir peur (de) to be afraid (of)
peut-être perhaps
phare m headlight ; lighthouse
pharmacie f chemist's ; pharmacy
phoque m seal *(animal)*
photo f photograph
photocopie f photocopy
photocopier to photocopy
piano m piano
pichet m jug ; carafe
pie f magpie
pièce f room *(in house)* ; play *(theatre)* ; coin
  pièce d'identité means of identification
  pièce de rechange spare part
pied m foot
  à pied on foot
pierre f stone

piéton m pedestrians
pignon m pine kernel
pile f pile ; battery *(for radio, etc)*
pilon m drumstick *(of chicken)*
pilote m/f pilot
pilule f pill
pin m pine
pince f pliers
  pince à cheveux hairgrip
  pince à épiler tweezers
  pince à linge clothes peg
  pince à ongles nail clippers
pipe f pipe *(smoking)*
piquant(e) spicy ; hot
pique-nique m picnic
piquer to sting
piquet m peg *(for tent)*
piqûre f insect bite ; injection ; sting
pire worse
piscine f swimming pool
pissenlit m dandelion
pistache f pistachio *(nut)*
piste f ski-run ; runway *(airport)*
  piste cyclable cycle track
  piste de luge toboggan run
  piste pour débutants nursery slope
  pistes tous niveaux slopes for all levels of skiers
pistolet m pistol
placard m cupboard
place f square *(in town)* ; seat ; space *(room)*
  places debout standing room
plafond m ceiling
plage f beach
  plage seins nus topless beach
plainte f complaint
plaisanterie f joke
plaisir m enjoyment ; pleasure
plaît: s'il vous/te plaît please
plan m map *(of town)*
  plan de la ville street map
planche f plank
  planche à découper chopping board
  planche à repasser ironing board
  planche à voile sailboard ; wind-surfing
  planche de surf surfboard
plancher m floor *(of room)*
plante f plant ; sole *(of foot, shoe)*
plaque f sheet ; plate
  plaque (d'immatriculation) f number-plate

plat m dish ; course (of meal)
  plat de résistance main course
  plat principal main course
  plats à emporter take-away meal
plat(e) level (surface) ; flat
  à plat flat (battery)
platane m plane tree
plateau m tray
plâtre m plaster
plein(e) (de) full (of)
  le plein! fill it up! (car)
  plein sud facing south
  plein tarif peak rate
pleurer to cry (weep)
pleuvoir to rain
  il pleut it's raining
plier to fold
plomb m lead ; fuse
plombage m filling (in tooth)
plombier m plumber
plonger to dive
pluie f rain
plume f feather
plus more ; most
  plus grand(e) (que) bigger (than)
  plus tard later
plusieurs several
pneu m tyre
  pneu de rechange spare tyre
  pneu dégonflé flat tyre
  pneus cloutés snow tyres
poche f pocket
poché(e) poached
poêle f frying-pan
poème m poem
poids m weight
  poids lourd heavy goods vehicle
poignée f handle
poignet m wrist
poil m hair ; coat (of animal)
poinçonner to punch (ticket, etc)
point m place ; point ; stitch ; dot
  à point medium rare (meat)
pointure f size (of shoes)
poire f pear ; pear brandy
poireau m leek
pois m pea ; spot (dot)
  petits pois peas
poison m poison
poisson m fish
poissonnerie f fishmonger's shop
poitrine f breast ; chest

poivre m pepper
poivron m pepper (capsicum)
police f policy (insurance) ; police
policier m policeman ; detective
  film/novel
pollué(e) polluted
pommade f ointment
pomme f apple ; potato
pomme de terre f potato
pompe f pump
pompes funèbres fpl undertaker's
pompier m fireman
  pompiers fire brigade
poney m pony
pont m bridge ; deck (of ship)
  faire le pont to have a long weekend
populaire popular
porc m pork ; pig
port m harbour ; port
portable m mobile phone ; laptop
portatif portable
porte f door ; gate
portefeuille m wallet
porter to wear; to carry
porte-bagages m luggage rack
porte-clefs m keyring
porte-monnaie m purse
porteur m porter
portier m doorman
portion f helping ; portion
porto m port (wine)
poser to put ; to lay down
posologie f dosage
posséder to own
poste f post ; post office
  poste de contrôle checkpoint
  poste de secours first-aid post
poste m radio/television set ; extension
  (phone)
poster m poster (decorative)
poster to post
pot m pot ; carton (yoghurt, etc)
  pot d'échappement exhaust pipe
potable ok to drink
potage m soup
poteau m post (pole)
  poteau indicateur signpost
poterie f pottery
poubelle f dustbin
pouce m thumb
poudre f powder
poule f hen
poulet m chicken
poumon m lung

7 **poupée** f doll
pour for
pourboire m tip
pourquoi why
pourri(e) rotten *(fruit, etc)*
pousser to push
poussette f push chair
pousser to push
poussière f dust
pouvoir to be able to
pré m meadow
préfecture de police f police head-
quarters
préféré(e) favourite
préférer to prefer
premier(-ière) first
 premier cru first-class wine
 premiers secours first aid
prendre to take ; to get ; to catch
prénom m first name
préparer to prepare ; to cook
près de near (to)
présenter to present ; to introduce
préservatif m condom
pressé(e) squeezed ; pressed
pressing m dry cleaner's
pression f pressure
 pression des pneus tyre pressure
prêt(e) ready
 prêt à cuire ready to cook
prêt-à-porter m ready-to-wear
prêter to lend
prêtre m priest
prévision f forecast
prier to pray
prière de... please...
prince m prince
princesse f princess
principal(e) main
printemps m spring
priorité f right of way
 priorité à droite give way to traffic
 from right
prise f plug ; socket
privé(e) private
prix m price ; prize
 à prix réduit cut-price
 prix d'entrée admission fee
 prix de détail retail price
probablement probably
problème m problem
prochain(e) next
proche close *(near)*
produits mpl produce ; product

professeur m teacher
profiter de to take advantage of
profond(e) deep
programme m schedule ; programme
(list of performers, etc)
 programme informatique computer
 program
promenade f walk ; promenade ; ride
(in vehicle)
 faire une promenade to go for a walk
promettre to promise
promotionnel(le) special low-price
prononcer to pronounce
propre clean ; own
propriétaire m/f owner
propriété f property
protège-slip m panty-liner
protestant(e) Protestant
provenance f origin ; source
provisions fpl groceries
province f province
provisoire temporary
provisoirement for the time being
proximité: à proximité nearby
prune f plum ; plum brandy
pruneau m prune
public m audience
public(-que) public
publicité f advertisement *(on TV)*
puce f flea
puissance f power
puits m well *(for water)*
pull m sweater
pullover m sweater
purée f purée ; mashed
PV m parking ticket
pyjama m pyjamas

quai m platform
qualifié(e) skilled
qualité f quality
quand when
quantité f quantity
quarantaine f quarantine
quart m quarter
quartier m neighbourhood ; district
que that ; than ; whom ; what
 qu'est-ce que c'est? what is it?
quel(le) which ; what

quelqu'un someone
quelque some
quelque chose something
quelquefois sometimes
question f question
queue f queue ; tail
  faire la queue to queue (up)
qui who ; which
quincaillerie f hardware ; hardware shop
quinzaine f fortnight
quitter to leave a place
quoi what
quotidien(ne) daily

R

rabais m reduction
raccourci m short cut
raccrocher to hang up (phone)
race f race (people)
racine f root
radiateur m radiator
radio f radio
radiographie f X-ray
radis m radish
rafraîchissements mpl refreshments
rage f rabies
ragoût m stew ; casserole
raide steep
raie f skate (fish)
raifort m horseradish
raisin m grape
  raisin sec sultana ; raisin ; currant
  raisins blancs green grapes
  raisins noirs black grapes
raison f reason
ralentir to slow down
rallonge f extension (electrical)
randonnée f hike
  randonnée à cheval pony-trekking
râpe f grater
râpé(e) grated
rappeler to remind
  se rappeler to remember
rapide quick ; fast
rapide m express train
raquette f racket ; bat ; snowshoe
rare rare ; unusual
raser to shave off
  se raser to shave

rasoir m razor
rater to miss (train, flight etc)
RATP f Paris transport authority
rayé(e) striped
rayon m shelf ; department (in store) ; spoke (of wheel)
  rayon hommes menswear
RC ground floor
reboucher to recork
récemment recently
récepteur m receiver (of phone)
réception f reception ; check-in
réceptionniste m/f receptionist
recette f recipe
recharge f refill
rechargeable refillable (lighter, pen)
recharger to recharge (battery, etc)
réchaud de camping m camping stove
réclamation f complaint
réclame f advertisement
recommandé(e) registered (mail)
recommander to recommend
récompense f reward
reconnaître to recognize
reçu m receipt
réduction f reduction ; discount; concession
réduire to reduce
refuge m mountain hut
refuser to reject ; to refuse
regarder to look at
régime m diet (slimming)
région f region
règle f rule ; ruler (for measuring)
règles fpl period (menstruation)
  règles douloureuses cramps
règlement m regulation ; payment
régler to pay ; to settle
réglisse f liquorice
reine f queen
relais routier m roadside restaurant
rembourser to refund
remède m remedy
remercier to thank
remettre to put back
  remettre à plus tard to postpone
  se remettre to recover (from illness)
remonte-pente m ski lift
remorque f trailer
remorquer to tow
remplir to fill ; to fill in/out/up
renard m fox
rencontrer to meet
rendez-vous m date ; appointment

79 **rendre** to give back

renouveler to renew

renseignements mpl information

rentrée f return to work after break
rentrée (des classes) start of the new school year

renverser to knock down (in car)

réparations fpl repairs

réparer to fix (repair)

repas m meal

repasser to iron

répondeur automatique m answer-phone

répondre (à) to reply ; to answer

réponse f answer ; reply

repos m rest
se reposer to rest

représentation f performance

requis(e) required

RER m Paris high-speed commuter train

réseau m network

réservation f reservation ; booking

réserve naturelle f nature reserve

réservé(e) reserved

réserver to book (reserve)

réservoir m tank
réservoir d'essence fuel tank

respirer to breathe

ressort m spring (metal)

restaurant m restaurant

reste m rest (remainder)

rester to remain ; to stay

restoroute m roadside or motorway restaurant

retard m delay

retirer to withdraw ; to collect (tickets)

retour m return

retourner to go back

retrait m withdrawal ; collection
retrait d'espèces cash withdrawal

retraité(e) retired

retraité(e) m/f old-age pensioner

rétrécir to shrink (clothes)

rétroviseur m rearview mirror
rétroviseur latéral wing mirror

réunion f meeting

réussir (à) to succeed

réussite f success ; patience (game)

réveil m alarm clock

réveiller to wake (someone)
se réveiller to wake up

réveillon m Christmas/New Year's Eve

revenir to come back

réverbère m lamppost

revue f review ; magazine

rez-de-chaussée m ground floor

rhum m rum

rhumatisme m rheumatism

rhume m cold (illness)
rhume des foins hay fever

riche rich

rideau m curtain

rides fpl wrinkles

rien nothing ; anything
rien à déclarer nothing to declare

rire to laugh

rivage m shore

rive f river bank

rivière f river

riz m rice

RN trunk road

robe f gown ; dress

robinet m tap

rocade f ringroad

rocher m rock (boulder)

rognon m kidney (to eat)

roi m king

roman m novel

roman(e) Romanesque

romantique romantic

romarin m rosemary

rond(e) round

rond-point m roundabout

rose pink

rose f rose

rossignol m nightingale

rôti(e) roast

rôtisserie f steakhouse ; roast meat counter

roue f wheel
roue de secours spare wheel

rouge red

rouge à lèvres m lipstick

rouge-gorge m robin

rougeole f measles

rougeur f rash (skin)

rouillé(e) rusty

rouleau à pâtisserie m rolling pin

rouler to roll ; to go (by car)

route f road ; route
route barrée road closed
route nationale trunk road
route principale major road
route secondaire minor road

routier m lorry driver
Royaume-Uni m United Kingdom
ruban m ribbon ; tape
rubéole f rubella
rue f street
  rue sans issue no through road
ruelle f lane ; alley
ruisseau m stream
russe Russian

S

SA Ltd ; plc
sable m sand
  sables mouvants quicksand
sabot de Denver wheel clamp
sac m sack ; bag
  sac à dos backpack
  sac à main handbag
  sac de couchage sleeping bag
  sac poubelle bin liner
sachet de thé m tea bag
sacoche f panniers (for bike)
safran m saffron
sage good (well-behaved) ; wise
saignant(e) rare (steak)
saigner to bleed
saint(e) m/f saint
Saint-Sylvestre f New Year's Eve
saisir to seize
saison f season
  basse saison low season
  de saison in season
  haute saison high season
saisonnier seasonal
salade f lettuce ; salad
  salade de fruits fruit salad
salaire m salary ; wage
sale dirty
salé(e) salty ; savoury
salle f lounge (at airport) ; hall ; ward (hospital)
  salle à manger dining room
  salle d'attente waiting room
  salle de bains bathroom
salon m sitting room ; lounge
  salon de beauté beauty salon
salut! hi!
samedi m Saturday
sandales fpl sandals
sandwich m sandwich
sang m blood

sanglier m wild boar
sans without
  sans alcool alcohol-free
  sans connaissance unconscious
  sans issue no through road
santé f health
  santé! cheers!
  en bonne santé well (healthy)
sapin m fir (tree)
SARL f Ltd ; plc
sauce f sauce
sauf except (for)
saumon m salmon
sauter to jump
sauvegarder to back up (computer)
sauver to rescue
savoir to know (be aware of)
  savoir faire quelque chose to know how to do sth
savon m soap
Scellofrais® m Clingfilm®
scène f stage
scie f saw
score m score (of match)
scotch m whisky
séance f meeting ; performance
seau m bucket
sec (sèche) dried (fruit, beans)
sèche-cheveux m hairdryer
sèche-linge m tumble dryer
sécher to dry
seconde f second (in time)
  en seconde second class
secouer to shake
secours m help
secrétaire m/f secretary
secrétariat m office
secteur m sector ; mains
sécurité f security ; safety
séjour m stay ; visit
sel m salt
self m self-service restaurant
selle f saddle
semaine f week
sens m meaning ; direction
  sens interdit no entry
  sens unique one-way street
sentier m footpath
  sentier écologique nature trail
sentir to feel
septembre September
séparément separately
série f series ; set
seringue f syringe
serré(e) tight (fitting)

serrer to grip ; to squeeze
  serrez à droite keep to the right-hand lane

serrure f lock

serrurerie f locksmith's

serveur m waiter

serveuse f waitress

servez-vous help yourself

service m service ; service charge ; favour
  service compris service included
  service d'urgences accident & emergency department

serviette f towel ; briefcase
  serviette hygiénique sanitary towel

servir to dish up ; to serve

seul(e) alone ; lonely

seulement only

sexe m sex

shampooing m shampoo

short m shorts

si if ; yes *(to negative question)*

SIDA m AIDS

siècle m century

siège m seat ; head office
  siège pour bébés/enfants car seat *(for children)*

signaler to report

signer to sign

simple simple ; single ; plain

site m site
  site web web site

situé(e) located

ski m ski ; skiing
  ski de randonnée cross-country skiing
  ski nautique water-skiing

slip m underpants ; panties
  slip (de bain) trunks *(swimming)*

snack m snack bar

SNCB f Belgian Railways

SNCF f French Railways

société f company ; society

sœur f sister

soie f silk

soif f thirst
  avoir soif to be thirsty

soin m care
  soins du visage facial

soir m evening

soirée f evening ; party

soja m soya ; soya bean

sol m ground ; soil

soldat m soldier

solde m balance *(remainder owed)*

soldes mpl sales
  soldes permanents sale prices all year round

sole f sole *(fish)*

soleil m sun ; sunshine

somme f sum

sommelier m wine waiter

sommet m top *(of hill, mountain)*

somnifère m sleeping pill

sonner to ring ; to strike

sonnette f doorbell

sonner to ring bell

sorbet m water ice

sorte f kind *(sort, type)*

sortie f exit
  sortie de secours emergency exit
  sortie interdite no exit

sortir to go out *(leave)*

soucoupe f saucer

soudain suddenly

souhaiter to wish

soûl(e) drunk

soulever to lift

soupape f valve

soupe f soup

souper m supper

sourcils mpl eyebrows

sourd(e) deaf

sourire to smile

souris f mouse *(also for computer)*

sous underneath ; under

sous-sol m basement

sous-titres mpl subtitles

sous-vêtements mpl underwear

souterrain(e) underground

soutien-gorge m bra

souvenir m memory ; souvenir

souvent often

sparadrap m sticking plaster

spécial(e) special

spécialité f speciality

spectacle m show *(in theatre)* ; entertainment

spectateurs mpl audience

spiritueux mpl spirits

sport m sport
  sports nautiques water sports

sportif(-ive) sports ; athletic

stade m stadium

stage m course *(period of training)*

standard m switchboard

station f station (metro) ; resort
  station balnéaire seaside resort
  station de taxis taxi rank
  station thermale spa
  station-service service station
stationnement m parking
stérilet m coil (IUD)
stimulateur (cardiaque) m pacemaker
store m blind ; awning
stylo m pen
sucette f lollipop ; dummy
sucre m sugar
sucré(e) sweet
sud m south
suisse Swiss
Suisse f Switzerland
suite f series ; continuation ; sequel
suivant(e) following
suivre to follow
  faire suivre please forward
super m four-star petrol
supermarché m supermarket
supplément m extra charge
supplémentaire extra
sur on ; onto ; on top of ; upon
  sur place on the spot
sûr safe ; sure
surcharger to overload
surchauffer to overheat
surf m surfing
  faire du surf to surf
  surf des neiges snowboard
  surf sur neige snowboarding
surgelés mpl frozen foods
surveillé(e) supervised
survêtement m tracksuit
sympa(thique) nice ; pleasant
synagogue f synagogue
syndicat d'initiative m tourist office

T

tabac m tobacco ; tobacconist's
table f table
tableau m painting ; picture ; board
  tableau de bord dashboard
tablier m apron
tache f stain
taie d'oreiller f pillowcase
taille f size (of clothes) ; waist
  taille unique one size
  grande taille outsize (clothes)

tailleur m tailor ; suit (women's)
talc m talc
talon m heel ; stub (counterfoil)
  talon minute shoes reheeled while
  you wait
tampon m tampon
  tampon Jex® scouring pad
tante f aunt
taper to strike ; to type
tapis m carpet
  tapis de sol groundsheet
tard late
  au plus tard at the latest
tarif m price-list ; rate ; tarif
tarte f flan ; tart
tartine f slice of bread and butter (or
  jam)
tartiner: à tartiner for spreading
tasse f cup ; mug
taureau m bull
tauromachie f bull-fighting
taux m rate
  taux de change exchange rate
  taux fixe flat rate
taxe f duty ; tax (on goods)
taxi m cab (taxi)
TCF m Touring Club de France (AA)
teinture f dye
teinturerie f dry cleaner's
télé f TV
télébenne f gondola lift
télécabine f gondola lift
télécarte f phonecard
télécommande f remote control
téléphérique m cable-car
téléphone m telephone
  téléphone portable mobile phone
téléphoner (à) to phone
téléphoniste m/f operator
télésiège m chair-lift
téléviseur m television (set)
télévision f television
température f temperature
tempête f storm
temple m temple ; synagogue ;
  protestant church
temps m weather ; time
tendon m tendon
tenir to hold ; to keep
tennis m tennis
tension f voltage ; blood pressure
tente f tent
tenue f clothes ; dress
  tenue de soirée evening dress
terrain m ground ; land ; pitch ; course

terrasse *f* terrace
terre *f* land ; earth ; ground
  terre cuite terracotta
tête *f* head
tétine *f* dummy *(for baby)*
TGV *m* high-speed train
thé *m* tea
  thé au lait tea with milk
  thé nature tea without milk
théâtre *m* theatre
théière *f* teapot
thermomètre *m* thermometer
ticket *m* ticket *(bus, cinema, museum)*
  ticket de caisse receipt
tiède lukewarm
tiers *m* third ; third party
timbre *m* stamp
tirage *m* printing ; print *(photo)*
  tirage le mercredi lottery draw on
  Wednesdays
tire-bouchon *m* corkscrew
tirer to pull
  tirez pull
tiroir *m* drawer
tisane *f* herbal tea
tissu *m* material ; fabric
titre *m* title
  à titre indicatif for info only
  à titre provisoire provisionally
titulaire *m/f* holder of *(card, etc)*
toile *f* canvas ; web *(spider)*
toilettes *fpl* toilet ; powder room
toit *m* roof
  toit ouvrant sunroof
tomate *f* tomato
tomber to fall
tonalité *f* dialling tone
tongs *fpl* flip flops
tonneau *m* barrel (wine/beer)
tonnerre *m* thunder
torchon *m* tea towel
tordre to twist
tôt early
total *m* total *(amount)*
toucher to touch
toujours always ; still ; forever
tour *f* tower
tour *m* trip ; walk ; ride
tourisme *m* sightseeing
touriste *m/f* tourist
touristique tourist *(route, resort, etc)*
tourner to turn
tournesol *m* sunflower
tournevis *m* screwdriver
  tournevis cruciforme phillips screw-

driver
tourte *f* pie
tous all (plural)
  tous les jours daily *(each day)*
Toussaint *f* All Saints' Day
tousser to cough
tout(e) all ; everything
  tout à l'heure in a while
  tout compris all inclusive
  tout de suite straight away
  tout droit straight ahead
  toute la journée all day
tout le monde everyone
toutes all *(plural)*
  toutes directions all routes
toux *f* cough
tradition *f* custom *(tradition)*
traditionnel(-elle) traditional
traduction *f* translation
traduire to translate
train *m* train
trajet *m* journey
tramway *m* tram
tranchant sharp *(razor, knife)*
tranche *f* slice
tranquille quiet *(place)*
transférer to transfer
transpirer to sweat
travail *m* work
travailler to work *(person)*
  travailler à son compte to be self
  employed
travaux *mpl* road works
travers: à travers through
traversée *f* crossing *(voyage)*
traverser to cross *(road, sea, etc)*
tremplin *m* diving-board
  tremplin de ski ski jump
très very ; much
triangle de présignalisation *m* warning
  triangle
tricot *m* knitting ; sweater
tricoter to knit
trimestre *m* term
triste sad
trop too ; too much
trottoir *m* pavement ; sidewalk
trou *m* hole
trousse *f* pencil case
  trousse de premiers secours first
  aid kit
trouver to find
  se trouver to be *(situated)*

tuer kill

tunnel *m* tunnel

tuyau *m* pipe *(for water, gas)*
  tuyau d'arrosage hosepipe

TVA *f* VAT

typique typical

U

UE *f* EU

ulcère *m* ulcer

ultérieur(e) later *(date, etc)*

un(e) one ; a ; an
  l'un ou l'autre either one

uni(e) plain *(not patterned)*

Union européenne *f* European Union

université *f* university

urgence *f* urgency ; emergency

urine *f* urine

usage *m* use

usine *f* factory

utile useful

utiliser to use

V

vacances *fpl* holiday(s)
  en vacances on holiday
  grandes vacances summer holiday

vaccin *m* vaccination

vache *f* cow

vagin *m* vagina

vague *f* wave *(on sea)*

vaisselle *f* crockery

valable valid *(ticket, licence, etc)*

valeur *f* value

valider to validate

valise *f* suitcase

vallée *f* valley

valoir to be worth
  ça vaut... it's worth...

vanille *f* vanilla

vapeur *f* steam

varicelle *f* chickenpox

varié(e) varied ; various

vase *m* vase

veau *m* calf ; veal

vedette *f* speedboat ; star *(film)*

végétal(e) vegetable

végétarien(ne) vegetarian

véhicule *m* vehicle

véhicules lents slow-moving vehicles

veille *f* the day before ; eve
  veille de Noël Christmas Eve

veine *f* vein

vélo *m* bike
  vélo tout terrain (VTT) mountain bike

velours *m* velvet

venaison *f* venison

vendange(s) *fpl* harvest *(of grapes)*

vendeur(-euse) *m/f* sales assistant

vendre to sell
  à vendre for sale

vendredi *m* Friday
  vendredi saint Good Friday

vénéneux poisonous

venir to come

vent *m* wind

vente *f* sale
  vente aux enchères auction
  vente-sauvage car boot sale

ventilateur *m* ventilator ; fan

verglas *m* black ice

vérifier to check ; to audit

vernis *m* varnish
  vernis à ongles nail varnish

verre *m* glass
  verres de contact contact lenses

verrouillage central *m* central locking

vers toward(s) ; about

versement *m* payment ; instalment

verser to pour ; to pay

vert(e) green

veste *f* jacket

vestiaire *m* cloakroom

vêtements *mpl* clothes

vétérinaire *m/f* vet

veuf *m* widower

veuillez... please...

veuve *f* widow

via by *(via)*

viande *f* meat
  viande hachée mince *(meat)*

vidange *f* oil change (car)

vide empty

videoclub *m* video shop

vie *f* life

vieux (vieille) old

vigile *m* security guard

vigne *f* vine ; vineyard

vignoble *m* vineyard

VIH *m* HIV

village *m* village

ville *f* town ; city

vin *m* wine

vin en pichet house wine
vin pétillant sparkling wine
vinaigre *m* vinegar
violer to rape
violet(-ette) purple
vipère *f* adder ; viper
virage *m* bend ; curve ; corner
vis *f* screw
  vis platinées points *(in car)*
visage *m* face
visite *f* visit ; consultation *(of doctor)*
  visite guidée guided tour
visiter to visit *(a place)*
visiteur(-euse) *m/f* visitor
visser to screw on
vite quickly ; fast
vitesse *f* gear *(of car)* ; speed
  vitesse limitée à... speed limit...
vitrail *m* stained-glass window
vitrine *f* shop window
vivre to live
VO: *en VO* with subtitles *(film)*
vœu *m* wish
voici here is/are
voie *f* lane (of road) ; line ; track
voilà there is/are
voile *f* sail ; sailing
voilier *m* sailing boat
voir to see
voisin(e) *m/f* neighbour
voiture *f* car ; coach (of train)
vol *m* flight ; theft
  vol intérieur domestic flight
volaille *f* poultry
volant *m* steering wheel
voler to fly *(bird)* ; to steal
volet *m* shutter *(on window)*
voleur(-euse) *m/f* thief
volonté *f* will
  à volonté as much as you like
vomir to vomit
v.o.s.t. original version with
  subtitles *(film)*
vouloir to want
voyage *m* journey
  voyage d'affaires business trip
  voyage organisé package holiday
voyager to travel
voyageur(-euse) *m/f* traveller
vrai(e) real ; true
VTT *m* mountain bike
vue *f* view ; sight

french–eng v/w/x/y/z

W

w-c *mpl* toilet
wagon *m* carriage ; waggon
wagon-couchettes *m* sleeping car
wagon-restaurant *m* dining car
web *m* internet

X

xérès *m* sherry

Y

yacht *m* yacht
yaourt *m* yoghurt
  yaourt nature plain yoghurt
yeux *mpl* eyes
youyou *m* dinghy

Z

zéro *m* zero
zona *m* shingles *(illness)*
zone *f* zone
  zone piétonne pedestrian area
zoo *m* zoo

HOW FRENCH WORKS

NOUNS

*A **noun** is a word such as **car**, **horse** or **Mary** which is used to refer to a person or thing.*

Unlike English, French nouns have a gender: they are either *masculine* (**le**) or *feminine* (**la**). Therefore words for *the* and *a(n)* must agree with the noun they accompany – whether *masculine*, *feminine* or *plural*:

	masc.	*fem.*	*plural*
the	**le chat**	**la rue**	**les chats**, **les rues**
a, an	**un chat**	**une rue**	**des chats**, **des rues**

If the noun begins with a vowel (**a**, **e**, **i**, **o** or **u**) or an unsounded **h**, **le** and **la** shorten to **l'**, i.e. **l'avion** *(m)*, **l'école** *(f)*, **l'hôtel** *(m)*.

NOTE: **le** and **les** used after the prepositions **à** (to, at) and **de** (any, some, of) contract as follows:

à + **le** = **au** (**au cinéma** but **à <u>la</u> gare**)
à + **les** = **aux** (**aux magasins** - applies to both *(m)* and *(f)*)
de + **le** = **du** (**du pain** but **de <u>la</u> confiture**)
de + **les** = **des** (<u>**des**</u> **pommes** - applies to both *(m)* and *(f)*)

There are some broad rules as to noun endings which indicate whether they are *masculine* or *feminine*:

Generally *masculine* endings:

-er, **-ier**, **-eau**, **-t**, **-c**, **-age**, **-ail**, **-oir**, **-é**, **-on**, **-acle**, **-ège**, **-ème**, **-o**, **-ou**.

Generally *feminine* endings:

-euse, **-trice**, **-ère**, **-ière**, **-elle**, **-te**, **-tte**, **-de**, **-che**, **-age**, **-aille**, **-oire**, **-ée**, **-té**, **-tié**, **-onne**, **-aison**, **-ion**, **-esse**, **-ie**, **-ine**, **-une**, **-ure**, **-ance**, **-anse**, **-ence**, **-ense**.

PLURAL

The general rule is to add an **s** to the singular:

        le chat   ➜   **les chats**

Exceptions occur with the following noun endings: **-eau**, **-eu**, **-al**

        le bat<u>eau</u>   ➜   **les bat<u>eaux</u>**
        le nev<u>eu</u>   ➜   **les nev<u>eux</u>**
        le chev<u>al</u>   ➜   **les chev<u>aux</u>**

Nouns ending in **-s**, **-x**, or **-z** do not change in the plural.

        le dos   ➜   **les dos**
        le prix   ➜   **les prix**
        le nez   ➜   **les nez**

ADJECTIVES

*An **adjective** is a word such as **small**, **pretty** or **practical** that describes a person or thing, or gives extra information about them.*

Adjectives normally follow the noun they describe in French,

e.g. **la pomme verte** (the green apple)

Some common exceptions which go before the noun are: **beau** beautiful, **bon** good, **grand** big, **haut** high, **jeune** young, **long** long, **joli** pretty, **mauvais** bad, **nouveau** new, **petit** small, **vieux** old.

e.g. **un bon livre** (a good book)

French adjectives have to reflect the gender of the noun they describe. To make an adjective *feminine*, an **e** is added to the *masculine* form (where this does not already end in an **e**, e.g. **jeune**).

NOTE: The addition of an **e** to the final consonant (which is usually silent in the *masculine*) means that you should pronounce the ending in the *feminine*.

masc. **le livre vert**	*fem.* **la pomme verte**
luh leevr vehr	*la pom vehrt*
(the green book)	(the green apple)

To make an adjective plural, an **s** is added to the singular form: *masculine plural* – **verts** (remember – the ending is still silent: *vehr*) or *feminine plural* – **vertes** (because of the **e**, the **t** ending is sounded: *vehrt*).

MY, YOUR, HIS, HER, OUR, THEIR

These words also reflect the gender and number of the noun (whether *masculine*, *feminine* or *plural*) they accompany and not on the sex of the 'owner'.

	with masc. *sing. noun*	*with fem.* *sing. noun*	*with plural* *nouns*
my	**mon**	**ma**	**mes**
your *(familiar, singular)*	**ton**	**ta**	**tes**
his/her	**son**	**sa**	**ses**
our	**notre**	**notre**	**nos**
your *(polite and plural)*	**votre**	**votre**	**vos**
their	**leur**	**leur**	**leurs**

PRONOUNS

*A **pronoun** is a word that you use to refer to someone or something when you do not need to use a noun, often because the person or thing has been mentioned earlier. Examples are **it**, **she**, **something** and **myself**.*

subject		*object*	
I	**je, j'**	me	**me, m'**
you *(familiar)*	**tu**	you	**te, t'**
you *(polite and plural)*	**vous**	you	**vous**
he/it	**il**	him/it	**le, l'**
she/it	**elle**	her/it	**la, l'**
we	**nous**	us	**nous**
they *(masculine)*	**ils**	them	**les**
they *(feminine)*	**elles**	them	**les**

In French there are two forms for you – **tu** and **vous**. **Tu** is the familiar form which is used with children and people you know as friends. **Vous**, as well as being the plural form for you, is also the polite form of addressing someone. You should probably use this form until the other person invites you to use the more familiar **tu** ('**on se dit 'tu'?**').

Object pronouns are placed before the verb:

e.g.　　　　**il vous aime** (he loves <u>you</u>)

　　　　　　nous la connaissons (we know <u>her</u>)

However, in commands or requests, object pronouns follow the verb,

e.g.　　　　**écoutez-le** (listen to <u>him</u>)

　　　　　　aidez-moi (help <u>me</u>)

NOTE: this does not apply to negative commands or requests,

e.g.　　　　**ne le faites pas** (don't do <u>it</u>)

The object pronouns shown above are also used to mean **to me**, **to us**, etc. except,

　　　　　　le and **la** which become **lui** (to him, to her)

　　　　　　les which becomes **leur** (to them)

e.g.　　　　**il le lui donne** (he gives it <u>to him</u>)

VERBS

*A **verb** is a word such as **sing**, **walk** or **cry** which is used with a subject to say what someone or something does or what happens to them. **Regular verbs** follow the same pattern of endings. **Irregular verbs** do not follow a regular pattern so you need to learn the different endings.*

There are three main patterns of endings for verbs in French – those ending -**er**, -**ir** and -**re** in the dictionary.

DONNER	TO GIVE
je donne	I give
tu donnes	you give
il/elle donne	he/she gives
nous donnons	we give
vous donnez	you give
ils/elles donnent	they give

past participle: **donné** (with **avoir**)

FINIR	TO FINISH
je finis	I finish
tu finis	you finish
il/elle finit	he/she finishes
nous finissons	we finish
vous finissez	you finish
ils/elles finissent	they finish

past participle: **fini** (with **avoir**)

RÉPONDRE	TO REPLY
je réponds	I reply
tu réponds	you reply
il/elle répond	he/she replies
nous répondons	we reply
vous répondez	you reply
ils/elles répondent	they reply

past participle: **répondu** (with **avoir**)

IRREGULAR VERBS

Among the most important irregular verbs are the following:

ÊTRE	TO BE
je suis	I am
tu es	you are
il/elle est	he/she is
nous sommes	we are
vous êtes	you are
ils/elles sont	they are

past participle: **été** (with **avoir**)

AVOIR	TO HAVE
j'ai	I have
tu as	you have
il/elle a	he/she has
nous avons	we have
vous avez	you have
ils/elles ont	they have

past participle: **eu** (with **avoir**)

ALLER	TO GO
je vais	I go
tu vas	you go
il/elle va	he/she goes
nous allons	we go
vous allez	you go
ils/elles vont	they go

past participle: **allé** (with **être**)

VENIR	TO COME
je viens	I come
tu viens	you come
il/elle vient	he/she comes
nous venons	we come
vous venez	you come
ils/elles viennent	they come

past participle: **venu** (with **être**)

FAIRE	TO DO
je fais	I do
tu fais	you do
il/elle fait	he/she does
nous faisons	we do
vous faites	you do
ils/elles font	they do

past participle: **fait** (with **avoir**)

VOULOIR	TO WANT
je veux	I want
tu veux	you want
il/elle veut	he/she wants
nous voulons	we want
vous voulez	you want
ils/elles veulent	they want

past participle: **voulu** (with **avoir**)

POUVOIR	TO BE ABLE TO
je peux	I can
tu peux	you can
il/elle peut	he/she can
nous pouvons	we can
vous pouvez	you can
ils/elles peuvent	they can

past participle: **pu** (with **avoir**)

DEVOIR	TO HAVE TO
je dois	I have to
tu dois	you have to
il/elle doit	he/she has to
nous devons	we have to
vous devez	you have to
ils/elles doivent	they have to

past participle: **dû** (with **avoir**)

PAST TENSE

*To make a simple past tense, you need an **auxiliary verb** with the past participle of the main verb, e.g. **I have** (auxiliary) **been** (past participle), **I have** (auxiliary) **eaten** (past participle). In French the basic auxiliary verbs are **avoir** (to have) and **être** (to be). A **reflexive verb** is one where the subject and object are the same e.g. **to enjoy yourself, to dress yourself**. These verbs take **être** as their auxiliary verb.*

To form the simple past tense, *I gave/I have given, I finished/I have finished*, combine the present tense of the verb **avoir** – *to have* with the past participle of the verb (**donné**, **fini**, **répondu**),

e.g.	**j'ai donné**	I gave/I have given
	j'ai fini	I finished/I have finished
	j'ai répondu	I replied/I have replied

Not all verbs take **avoir** (**j'ai...**, **il a...**) as their auxiliary verb. The reflexive verbs (**s'amuser**, **se promener**, etc) take **être** (**je me suis...**, **il s'est...**), and so do a dozen or so other verbs which generally express the idea of motion or staying such as **aller** (to go) and **rester** (to stay),

e.g.	**je me suis amusé**	I had fun
	je suis allé	I went
	je suis resté	I stayed

When the auxiliary verb **être** is used, the past participle (**amusé**, **allé**, **resté**, etc) becomes like an adjective and agrees with the subject of the verb in number and gender:

e.g.	**je me suis amusée**	I had fun *(female)*
	nous nous sommes amusés	we had fun *(plural)*
	je suis allée	I went *(female)*
	nous sommes allés	we went *(plural)*
	je suis restée	I stayed *(female)*
	nous sommes restés	we stayed *(plural)*

To make a sentence negative e. g. *I am not eating*, you use **ne ... pas** around the verb or auxilliary verb.

| e.g. | **je ne mange pas** | I am not eating |
| | **je ne suis pas amusé** | I did not have fun |